Effort and Grace

Re-inventing Philosophy as a Way of Life

Series editors: Keith Ansell-Pearson, Matthew Sharpe and Michael Ure

For the most part, academic philosophy is considered a purely theoretical discipline that aims at systematic knowledge; contemporary philosophers do not, as a rule, think that they or their audience will lead better lives by doing philosophy. Recently, however, we have seen a powerful resurgence of interest in the countervailing ancient view that philosophy facilitates human flourishing. Philosophy, Seneca famously stated, teaches us doing, not saying. It aims to transform how we live. This ancient ideal has continually been reinvented from the Renaissance to late modernity and is now central to contemporary debates about philosophy's role and future.

This series is the first synoptic study of the re-inventions of the idea of philosophy as an ethical pursuit or 'way of life'. Collectively and individually, the books in this series will answer the following questions:

1. How have philosophers re-animated the ancient model of philosophy? How have they revised ancient assumptions, concepts and practices in the light of wider cultural shifts in the modern world? What new ideas of the good life and new arts, exercises, disciplines and consolations have they formulated?
2. Do these re-inventions successfully re-establish the idea that philosophy can transform our lives? What are the standard criticisms of this philosophical ambition and how have they been addressed?
3. What are the implications for these new versions of philosophy as a way of life for contemporary issues that concern the nature of philosophy, its procedures, limits, ends and its relationship to wider society?

Also in the series
The Selected Writings of Pierre Hadot: Philosophy as Practice,
trans. Matthew Sharpe and Federico Testa

Also available from Bloomsbury
Maine de Biran's 'Of Immediate Apperception', Maine de Biran
Bergson: Thinking beyond the Human Condition, Keith Ansell Pearson
Félix Ravaisson: Selected Essays, ed. Mark Sinclair

Effort and Grace

On the Spiritual Exercise of Philosophy

Simone Kotva

BLOOMSBURY ACADEMIC
LONDON • NEW YORK • OXFORD • NEW DELHI • SYDNEY

BLOOMSBURY ACADEMIC
Bloomsbury Publishing Plc
50 Bedford Square, London, WC1B 3DP, UK
1385 Broadway, New York, NY 10018, USA
29 Earlsfort Terrace, Dublin 2, Ireland

BLOOMSBURY, BLOOMSBURY ACADEMIC and the Diana logo are
trademarks of Bloomsbury Publishing Plc

First published in Great Britain 2020
This paperback edition published in 2022

Copyright © Simone Kotva, 2020

Simone Kotva has asserted her right under the Copyright, Designs and
Patents Act, 1988, to be identified as Author of this work.

For legal purposes the Acknowledgements on p. xiii constitute
an extension of this copyright page.

Series design by Charlotte Daniels
Cover image: Greek classical sculpture of Nike of Samothrace
(Photo by Panagiotis Karapanagiotis / Alamy)

All rights reserved. No part of this publication may be reproduced or
transmitted in any form or by any means, electronic or mechanical, including
photocopying, recording, or any information storage or retrieval system,
without prior permission in writing from the publishers.

Bloomsbury Publishing Plc does not have any control over, or responsibility for,
any third-party websites referred to or in this book. All internet addresses given
in this book were correct at the time of going to press. The author and publisher
regret any inconvenience caused if addresses have changed or sites have ceased
to exist, but can accept no responsibility for any such changes.

A catalogue record for this book is available from the British Library.

Library of Congress Cataloging-in-Publication Data

Names: Kotva, Simone, author.
Title: Effort and grace: on the spiritual exercise of philosophy / Simone Kotva.
Description: New York: Bloomsbury Academic, 2020. |
Series: Re-inventing philosophy as a way of life | Includes bibliographical references and index. |
Summary: "Philosophy and theology have long harboured contradictory views on spiritual practice.
While philosophy advocates the therapeutic benefits of daily meditation, the theology of
grace promotes an ideal of happiness bestowed with little effort. As such, the historical juxtaposition
of effort and grace grounding modern spiritual exercise can be seen as the essential tension between
the secular and sacred. In Effort and Grace, Simone Kotva explores an exciting new theory of spiritual
endeavour from the tradition of French spiritualist philosophy. Spiritual exercise has largely been studied
in relation to ancient philosophy and the Ignatian tradition, yet Kotva's new engagement with its more
recent forms has alerted her to an understanding of contemplative practice as rife with critical potential.
Here, she offers an interdisciplinary text tracing the narrative of spiritual exertion through the work of seminal
French thinkers such as Maine de Biran, Fe´lix Ravaisson, Henri Bergson, Alain (E´mile Chartier), Simone Weil
and Gilles Deleuze. Her findings allow both secular philosophers and theologians to understand how the
spiritual life can participate in the contemporary philosophical conversation"– Provided by publisher.
Identifiers: LCCN 2020009689 (print) | LCCN 2020009690 (ebook) | ISBN 9781350113657 (hardback) |
ISBN 9781350113640 (ebook) | ISBN 9781350113664 (epub)
Subjects: LCSH: Spiritualism. | Philosophy and religion.
Classification: LCC B841.K68 2020 (print) | LCC B841 (ebook) | DDC 102.3–dc23

LC record available at https://lccn.loc.gov/2020009689
LC ebook record available at https://lccn.loc.gov/2020009690
Edit

ISBN: HB: 978-1-3501-1365-7
PB: 978-1-3501-9475-5
ePDF: 978-1-3501-1364-0
eBook: 978-1-3501-1366-4

Series: Re-inventing Philosophy as a Way of Life

Typeset by Integra Software Services Pvt. Ltd.

To find out more about our authors and books visit www.bloomsbury.com
and sign up for our newsletters.

For John Hughes, in memory

Contents

Preface		viii
Acknowledgements		xiii
Note on text and translations		xv
1	The spiritual exercise of philosophy: Two ideals	1
2	The spiritual life: Maine de Biran	27
3	Grace: Félix Ravaisson	59
4	Effort: Henri Bergson and Alain (Émile Chartier)	97
5	The paradox of attention: Simone Weil	131
6	Epilogue: Reclaiming attention	173
Notes		181
Bibliography		213
Index		227

Preface

In *Waiting on God* (1950), the posthumous collection which first drew the world's notice to Simone Weil, the author compared philosophical enquiry to prayer, 'the greatest of all efforts perhaps, but … a negative effort'.[1] The comparison indicated a close connection between the work of philosophy and the activity of spiritual exercise, even claiming that the two were not fundamentally opposed and urging a reappraisal of the assumed differences between philosophy and theology in light of a shared practice.

For Weil, the purpose of scrutinizing philosophy in light of spiritual exercise was to expose the presumptions of the 'secular morality' which had created the rupture between philosophy and theology in the first place.[2] Where secular morality had elevated effort by praising the virtue of activity and the grandeur of human endeavour – 'muscular effort' – it had rejected religion and allied itself to Stoicism.[3] But this modern Stoicism, Weil contended, failed to recognize that other side of Stoic teaching which had influenced the early church and the whole tradition of mystical prayer: the recognition that while some things are in our control, others are not.[4] A farmer pulls up weeds, but it is rain and sun which make the seed grow.[5] The good both is and is not up to us; it is both activity and passivity, willing and waiting, effort *and* grace – for while nothing is achieved without effort, effort on its own cannot achieve everything. For Weil, modern Stoicism lost its purpose when it failed to account for the grace at stake in effort; analogously, spiritual exercise became secular when it forgot the significance of effortlessness in the search after truth. If philosophical method and spiritual exercise were to converge again, the spirit of exercise must be seen to depend not on raw effort – the will to power – but on effort co-extensive with passivity, on Stoicism *with* Christianity, or (what to Weil amounted to the same thing) on Stoicism *with itself.*

Weil's challenge to the philosophy of spiritual exercise lies at the core of this book. It argues that an unexamined valorization of effort has for several centuries muddied the waters of the Western imagination, shaping the way philosophers have thought about spiritual exercise and its relation to philosophical method. It has forced a divide between effort and passivity, strength and weakness, independence and dependence, Stoicism and Christianity. In Weil's work this challenge receives an explicitly religious articulation, and yet the paradox for which she argues – the paradox of strength co-extensive with impotence, of action with passivity – need not be expressed as 'theology'. For this reason, Weil's ideas will be explored against the backdrop of the nineteenth-century intellectual tradition to which she owed her early formation. This tradition, known as French spiritualism, drew on an Augustinian understanding of mystical prayer in which grace is a key feature and in which the value of spiritual exercise lies not principally in exertion but in the ability to let go of effort and abandon the will. But the purpose of French spiritualism was to understand the nature of human experience as such and to this extent it relied on a psychological approach distinct from doctrinal concerns.

Fundamental to Weil's ideas and to spiritualism more broadly is the concept and practice of 'attention'. It is a concept which has become singularly important for the philosophy of spiritual exercise today. 'Attention' is used to indicate a state of concentration distinct from and superior to everyday attitudes, a claim which is often cited but rarely interrogated or validated. Frequently, attention is contrasted to passivity and opposed to every form of inactivity.[6] But in Augustinian mysticism, attention (at its most intense) is analysed in terms of passivity, and when Maine de Biran, the father of French spiritualism, first argued for the centrality of attention in the constitution of conscious life – a riposte to the passivism of Condillac's statue – it was to unsettle any valorization of effort and insist on the irreducible presence of both action and passion in every psycho-physical operation.[7] Similarly, when Weil needed to name the 'negative effort' characteristic of both philosophy and spiritual exercise, she called it 'attention'.[8] To arrive at such definitions of attention both Biran and Weil drew on Augustinian methods of introspection, mediated to them through the writings of François Fénelon, Jean-Jacques Rousseau and John of the Cross, among many other figures. It is the argument of this book that the concept best capable of interrogating the philosophy of spiritual exercise will be recovered through a re-engagement with the paradox of passive attention.

To understand spiritual exercise and philosophical practice in this way, as formations of 'negative effort', is to ask difficult questions of the critical theory which, in the twentieth and twenty-first centuries, has wanted to reclaim spiritual exercise as positive technique. To this end, I address the pivotal role which effort has played in the recent philosophical retrieval of spiritual exercise. Principal in this movement has been Pierre Hadot, but, unusually for a book on philosophy and spiritual exercise, mine is not an extended response to his work. Turning to Weil rather than Hadot, I argue that much contemporary theorization of spiritual exercise is based on a selective reading of ancient practices that leaves out the crucial element of passivity – of relaxation, effortlessness and desire – without which exercise alone is merely tiredness and so much passion spent. This is where Weil's background and intellectual thought-world become important. In French spiritualism a guiding question was how the mystics' ideal of grace related to and questioned the Stoics' ideal of effort, both morally and psychologically; and this is the question unasked by the philosophy of spiritual exercise today. But the decision to read with Weil rather than Hadot matters for historical as well as philosophical reasons. Hadot's ideas, though now often treated as *sui generis,* emerged out of the same intellectual milieu as did those of Weil, his older contemporary. My interest in the subject of philosophy and spiritual exercise began during my doctoral work as I set out to understand how two such different approaches – those of Hadot and of Weil – could have emerged from the same thought-world. I had discovered by then that there was some philosophical connection between Hadot and Henri Bergson, for whom effort was a central idea and the key to understanding the connection between philosophy and spiritual exercise. I also knew that Weil had disliked Bergson's philosophy. Spurred on by these findings, I began to write the history of effort as a governing ideal in modern French thought. This work was reflected in an article on 'The God of Effort: Bergson and the Stoicism of Modernity', which was published in *Modern Theology* 32:3 (2016) and which became Chapter 4 of the present book. After this, the problem that remained was to work out the genealogy of Weil's alternative approach to spiritual exercise. I returned to the study of Weil's precursors and found that the origin, ultimately, of Weil's understanding of spiritual exercise – via some considerable detours, one of them being Weil's teacher, Alain (Émile Chartier) – was Biran's spiritualism. It also became obvious to me that it would be necessary to write more about Biran, his influences and the fate of his thought during the late nineteenth century. How did this Augustinian current survive; but, equally, what were the reasons it met with such resistance? The presentation of Biran and his main follower, Félix Ravaisson, in Chapters 2 and 3, is the result of that research, and will prepare the reader for my interpretation of Weil's philosophy in Chapter 5, and for my comparison of Weil and Hadot at the end of that chapter. I had thought to leave out of this work the question of passivity in the philosophy of spiritual exercise after Weil, as I treat of it separately elsewhere. But I saw that this was not possible. There are a number of ways in which recent philosophers, realizing how urgent is the need now for better, more sustainable, practices of attention, are rediscovering the concept of spiritual passivity independently of its traditional context yet in ways that mark the current epoch as, in many respects, a very late spiritualism or, perhaps better, a new Augustinianism in matters of ethics. My remarks on the critique of effort and the role of a spiritualist approach to spiritual exercises today are given in the Epilogue and build on an article, 'Attention in the Anthropocene: On the Spiritual Exercises of Any Future Science', published in *Political Geology: Active Stratigraphies and the Making of Life*, edited by Adam Bobbette and Amy Donovan (2018).

There is no recent study in English on the significance of French spiritualism as a whole and very few books in any language that deal with it as a philosophy of spiritual exercise. When I began, my principal guide was Henri Gouhier's *Les conversions de Maine de Biran* (1948), which includes a remarkable study of Biran and Fénelon. In 2014, Clare Carlisle's *On Habit* was published. This book investigates a central question of spiritual exercise – habit – through (among others) spiritualist philosophers; it discusses the ideas of Biran, Ravaisson and Bergson, and places them in the context of current debates. It has been important to me, particularly in its appreciation for grace and passivity, though its arguments follow lines that are quite different from this book. I have also benefitted immensely from David Marno's *Death Be Not Proud: The Art of Holy Attention* (2016), an archaeology of passivity in early modern spiritual exercise with special relevance to the French context. Other books and articles that I have found particularly helpful are: Michel Spanneut, *Permanence du Stoïcisme de Zénon à Malraux* (1973); William J. Bouwsma, 'The Two Faces of Humanism: Stoicism and Augustinianism in Renaissance Thought' in *A Usable Past: Essays in European Cultural History* (1990); Gavin Flood, *The Ascetic Self: Modernity, Subjectivity and Tradition* (2004); Christopher Brooke, *Philosophic Pride: Stoicism and Political Thought from Lipsius to Rousseau* (2012); Charly Coleman, *The Virtues of Abandon: An Anti-Individualist History of the French Enlightenment* (2014).

The present book is motivated by a concern to place Weil's idea of spiritual exercise in an historical context but it also aims to provide an alternative way for thinking about philosophy as spiritual exercise and art of living. It especially aims to clarify, through the history of French spiritualism, the significance of passivity for philosophical practice today. Weil's contemporary, the cultural critic Josef Pieper, once identified a suspicion of passivity orienting modernity's all-encompassing fascination with work. When leisure is refused as laxity, so is the joy which comes with leisure and the recognition that, as Weil puts it in one of her essays, 'we have to press on and loosen up alternatively, just as we breathe in and out'.[9] For thinkers such as Pieper and Weil, the purpose of writing about passivity and interrogating effort was not to deny effort's significance, but, to the contrary, show that while effort is a factor in life, effort is not the only factor. In the organic as well as the moral life, active effort and passive receptivity depend upon one another. Yet many philosophers, from the ancient Cynics to Kant, have insisted that the good was equivalent to effort.

> So, effort is good. Now, this is an image that still (or, once more?) has a certain compelling attraction: from the motto of Erasmus to the philosophy of Kant, who used the word 'Herculean' to praise the heroism of the philosophers, and on to Thomas Carlyle, the prophet of the religion of Work: 'You must labour like Hercules.'[10]

The fascination with effort recognized by Pieper in the 1940s shows no sign of abating. When, today, spiritual practice and meditation are proving more popular than ever before, what attracts is rarely the leisure that celebrates the end of work and more often the rigours of self-improvement which make effort its own end and reward. As one critic points out, for modernity there is properly no religion, only 'misunderstood regimens'.[11] Whether such reduction of religion to the effort of self-improvement is a general truth or a necessary consequence of how spiritual exercise has evolved is the subject of this book.

SIMONE KOTVA
Cambridge, Emmanuel College, 20 May 2020

Acknowledgements

This book began as a doctoral dissertation and I would like to thank especially Douglas Hedley and Catherine Pickstock, my supervisors, for their support and encouragement. Jacob Sherman and Clare Carlisle Tresch, my doctoral examiners, provided invaluable comments, and John Milbank and Boris Gunjević offered helpful criticism at key moments; Keith Ansell-Pearson and the series editors gave perceptive criticism of the manuscript as a whole. I am grateful to Oliver Soskice for instructing me in the art of attention and to David Jackson, Michael Martin Badier and Samuel Järnegard Fogelvik for checking translations (all remaining faults are my own). Victor Emma-Adamah's generous reading has saved me from numerous errors. Simon Jackson and Freja Simonsdotter share my work and make it a joy, as do my family in Sweden and North America.

Over the years many people have contributed to the form of my research: Marco Andreacchio, Silvianne and Barnabas Aspray, Hjördis Becker-Lindenthal, Jack Belloli, Mårten Björk, Adam Bobbette, Patricia Boulhousa, Christopher Burlinson, Johannes Börjesson, Raphael Cadenhead, Christian Coppa, Gwendolen Dupré, Melissa and Zachary Guiliano, Ryan Haecker, Alexander Hampton, Emelie Hasselgren, Simon Henriksson, Isidoros Katsos, Laura McCormick Kilbride, Robin Kirkpatrick, Jon Mackenzie, Robert Macfarlane, Philip McCosker, Mary-Ann Middelkoop, Ragnar Misje Bergem, Sebastian Milbank, John Munns, Elizabeth Powell, Ruth and Simon Ravenscroft, Arabella and James Robinson, Jon Sanders, Ola Sigurdson, Alice Tarbuck, Hugo Ticciati, Alica Tserkovnaja, Diederik Vergunst, Giles Waller, Hanna Weibye, Feronia Wennborg and Nicola Wilkes. Early versions of chapters were presented at seminars in Cambridge, Gothenburg, London and Durham, and I am thankful to the conveners for their invitations and to the helpful comments from the staff and students present. The Bill and Melinda Gates Foundation, and the Gwyn funds at Emmanuel College, funded my time at Cambridge as a doctoral student, and a Research Fellowship at Emmanuel College allowed me to complete this book. Particular thanks are due to the Master and Fellows of Emmanuel College for providing a generous and caring environment.

The late John Hughes, who supervised the MPhil essay which was to become the germ of the present work, was a significant influence and now much missed. He commented on an early outline of my doctoral research, and, at the time of his death, had challenged me to think more deeply about the philosophy of Simone Weil. The present book – a contribution to our unfinished exchange – is dedicated to his memory, and I would like to thank Jeremy Caddick for inviting me to give the sermon in honour of John, 'Work and Rest', from which the theme of this book emerged.

The publishers thank Mark Sinclair for permission to cite from Félix Ravaisson, *Selected Essays* (London: Bloomsbury, 2017).

Note on text and translations

This book is concerned with French intellectual and literary culture; my aim has been to write for an Anglophone audience and wherever possible I have made use of existing translations. Where no English translation has been to hand I have supplied my own version. I have given the English translation of any untranslated titles in brackets, and, when first cited, have indicated the original year of publication or the date of composition in the case of works posthumously edited. For standard texts where many translations exist, I have added section references in brackets. All translations from the Bible are from the New Revised Standard Version.

1

The spiritual exercise of philosophy: Two ideals

Spiritual exercise has been used to understand the method of philosophy ever since the early modern period and retains to this day its hold upon the imagination. The motivation is not difficult to fathom. In its most general sense, spiritual exercise is a means of focussing attention, and philosophy is said to begin with attention, or the ability to wonder and look closely at the world.[1] The father of the modern discipline of spiritual exercise, Ignatius of Loyola, for this reason contrasted the concentration demanded by spiritual exercise with distraction, arguing that periodic retreat allowed the practitioner to avoid 'having his [sic] understanding divided on many things, but concentrating his care on one thing only, namely, on serving his Creator and benefiting his own soul'.[2] Necessarily, the philosophical innovators of the sixteenth and seventeenth centuries were enthralled by the idea. Suspicious of scholastic logic and book-learning, René Descartes nonetheless desired the same clear vision of truth aimed at by the pre-moderns. And now here was a simple method. Relying on nothing but attention, how easily might not humanity become, at last, masters and possessors of nature. With the early modern transformation of spiritual exercise into a scientific method, philosophy would realize what had previously been considered a wholly religious enterprise. Soon the desire to converse with God in prayer was removed from its contemplative context. In these two forms – the one religious and the other in effect methodological – spiritual exercise has been represented in modern European philosophy which is, in the broadest sense, the subject of this book.

Spiritual exercise is a tradition with a long history. Yet most of the authors I will be considering here wrote in the nineteenth century. It is my claim, however, that the tradition of nineteenth-century philosophy that frames my discussion – French spiritualism – draws on spiritual exercise in ways that address directly the question of philosophical method which has become significant in recent years. There are today many studies which, following the example of Pierre Hadot, use spiritual exercise to question the notion that philosophy begins with theory. Presentations of philosophy as 'therapy', 'practice' and 'technique' point to a growing sense that knowledge does not resemble a Newtonian constant but a morphic field, its evolving outlines shaped by habits, accumulated actions and unconscious desires. Such studies, however, begin with the assumption that philosophy, presented as exercise, prioritizes practice over theory; even that practice and theory are fundamentally opposed. My purpose is to show both the potency of this opposition – how it has come to organize everyday life – and with what resistance it has been met. It is my claim that in order to appreciate the questioning which spiritual exercise brings to bear on philosophy it is necessary to study the relation between the ethical and the way of thinking called 'metaphysics'. As such, this book is aimed at both philosophers and theologians, with the hope that it will clarify how exercise – skilled, failed and resumed – has shaped and continues to shape the modern condition.[3]

I

First, however, the claim that the significance of spiritual exercise today rides on an apparent opposition between ethics and metaphysics demands justification. For it would seem that any exercise qualified by 'spirit' is already pointing towards the invisible and so admits to principles and foundations in excess of practice.[4] What, then, are the motivations, in past centuries and our own, that could lead spiritual exercise to detach itself from the spiritual? The answer to this question will begin with a distinction between two ideals of spiritual exercise: one that tends to emphasize effort, or what a person can achieve of their own volition, the other that tends to focus instead on passivity, or what a person can achieve by letting go of the will and surrendering to a more-than-human power. How the two ideals are weighed and related to one another will determine the way the 'spiritual' in 'spiritual exercise' is understood. In brief, where effort is the principal interest, spirit tends to diminish in significance. Conversely, where passivity is recognized – and its associated affects, such as receptivity, relaxation and abandonment – the sense of the 'spiritual' typically will increase.

The first, active and exertive interpretation of spiritual exercise is not easy to grasp as it has become very widespread. The idea that happiness is the result of the hard work applied by an individual to themselves makes itself known in a variety of ways. The influential work of Pierre Hadot is one straightforward example. In *Philosophy as a Way of Life: Spiritual Exercises from Socrates to Foucault* (1981–7), Hadot chose to refer to ancient philosophy as a form of *spiritual* exercise. 'Attention (*prosoche*)', he claimed, 'is the fundamental Stoic spiritual attitude.'[5] It was a bold statement, claiming an affinity between the spiritual exercise tradition of Christian writers like Ignatius of Loyola and Stoic philosophers like Epictetus and Marcus Aurelius. Yet for Hadot the appeal of identifying Stoicism with spiritual exercise lay precisely in the degree to which it could show philosophy to be quite distinct from metaphysical concerns – concerns which, in the case of the Stoics no less than Ignatius, involved all manner of cosmological and theological beliefs. 'This, of course', he admits, 'presupposes that we reduce these philosophies to their spirit and essence, detaching them from their outmoded cosmological or mythical elements, and disengaging from them the fundamental propositions that they themselves considered essential.'[6] In other words, while Hadot recognized the significance of 'spiritual' matters for the originators of spiritual exercise, he contended that it was possible to perform spiritual exercises without the spiritual elements fundamental to the context for which they were written. From this striking shift in perspective, two results follow. In the first place, the 'spirit and essence' of spiritual exercise are perceived to be distinct from the concerns one might otherwise recognize as 'spiritual': belief in spirits, gods and more-than-human powers – the sort of concerns that occupied the ancient Stoics and Ignatius. In the second place, and in lieu of the 'spiritual' in the sense of the more-than-human, Hadot's definition of spiritual exercise becomes centred on the sphere of the individual human and what the individual may achieve through their own efforts. 'Philosophy was a way of life, both in its exercise and effort to achieve wisdom,' writes Hadot.[7] In an interview with his English translator, Hadot stated succinctly the purpose of spiritual exercises as a form of internal work: 'We must ... fortify ourselves by preparing ourselves against hardships in advance.'[8] In other words, where the spiritual in spiritual exercise was concerned, metaphysics would proceed from ethics, or, what for Hadot came to the same thing, from effort.[9]

We shall have occasion to return to Hadot; for now, I will remark that although the idea of achieving wisdom through individual effort certainly is not foreign to ancient philosophy and forms an important part of the overall method of spiritual exercise, even Socrates – the perennial model for philosophers and Hadot's principal source of inspiration – did not consider such wisdom possible by effort alone. After all, to argue that human reason, and so human effort, may be limited in relation to wisdom and unable to comprehend it fully is the philosophical meaning behind the *daimon* or 'spirit' that in Plato's dialogues interrupts Socrates' thoughts at crucial points; as it is, also, the philosophical meaning behind the gods and oracles from which Socrates (much to the embarrassment of his interlocutors) claims to receive knowledge.[10] 'Receive' is the key word here, for what *spiritual* exercise – as distinct from human effort – draws attention to is the significance, for wisdom, of a style of thinking and doing that is different from effort and yet not separate from it; a style of thinking and doing that the handbooks of spiritual exercise would call 'receptive' and would associate, closely, with the experience of intuition, inspiration, illumination and other 'passive' modes of knowing distinct from the 'active' modes associated with reason and intellect. As David Marno has shown in a recent series of important studies, even when a writer like Ignatius praises effort and encourages a strict discipline of meditation, the *Spiritual Exercises* (1522–4) acknowledges that the 'spiritual relish and fruit' of meditation may arrive through divine illumination – spontaneously, and with no effort on the part of the meditator.[11] Spiritual relish might be achieved by effort, but it might also be received unsolicited, through grace. Here it is deliberately unclear whether what the spiritual exercise does is to prepare for, rather than directly solicit, grace. Several later writers in the same tradition responded keenly to this problem. The guided meditations of Francis de Sales, John of the Cross and François Fénelon, for instance, argue that to present prayer as a voluntary effort was to ignore entirely the weakness of the will, for no amount of voluntary effort could conjure up God or happiness or virtue. They addressed this *aporia* by understanding meditation as an activity that was easy as well as difficult, more like 'waiting' than willing. Instead of attention achieving grace by its own efforts, a degree of passivity ensured that attention, in Marno's words, 'prepare[d] for divine grace without taking any action to solicit it'.[12]

Such alternative traditions of spiritual exercise, Marno argues, in which effort is not elevated but subjected to scrutiny, and in which passivity serves as the metaphor for thinking through the idea of wisdom, remained significant throughout the early modern period and persisted into the twentieth century. And Marno mentions what is undoubtedly the most famous example: the work of the French philosopher and mystic Simone Weil.[13] When Weil wanted to explain the practice of prayer she drew on John of the Cross, calling 'attention' (*l'attention*) 'waiting' (*l'attente*).[14] Weil's most striking idea, attention as 'waiting' was an attempt to understand the nature of spiritual exercise in ways that did not rely wholly on the will. In prayer a person makes an effort to meditate and pay attention, and yet there is no expectation that attention itself will produce grace, for grace arrives unsolicited. So attention is both active and passive; it is, she explained, a 'kind of passive activity' or a 'negative effort'.[15] Weil took this concept of passive attention very far, using it to question what she saw as modern culture's valorization of the will and of 'muscular effort' more generally. We tend, said Weil, to think about attention as something one does in order to achieve a goal, when in fact any philosopher will tell you that they arrived at their greatest discoveries not when they were exerting themselves to the utmost but when they were no longer trying and had as it were become unconscious of the fact of paying attention. Prayer, she thought, operated in exactly the same way, and so did philosophical method. In order to find the truth, it is necessary to set out in search for it, but it is also necessary to desist from trying too hard. Neither action nor passivity grounds spiritual exercise; it is the paradox of effort and grace that shapes it.

Weil's intuitions guide the enquiry into the philosophy of spiritual exercise undertaken in this book. While few now read her as a philosopher of spiritual exercise, recent developments in the study of attention have rediscovered her ideas and offer an opportunity to address philosophy's ambivalence over passivity, and more importantly to better our understanding of the nature of spiritual exercise itself. In the last two decades, philosophers and critics have begun to take seriously the idea of passivity in attention and to theorize it, often with particular reference to Weil. Marno we have already mentioned. In his study of John Donne's poetry, *Death Be Not Proud: The Art of Holy Attention* (2016), Marno discusses the dynamics of what he calls 'easy attention', a concept drawn from the same early modern sources that also inspired Weil. Marno's idea of 'easy attention' is very close to Weil's idea of 'passive activity', and I will be returning to it later on when thinking about the togetherness of action and passivity in spiritual exercise.[16] I will also consider, briefly, the work of Iris Murdoch, who drew on Weil's concept of passive attention in her moral philosophy, using it to scrutinize not only what she – like Weil – recognized as modernity's tendency to valorize human effort, but also what she perceived to be modernity's tacit (and sometimes not so tacit) elevation of chauvinist ideals.[17] And there are other thinkers one might discuss: at around the same period that Murdoch took impression from *Waiting on God*, Weil was the subject of Giorgio Agamben's earliest scholarship, which has since been characterized by a concern for passivity and a recognition of weakness at the centre of human experience. Although Agamben is not dealt with here, many of the arguments in the present chapter will be found to resonate with the 'weak thought' and philosophy of radical passivity that has developed around and beyond Agamben's thought in the work of figures like Gianni Vattimo and, more recently, Marika Rose.[18]

II

But quite aside from Weil and the influence of her ideas on later thinkers, the questions she raises speak to a long history of philosophers choosing to think with passivity as a way of kicking back against the norms of modern Western culture. From Jean-Jacques Rousseau, Friedrich Schelling and the Romantic philosophers, to the Frankfurt school and the phenomenology of Michel Henry, there are many who have challenged modernity's fascination with effort. Whenever Enlightenment ideals are questioned, whenever philosophers confront the prerogatives of the 'active' faculties of reason, renewed attention will be given to the 'passive' faculties of intuition, feeling and pleasure; the ascetic's fear of the body and desire to conquer its passions thus becomes contrasted, typically, with another kind of asceticism, one that would cultivate instead an intense enjoyment of 'passive' embodiment.[19] Even, Friedrich Nietzsche, who celebrated the will and self-discipline (and who, like Hadot, praised the Stoics), was suspicious of self-discipline when allied to power. For those thinkers who have followed on from Nietzsche's approach to philosophy as an imperative to work on oneself – such as Gilles Deleuze, Michel Foucault and Peter Sloterdijk in particular – asceticism operates as both ideal and caution. The question of recovering the exercise of the will and of self-discipline, of recovering the practice of philosophy in order to think with its concepts – these are seen as mostly inseparably from the realization that discipline for its own sake does not cross paths with wisdom. Effort without repose is like work without pleasure.[20] The researches of Josef Pieper – a philosopher contemporaneous with Weil, and, like her, a keen reader of mysticism – are particularly relevant to this discussion. Pieper's *Leisure: The Basis of Culture* (1948) showed how, in the wake of social Darwinism, twentieth-century culture has tended to equate virtue with strength and, concomitantly, to regard relaxation as a sign of weakness and inferiority.[21] Like Max Weber, Pieper traces modernity's suspicion of relaxation to the success of the protestant work ethic, but he also reaches further back into the centuries. He sketches a long history of philosophers viewing the 'passive' faculties of intuition, feeling and inclination negatively as belonging to 'animal' nature, above which human beings were thought to be elevated precisely through their ability to *exercise* reason 'actively'. He also points to the misogyny implicit in such divisions, evident whenever the active/passive distinction is mapped onto gender binaries and women's thinking becomes associated essentially with the opposite of reason.[22] For Pieper a good example of this modern position in which the good is equated not only with effort but with reason is Immanuel Kant's moral philosophy: 'Indeed, according to Kant, the moral law by definition is opposed to natural inclination.'[23] As a consequence, whatever is good is so through the effort of the will to rise above and conquer 'animal' nature: 'It is simply part of the nature of things that the Good is difficult and that the voluntary effort put into forcing oneself to do something becomes the standard for moral goodness.'[24] Pieper saw a connection here between Kant's account of morality free from leisure and his account of intellectual labour. Kant interpreted philosophy as the result of hard work, likening self-knowledge to a 'Herculean labour'.[25] As a consequence, he was uneasy about intuition, traditionally viewed as a mode of knowledge distinct from ratiocination and from the efforts of the will. Thus, in Aristotle's *Nicomachean Ethics*, the happy life is also the most leisurely life; it is the contemplative life (*bios theoretike*) of the philosopher. For Augustine, Thomas Aquinas and the whole Christian tradition of mystical theology, to be happy was to receive, through intuition, a vision of truth.[26] Commenting on the distinctive feature of intuition – its apparent independence from human effort – when compared to Kant's ideal of intellectual labour, Pieper reflects: 'We have to be awake and active ... [b]ut all the same, it is a "relaxed" looking ... receiv[ing] the things that present themselves to us that come to us without any need for "effort" on our part to "possess" them.'[27] Here the idea of contemplation as a mode of receptivity comes very close to scholastic ideas of grace, and Pieper makes explicit the connection. 'Relaxed looking' is like grace because, just as when receiving a gift, contemplation requires an attitude of receptivity: 'in knowing', argues Pieper, 'the highest form ... comes to one like a gift: it is effortless and not burdensome'.[28]

What is distinct about Pieper's account of philosophy is the way it gives importance not only to spiritual exercise – which is what contemplative or 'relaxed looking' amounts to – but to relaxation. The idea was central to Christian writers for obvious reasons – in Genesis God concludes the work of creation by resting on the seventh day, and repose was considered the form of the divine life and of grace – but it is already there among the philosophical schools that preceded Christianity. The Stoics revered Hercules' labours but they also praised leisure or *skhole* and celebrated as a state of blessedness (*makaria*) effortless repose. Wisdom was to remain constant and act always in moderation. Indeed, tranquillity or *ataraxia* was seen by both Stoic and Epicureans as the purpose of philosophy.[29] Yet in the literature on philosophy as a way of life and spiritual exercise, especially the popular work that has developed from Hadot, Stoicism has more often been associated with effort than with repose, even though, as Hadot acknowledges in *Philosophy as Way of Life*: 'To cure the soul, it is not necessary, as the Stoics would have it, to train it to stretch itself tight, but rather to train it to relax'.[30] And, as André-Jean Festugière – another writer contemporaneous with Weil – once argued, it is possible to see in Epicurus a 'spiritual director' offering perennial resistance to the cult of the hero, wherever and whenever it takes form.[31] 'Always, from age to age Hercules and his labours kept their value as an example', reflected Festugière in *Epicurus and His Gods* (1946), and thus 'called forth an ethic of struggle and effort'.[32] By training the soul to relax Epicurus challenged the heroic equivalence between virtue and effort and pointed, instead, to the equal importance of leisure when it comes to happiness. Moreover, Festugière thought, Epicurus' spiritual direction was not the decadent affair evident even in Hadot's juxtaposition of Stoicism with Epicureanism. Epicurean pleasure is frugal; at the heart of the Epicurean life was the practice of holding common meals and modest banquets among friends. Seen from the point of view of the communal meal, relaxation and pleasure are not indulgences but necessities.[33]

With the help of Pieper and Festugière – and Weil, Murdoch, Marno and other critics of effort – we can start to understand better the reasons and unspoken assumptions behind the modern outlook on philosophy as a spiritual exercise. It may be said to be motivated by a desire to improve the self through the cultivation of good habits. This is its positive attraction, for what spiritual exercise promises is a happy life and a virtuous disposition. Work is essential to this image; work which the individual performs on themselves for the sake of their own and others' benefit. The impulse towards exercise presents, in this way, a portrait of the individual labouring as part of a flourishing community. But this image, hedged about, as it so often is, with goodness couched as self-fortification, valour and struggle, easily degenerates into a single-minded pursuit of power. In what follows, I will propose an alternative way of thinking about the nature of spiritual exercise and its relation to philosophical method. Crucial to this alternative account is the now mostly neglected tradition of mystical prayer significant to Weil as it was also to Pieper, and key figures from this tradition will appear throughout what follows. But before Weil learnt about mystical prayer from John of the Cross her thinking on passive attention had already been shaped by an intervening tradition of nineteenth-century thought. Known as French spiritualism, it combined elements of mystical spirituality with a psychological approach, challenging the heroic ideal in philosophy and proposing new critiques of philosophical method in light of passivity and the concept of grace. It is this tradition which forms the basis for the present enquiry into the spiritual in exercise.

What is the significance of French spiritualism for the philosophy of spiritual exercise? Instead of addressing the question in broad strokes, I want to sketch an incident that may indicate an answer. It is a brief event in the life of a young philosopher who was to become the inspiration for French spiritualism, but it is also a paradigmatic description of philosophical therapy considered as a dialectic of activity and passivity. His later readers (for this event was recorded in a diary that became known first after the author's death) would have been familiar with both the style and the content of the incident described. As such, the incident becomes significant for thinking about spiritual exercise as a whole, and for those who, like Weil would later do, sought to resist the sanguine claims of effort when it came to philosophy's cure.

III

At sundown on 27 May 1794 Maine de Biran took a solitary stroll on his family estate at Grateloup, near Bergerac. Later that same evening Biran recorded the walk in his *journal intime* or private journal. The purpose of this journal was therapeutic: Biran, who suffered from a chronically impaired digestion, used literary introspection to understand and improve his condition. The entry dated 27 May is long, covering half a dozen pages of close script. Though it is a fragment never intended for publication, the account is detailed and follows a clear line of argument. At its centre, and the reason Biran gives for committing the walk to writing, is an experience: a 'state of rapture' (*état de ravissement*) which overcame the twenty-eight-year-old walker unexpectedly as he took in the fair weather and beauty of spring. The event caused Biran to feel physically at ease, and in response to this rapturous state there transpires, over the course of the entry, a whole psychology of happiness.

Biran begins the entry by describing the *mise en scène*:

> Today, the 27th of May, I experienced an occasion too sweet, too remarkable in its rarity that I should ever forget it. I was walking alone, a few moments before sundown: the weather was very beautiful; the freshness of things, the charm which, together, they offer in this brilliant period of spring that is felt so keenly by the soul but which is always weakened as one seeks to describe it; everything that struck my senses carried to my heart something sweet and sad; there were tears in the corners of my eyes.[34]

Biran then attempts to relate what he experienced during these brief and unforgettable moments, but finds it difficult. 'How many rapturous sensations have succeeded one another!' he exclaims, 'And now that I would like to give an account, how cold I feel!' If, Biran reasons, he could secure the state of rapture permanently, he would have gained the joys of heaven on earth. 'But', he confesses, 'an hour of this sweet calm will be followed by the usual agitation of my life; I already feel that this state of rapture is far from me: it is not made for a mortal.' With the return of physical discomfort, happiness, he concludes, is not permanent:

> Everything influences us and we constantly change with what surrounds us. I am often amused to observe the various situations of my soul flow by; they pass like the waves of a river, sometimes calm, sometimes agitated, but always succeeding one another without permanence.[35]

In the pages that follow we are impressed by a person for whom true happiness is above all rest, calm and repose. Such a position, Biran is aware, questions the commonplace notion that happiness may be achieved through voluntary effort. Mostly, Biran – the *malade* weakened by illness – rejects the idea that happiness is procured through effort and employs tranquillity to resist the 'pride' (*orgueil*) that seemed to come with effort.[36] During the solitary stroll, he had done nothing to solicit rapture; happiness had arrived spontaneously, by 'instantaneous access'. In relation to happiness, then, Biran finds himself entirely passive:

> But to procure for myself these delicious feelings, this peace of the soul, this interior calm which I experience through instantaneous access, I feel that I can do nothing, my activity is null, I am absolutely passive in my sentiments: almost always I am that which I would not want to be and almost never am I that which I aspire to be. On what, then, does the state of my soul depend; whence come these confused, tumultuous feelings through which I no longer know myself? I flee agitation and in spite of my efforts ceaselessly it is reproduced within me; my will exercises no power over my moral state.[37]

And so on. What is significant here is less the setting (the walk itself is nowhere detailed) than the philosophical reflection that arises from it. Biran is using the evidence of his solitary stroll to cast light on human nature. As he affirms his passivity and powerlessness, we hear echoes of St Paul. 'For I do not do the good I want, but the evil I do not want is what I do.'[38] Like Paul, Biran knows the good – rest, repose – but cannot achieve it, for embodied life is all effort, not least in the situation where one uses effort to *remain* calm! At the same time, Biran, like Paul, is convinced that happiness is not unattainable, for he has experienced it. The rapture was real; the question is simply what role, if any, effort played in its realization.

Towards the end of this journal entry Biran broadens his analysis of happiness. A different kind of effort enters into view. Biran considers that there are those who do not experience the same inner struggle as himself; persons for whom virtue is not an effort and to whom happiness comes spontaneously. Yet if life is unthinkable without effort, then how to explain the state of these happy persons?

Biran's response is to examine the whole life of the happy person. He finds that what makes a person virtuous is a formation of character that begins in childhood. 'Happy are those', he writes, 'who in their youth and when their character is not yet formed, can enjoy the society of truly enlightened people who direct them.'[39] A child surrounded by good persons will imitate the good and so become good themselves. What for Biran is significant in this idea is that imitation is an effort, and yet it is quite different from the kind of effort which characterizes the miseries of his own life. By imitating another's example, the effort which began as a voluntary activity eventually becomes, through habit, a second – or 'good' – nature. 'These [wise persons] are models he has before him', Biran explains, referring to the imagined youth: 'he makes efforts to get closer to them and to put himself in unison with them, he is forced to cultivate his good nature … By dint of work to be equal to them, he would probably end up becoming better.'[40] In other words, what Biran is describing as happiness is not a complete absence of effort but effort that is not experienced as a struggle; work which is motivated by desire and so is easy despite the labour involved. Fascinated, like all his contemporaries, by education, much of what Biran explains as the roots of his misery thus is traced to bad schooling, to a lack of good examples and an absence of proper habituation:

> If I had possessed and if I still possessed such happiness, maybe I would derive some fruit from it? But without help, delivered to myself and to vices maintained through so many years of dissipation (and forgetfulness of myself), what continual and repulsive work I must undertake in order to achieve the goal of wisdom that I propose! Everything I see turns me away from my projects. Even when I am isolated and retired, there are still too many bad examples. I have enough to do, when on my own, to reform, to exclude all the pitiful thoughts, all the senseless desires which present themselves to my imagination and oppose the exercise of my reason … I am no longer myself, I lie to myself, I say stupid things with conviction, I make a thousand mistakes.[41]

With the raptures of his solitary stroll momentarily forgotten, Biran returns to his own present state. Deprived of good habits, burdened by a misspent youth, wisdom becomes difficult and the good seems remote. 'What a torment to see the good, to love it', he complains, 'when one does not have enough character to embrace virtue and hold it there without any encouragement!'[42] Part of his difficulties he blames on the distractions of society, for even when retired to his country estate there are too many people, too many 'bad examples'. Wistfully he looks back to a time when public life was oriented to the good; he yearns for the academies and schools of the ancient Greeks, for Plato and Socrates. In lieu of such living examples there are books, but books, writes Biran, cannot speak and are in themselves powerless to change the reader. Desultorily he walks through the masters then fashionable and admired: Rousseau, who 'speaks to his heart' but whose reasoning distresses him; Michel de Montaigne, who 'pleases' him but whose doubts leave him in a 'painful state'; Gabriel Bonnot de Mably, who makes Biran 'love the good' but whose example tires him; Blaise Pascal, who 'elevates his thoughts' but whose melancholy temper 'penetrates everywhere'. Then, in a turn characteristic of Biran's style, he proposes a solution: 'O good Fénelon, come and console me! Your divine writings will dispel the veil with which your Jansenist adversary had covered my heart, as the sweet purple of the dawn hunts the sad darkness.'[43] Such writings as Fénelon's, he concludes, come closest to the divine examples of the ancients.

Biran's entry summarizes the dilemmas facing the philosopher for whom wisdom is an exercise and for whom happiness, well-being and health are the result of habit. He presents no new ideas; indeed, the entry is replete with commonplaces regarding the philosopher's need for isolation and retreat in order to cultivate good habits. Nonetheless, there is something striking about the scene and about Biran's analysis of it. This is borne out by the invocation to Fénelon with which Biran ends his account. As Charly Coleman has shown, the Bishop of Combrai represents the impetus to a reactionary current in French thought. This current, which would become important in the Romantic period, was closely associated with Quietism and a pre-existing tradition of mystical prayer. Fénelon, though he repelled the charges of Quietism levelled against him, presented a strong argument for the Quietist notion of 'abandonment': in order to achieve the good, a person should abandon their soul to the inspiration of God's grace. Such abandonment, argued Fénelon, would lead to a state of quiet repose and peace. Coleman has demonstrated how important Fénelon's ideas were for shaping French thought up until and including Rousseau, for whom the relationship of the individual to the general will was modelled on Fénelon's idea of abandonment to God.[44] But Fénelon's widely read *Maxims of the Saints* (1697) and spiritual letters also left lasting marks on French philosophy as a whole, and nowhere as clearly as on spiritualism.

'Spiritualism', a term that first appears at the end of the seventeenth century, was from the very beginning associated with Fénelon's mystical theology. References to Fénelon's spiritual writings are frequent in Biran's diaries, and key allusions also appear in the oeuvre of Félix Ravaisson, the thinker who succeeded in attaching Biran's philosophy definitively to the banner of 'spiritualism'. In 1867, Ravaisson famously recognized the future of French philosophy as a 'realism or positivist spiritualism', and what he had in mind then was a vision of universal peace along Fénelon's lines: 'beneath the disorder and antagonisms that agitate the surface where phenomena occur, at bottom, in the essential and eternal verity, everything is grace, love and harmony.'[45] While spiritualism has since been interpreted in a variety of ways, to Ravaisson's contemporaries, at least, the connection between Biran's spiritualism and Fénelon's theology of spiritual exercise was conspicuous. In 1883 Paul Janet, the historian of philosophy, even remarked how spiritualism showed 'that Quietism and mysticism are true'.[46] But Quietism was never an uncontested term (in France, it was associated with divisive politics) and those same Quietist notions of passivity – of grace, repose and abandonment – that provided Biran's philosophy with its founding moment are also the concepts from which later spiritualism sought to free itself. This is evident in the first major modern study of French spiritualism, Dominique Janicaud's *Ravaisson et la métaphysique: une géneaologie du spiritualisme français* (1969), which argued that despite some superficial similarities, nineteenth-century spiritualism remained quite different from the work of early modern 'spiritual' writers such as Fénelon.[47] This was a significant statement, for it left out the whole tradition of mystical prayer that had influenced spiritualist methods. In part Janicaud's approach is explained by the fact that his study is a genealogy of the philosophy of Henri Bergson, Ravaisson's successor at the Académie de Sciences Morales et Politiques and perhaps the most influential thinker ever to work with spiritualist ideas. Bergson's interest in mysticism and his conviction that philosophy was a form of spiritual work (the word he often chose to describe philosophical method was 'attention') are well known and need not be repeated here.[48] As Janicaud says, in Bergson's work philosophy continues to be figured as 'a profound methodology of the interior life'.[49] What is less widely recognized is the extent to which Bergson's interpretation of mysticism was quite distinct from earlier spiritualism. The most obvious difference was the importance Bergson assigned to effort in the spiritual life, a fact not unconnected to his interest in vitalism. For Bergson, spirit was the self-expression of effort, and the spiritual life was not really conceivable outside of effort. 'In our eyes', writes Bergson in *The Two Sources of Morality and Religion*

(1932), 'the ultimate end of mysticism is the establishment of a contact ... with the creative effort which life itself manifests. This effort is of God, if it is not God himself. The great mystic is to be conceived as an individual being, capable of ... continuing and extending the divine action.'[50] Ideas like these had an extraordinary impact on French philosophers, not least on Pierre Hadot, whose sense of spiritual exercise we have already mentioned as one deeply preoccupied with effort. I will have opportunity to return to Hadot further on; at present, I note only the echoes of Bergson's sense of the spiritual life in Hadot's work, a debt that Hadot readily acknowledges. What is contemplation, writes Hadot in his study of Plotinian thought, but 'the effort of attention through which the soul tries to maintain herself at the level to which God has raised her ... the ever-renewed effort to remain in a state of contemplation of the Good'.[51] The ideal of unwavering vigilance and perpetually renewed effort, like the image of the mystic who achieves apotheosis in Bergson's *Two Sources*, continues to appear in the philosophy of spiritual exercise descended from Hadot. It is there in Foucault's *History of Sexuality* and his writing on philosophy as a whole; it is there in the work of Sloterdijk.[52] Indeed, it is difficult to think of a major philosopher of spiritual exercise on whom Hadot's image of ever-renewed mental vigilance has not exerted its fascination.

My claim, then, is that Biran's rapture on 27 May 1794 announces, *in nuce*, an alternative philosophy of spiritual exercise that marks the beginning of an uneasiness (articulated in an intimate, personal, voice certainly) with the ideal of effort; an ideal that has since become so ever-present it is rarely questioned. It is a form of the second kind of spiritual exercise sketched earlier, the spiritual exercise caught in the tension between effort and repose and arrested by grace; the spiritual exercise that shaped spiritualism and that drew the interest of Simone Weil. If we study more closely how Biran puts together his account, we will begin to make better sense of the nature of the critique which his 'rapture' announces.

IV

From the very beginning of his diary entry, what strikes the reader about Biran's experience of happiness is the air of tranquillity and calm which surrounds it. Though Biran has not been cured of his bodily discomfort, in the moment of rapture he is no longer troubled by any pain. This is the therapeutic key to the extended framework of Biran's psychology, attractive because it presents the ideal state as one that is embodied yet free from bodily agitation: relaxed and pleasurable.

At first glance, such a presentation of human nature is far from unusual; indeed, it is typical of the period. Though French spiritualism often traces via Ravaisson its inspiration to Biran, the real originator of the philosophical introspection developed by Biran is, *pace* Biran's own caveats, Jean-Jacques Rousseau.[53] The account of Biran's solitary stroll – the events experienced as well as the analysis which Biran gives – evokes in particular Rousseau's *Reveries of a Solitary Walker* (1776–8). This volume, conceived as a recommencement of the *Confessions* (1765–9), continues the rigorous self-examination of that work, but does so in a new register. Exiled and banished from society, Rousseau finds himself depressed by his inability to improve his situation. After a time, however, Rousseau discovers that the cause of his frustration is the result not of his circumstances (which he cannot change) but of his attitude. '[R]ealising eventually that all my efforts were in vain and my self-torment to no avail,' he writes: 'I took the only course left to me, that of submitting to my fate and ceasing to fight against the inevitable.'[54] Once Rousseau learns to accept his new position and ceases to struggle against necessity, he finds himself the master of his own happiness: 'This resignation has made up for all my trials by the peace of mind it brings me, a peace of mind incompatible with the unceasing exertions of a struggle as painful as it was unavailing.'[55] At the core of this conversion is a serious critique of effort. From the perspective of tranquillity, freedom is not the result of effort, but rather the outcome of a negative kind of action. In Rousseau's expression: 'never doing what [one] does not want to do.'[56] This freedom Rousseau contrasts directly with the ideal of effort, for such an ideal, he reflects, connects virtue only with strength and endurance, even making persons slaves to endurance. In Rousseau's Pauline gloss: 'For they, being active, busy, ambitious, detesting freedom in others and not desiring it for themselves, as long as they can sometimes have their way, or rather prevent others from having theirs, they force themselves all their lives to do what they do not want to do and are willing to endure any servitude in order to command.'[57]

The key moment in the *Reveries* appears during the second walk when, awakening to the world after a spell of amnesia (Rousseau has just been run over by a charging Great Dane), he undergoes an epiphany very like the one later experienced by Biran:

> Night was coming on: I saw the sky, some stars, and a few leaves. This first sensation was a moment of delight. I was conscious of nothing else. In this instant I was being born again, and it seemed as if all I perceived was filled with

my frail existence. Entirely taken up by the present, I could remember nothing; I had no distinct notion of myself as a person, nor had I the least idea of what had just happened to me. ... I felt throughout my being such a wonderful calm, that whenever I recall this feeling I can find nothing to compare with it in all the pleasures that stir our lives.[58]

A substantial part of the *Reveries* is spent detailing ways in which Rousseau recreates similar states of rapture as he finds ways in which to concentrate and absorb the self, usually through meditation or a close study of the natural world. In the act of 'attention', a word which Rousseau invests with devotional significance, the solitary walker finds the source of his happiness. Here there is, he says, 'nothing external to us, nothing apart from ourselves and our own existence'. 'As long as this state lasts', he explains, 'we are self-sufficient like God.'[59]

The conditions for Biran's rapture, then, were put in place by Rousseau and the mysticism of tranquillity. Though Rousseau does not refer to Fénelon in the *Reveries*, his indebtedness to the author of the *Maxims of the Saints* is well known, and the *Reveries* in particular evoke Quietist themes to a striking degree.[60] Moreover, Rousseau's reveries are spiritual exercises in the classical sense: they are meditations the purpose of which is virtue, happiness and communion with God.[61] Over the course of them Rousseau reassesses happiness entirely in light of the rapture of awakening to a state of total calm. Like Biran echoing Paul and Fénelon, Rousseau concludes that happiness is repose, and that solitude is of the essence for achieving such states: 'the task I had set myself could only be performed in absolute isolation; it called for long and tranquil meditation which are impossible in the bustle of society life.'[62] It is when distracted by society that happiness becomes impossible and the interior struggle begins:

> When I ought to do the opposite of what I want, nothing will make me do it, but neither do I do what I want, because I am too weak. I abstain from acting, because my weakness is all in the domain of action, my strength is all negative, and my sins are all sins of omission, rarely sins of commission.[63]

How significant such attitudes were for the thinkers to come is clear when we consider the extent to which not only tranquillity and rapture but also meditation – particularly, of course, in close proximity to the natural world – would become ideals for the Romantic generation. In the *Reveries*, Rousseau succeeds in transforming Fénelon's spiritual prayer into a popular way of life that depended on no church – indeed, demanded rather the total isolation of the individual from society – and yet subscribed to the religion of the heart. We may thus see Rousseau as the originator of a modern form of spiritual exercise in which passivity and repose are given important roles.[64]

It would, however, be false to conclude that Biran's style of philosophising sprang fully formed from Rousseau's reveries. For one thing, the key word in Rousseau's account of tranquillity – self-sufficiency – does not figure in Biran's diary entry, nor is Rousseau's name mentioned without being challenged. 'Rousseau speaks to my heart', writes Biran, and yet his 'errors afflict me'.[65] What the errors of Rousseau were Biran does not say, but from his account of the rapture on 27 May 1794 they are not difficult to surmise. Was Biran's experience produced, as Rousseau put it, by 'nothing external to us, nothing apart from ourselves'? Not at all. The rapture of tranquillity arrested Biran from without; in relation to it he felt himself 'entirely passive'. If we look past the vaguely Romantic *mise en scène* in Biran's entry we find a different paradigm of spiritual exercise, older than Rousseau's, and more complex. For though Biran recognizes that there exist, indeed, people capable of preparing themselves for rapture through habit and training, he does not concede, with Rousseau, that such happiness is entirely up to our own efforts. Human nature is deeply paradoxical: both active and passive, at the same time but not in the same way. In light of Biran's appeal to Fénelon, this makes sense, for it is Fénelon who, aside from recognizing repose, is sensitive also to the tension between repose and effort. Seen from this perspective, Biran's philosophical exercise is a late gloss on an ancient theme. This is the theme of struggle co-extensive with repose, of effort with grace, of body with spirit, which we find in every writer attempting spiritual exercise from the time of Augustine onwards.

V

While, in the French tradition, Fénelon is the spiritual instructor of repose *par excellence* it was Augustine who laid the real foundation for this ideal of spiritual exercise. In the *Confessions* Augustine establishes the signposts of a spiritual journey that begins with effort and self-sufficiency, but ends in repose and dependence. What Augustine discovers in his meditations is not, as is so often affirmed, the self (arguably the Stoics, with their sophisticated methods for daily examining the self, had been there long before him) but that on which the self depends for its ability to meditate, attend and reflect: grace. In the background of all of Augustine's work is the challenge posed, to human effort, by grace. Ancient philosophy, including Stoicism (and later in Augustine's career, Pelagius' interpretation of Christianity), proposed that it was possible for a person to be free from fault by their own efforts. This context, we may infer, increased the necessity to defend grace, at the same time as it clarified to Augustine the unavoidable importance of effort when it came to human nature. The *Confessions* are framed by these two insights, especially the final book.[66]

The *Confessions* are written in the form of a prayer addressed to God. By examining his own life before God Augustine hopes to put to rest his inner struggle and attain peace: 'For thou hast created us for thyself', writes Augustine in Book 1, 'and our heart cannot be quieted till it may find repose in thee.'[67] By the time we reach the thirteenth book, the focus has turned wholly to the repose with which restlessness contrasts. Here is Augustine praying to God for 'the peace of quietness':

> Grant, O Lord God, thy peace unto us: for thou hast given us all things. Give us the peace of quietness, the peace of the Sabbath, peace without any evening. For all this most goodly array of things so very good, having finished its course, is to pass away, for both a Morning and an Evening was made in them.[68]

Before Augustine reaches this point in his prayer, however, he submits repose to careful scrutiny: its nature, and, in particular, its relation to effort. Before the Sabbath was, work began. Indeed, human beings were made to serve God, and so to work; in Genesis they are put in the garden of Eden to 'till it and keep it'.[69] Yet God himself is at rest. Moreover, God is not like a garden and has no need of human service: 'I [am not] made to be so assistant to thee with my service as to keep thee from tiring in their working (*in agendo*)', writes Augustine to God, 'or for fear thy power might be less if my service should be wanting: nor so to ply thee with my service, as a man [sic] does his land, that unless I tilled thee thou must lie fallow.'[70] Work, it seems, is both that which characterizes human life as a gift from God and that which separates God from creatures.

The final book of the *Confessions*, then, does not present repose as an uncomplicated ideal for the one who meditates. Give us peace, prays Augustine, and yet creation itself is the result of work, and everything within it – including the meditator – is a busy, working creature. It is as if the meditator lived in two worlds at once, the world of work and the world of the Sabbath. From the vantage of the first world, what God gives to creatures is work; thus, grace appears as effort. Within the *Confessions*, prayer especially is an effort. Throughout, Augustine describes his prayer in several ways that all involve activity: he 'invokes' God, 'attends' to him, 'calls out' to him and so forth. Nowhere does he intimate that such work is useless. It is as essential to Augustine's spiritual journey as the vigilant attention was to the ancient philosophers. But from the vantage of the second world, the world of rest, what God gives to creatures on the final day of creation is peace; thus, grace appears as repose. Now the world of effort looks degenerate and fallen:

> And all things are fair that thou has made; and lo, thyself art ineffably fairer, that madest all these: from whom had not Adam fallen, this brackishness of the sea had never flowed out of his loins: namely, this mankind [sic], so profoundly curious, and so tempestuously swelling, and so restlessly rumbling up and down.[71]

The purpose of the *Confessions* is to reintegrate the world of work with the world of repose. Reflecting on the opening verses of the Genesis narrative, Augustine reasons that the two are not opposed, for otherwise why would God's spirit be said to move over the waters?[72] This means that repose is not the absence of movement but a form (or better, the form) of movement. 'Thy spirit', explains Augustine, is that 'which Moves unchangeably over everything that is changeable.'[73] Spirit is also said to be the gift of God, meaning that neither is grace opposed to movement, because spirit is what moves as such. But to qualify movement as 'unchangeable', is that not to separate it from work? Not so, argues Augustine. 'Our rest is thy gift, our life's place', but some effort must still be made in order to reach it.[74] The difficulty lies in interpreting the effort. If it is voluntary, then virtue is up to us and grace is not freely given. Such a position, as Augustine well knew, would come close to Stoicism. Thus Augustine likens spirit instead to a movement caused by desire: 'My weight is my love: by that I am carried, whithersoever I be carried.'[75] What is different about desire when compared to volition is that it moves a person involuntarily. It is thus possible to perform an effort without trying to, that is, without experiencing effort as something difficult or even intentional. Effort then becomes easy, and it is possible to say, 'In thy good pleasure lies our peace' without contradicting the evident fact of movement and effort. If this is the case with human nature, so much the more in God, the image in which humans were created:

> For then also shalt thou rest in us, as thou now workest in us: and so shall that rest be thine, through his; even as these works are thine through us. But thou, O Lord, dost work always, and rest always too. Nor dost thou see for a time, nor art thou moved for a time, nor dost rest for a time; and yet thou makest those things which are seen in time, yea, the very times themselves, and the rest which proceeds from time.[76]

Augustine's prayer is positioned precariously between the two ideals of effort and repose. Like every spiritual exercise, the *Confessions* seeks to resist distraction through effort, and so achieve a kind of interior harmony or peace. Yet as long as that peace is conceived of as a state opposed to effort, the exercise becomes contradictory. Then it is a question either of using spiritual repose to resist a natural inclination towards effort, or of using natural effort to attain, impossibly, a supernatural state to which effort is in no wise related. In either case the boundary between effort and repose, the natural and the supernatural, would become very rigidly drawn. Hence the importance of Augustine's suggestion that spirit be understood as desire, for desire is natural movement. If spiritual movement is natural, its effort cannot be opposed to the supernatural. This is a paradoxical relationship. What is good is the involuntary movement; at the same time, only the will habituated to see the good will be able to recognize what it loves. This paradox, a familiar device in spiritual exercise, is common in the guided meditations of the early modern writers. In Fénelon's letters of spiritual direction, for instance, though effort is distinct from repose, the two are not divided. Peace does not destroy effort but alters its quality from strain to relaxation: 'You will be happy', advises the author, 'when a true love to Him shall make this duty easy.'[77] The paradox of the spiritual life challenges any sense in which the performance of exercise might be thought to guarantee its result, as it also resists the pessimistic conclusion that effort is useless in relation to repose. It would be absurd to imagine rest without effort, but it would be absurd, likewise, to imagine effort without rest. This allows spiritual exercise to be supernatural or metaphysical without separating itself from effort. Augustinian spiritual exercise is thus an instance of what Pieper called 'receptivity': an ability which is at the same time an inability, evident in the mysterious half-light of spontaneity in which every animal inclination becomes indistinct from supernatural movement.

What is striking, when we read the thirteenth book of the *Confessions* beside Biran's account of his rapture, is the resemblance between the dilemmas posed and the answers given. Augustine's meditator knows what he desires but is constantly thwarted in his ambition to achieve repose. The situation produces an uncertainty which challenges the reliability of his own method in achieving happiness. This leaves only one definite response, definite insofar as it is indefinite: to judge the effort by its spontaneous quality. In other words, to judge the effort by its degree of relaxation. Biran gives his own solitary stroll the same meaning. The 'state of rapture' showed him happiness and yet Biran is incapable of procuring the experience a second time through his own efforts. He is, like Augustine or Paul, contradicted by the efforts of his own will. Like them Biran realizes that what he needs is a character habituated in such way that he would be able to assume the good without struggle. Again, the same response: to procure happiness it is necessary to work well without labouring deliberately for the good. Biran's rapture may be shorn of the spiritual language of prayer, devotion and supplication that we find in Augustine, but it shows, nonetheless, the same basic impulse.[78] The key in this transformation of spiritual exercise is to confront the ideal of repose with a context that is modern without being 'secular'. This transformation is as essential to Biran as it is for spiritualism as a whole. Biran's philosophy has been characterized as a defence of metaphysics in an age of positivism, materialism and scientism. Yet as Biran's example shows, no less than modern science his philosophy attempts to discover truth through experience rather than tradition. The difference is that tradition is not for this reason forgotten or rejected. Such spiritual empiricism, I submit, is the relevance also of spiritualism for today's exercitant.[79]

VI

These paradoxical presentations of effort co-extensive with repose suggest that the nature of a spiritual exercise is more complex than would seem at first glance, perhaps a question of qualitative differences and shifts in intensity rather than one of either relinquishing or making the effort. In any case, it is difficult to avoid passivity, even if the idea of passivity seems to reject everything that is practicable about exercise.

For activity to be passive, it must receive something from beyond itself; it must be in excess of itself. By the *spiritual* I mean this fact of experience in excess of voluntary effort, of which *exercise* is a part. This distinction, it seems to me, is crucial. To a large part, the confusion which surrounds spiritual exercise today emerges from a failure to relate the involuntary to the voluntary when it comes to the effort involved in practices such as meditation, attention or prayer. Confusion is exacerbated when exercise is removed from a context originally metaphysical or 'religious'. As Peter Sloterdijk has seen so clearly, neither a religious nor a secular context saves exercise from becoming, through misuse, utile to regimes of power.[80] Nonetheless, exercise without spirit risks staking its claims wholly on effort; in a word, on power. By contrast, what is conveyed in concepts such as tranquillity, repose and grace are metaphors by means of which the absolute elevations of effort that underwrite every misuse of power might be resisted. Where philosophy, by presenting itself simply as effort, continues to affirm the very category it attempts to avoid, it may be hazardous to reject a spiritual turn that is also cognisant of the 'metaphysical'. It is this fact that, I hope, will allow us to understand better the nature of a spiritual exercise, and the distinction between effort and repose which I have been drawing out.

We have seen several ways in which to consider the relationship between effort and repose when it comes to spiritual exercise. It is possible to construe the relationship as an opposition. Thus one might pit Epicureanism against Stoicism, Augustine against Pelagius, the contemplative life against the active, the pre-modern against the modern and so on. But such dichotomies, with their implications of exclusivity, are useful only to a point. Stoicism, historically the most significant ancient school to be associated with spiritual exercise, demonstrates this well. From the early modern period onwards Stoicism played an important role in French thought. Christopher Brooke has given an account of the original motivations, which we may summarize as being twofold.[81] On the one hand, the influence of Augustine on French intellectual life meant that there were few who sided openly with the Stoics. Both Jerome and Augustine had written against the Stoics, and the well-known comparison between Stoicism and Pelagianism made the ancient school the perennial subject of disparaging remarks. At the core of this criticism was the ideal of *effort*: Stoicism, like Pelagius, was thought to encourage hubris and 'pride' (*orgeuil*) when it promised virtue through effort. On the other hand, new translations of Marcus Aurelius' *Meditations* reminded readers of the many similarities between Stoicism and Christianity. At the heart of this comparison was the ideal of *tranquillity*: both Stoicism and Christianity argued that true valour was to be moderate and patient – like Socrates facing his execution, or Christ on the cross.

In the eighteenth and nineteenth centuries, a double attitude towards Stoicism continued and increased in prominence.[82] We see it in Biran's invocation of tranquillity and his rejection of the Jansenists and of Pascal, both representatives of an extreme Augustinianism, and both overtly anti-Stoical. Ever since Biran, much of the peculiar attraction of spiritualism has been its unique ability to recognize the relevance of Stoicism as a critique of Augustinian spirituality, while at the same time resisting either a naïve return to Stoic ideas or a simple rejection of the Augustinian tradition. Ravaisson, for instance, wrote a seminal study on Stoicism, incorporated many Stoic ideas into his own philosophy, but also wrote against the Stoics and continued to read Fénelon and the mystics. During the 1880s, however, Stoicism became increasingly popular and its significance to spiritualist philosophy, as a consequence, was amplified. This is evident in Bergson's work and in the popular philosophy of his contemporary Alain (Émile Chartier), a thinker treated together with Bergson in this book.

Bergson and Alain shared this in common that they admired Stoicism as well as spiritualism, and found several ways in which to 'spiritualize' Stoicism, if not Stoicize spiritualism itself. The influence, via Bergson, of this spiritualized Stoicism is noticeable in Pierre Hadot's work, but its most interesting and still overlooked example must be Alain's student Simone Weil, whose entire religious philosophy revolves around an interrogation of Christian values in light of Stoicism. In Weil's work we see Stoicism used to think through the nature of spiritual exercise, and yet the context and purpose of Weil's religious philosophy are to understand and practise a mysticism of the Augustinian kind. Her position thus recapitulates independently the way Stoicism and Christianity appear together in early spiritualism, and I have for this reason chosen to approach Weil here as a post-Biranian thinker in the tradition of Biran and Ravaisson, rather than merely as a disciple of Alain.

Biran's own cognizance of the critical potential of Stoicism cannot be doubted. It has been remarked on by many commentators, and is an important part of the early notes found together with the diary entry in which the 'state of rapture' is detailed.[83] One fragment in particular, 'Portrait of the Sage', is significant. It follows closely the argument of Biran's account of his solitary stroll on 27 May 1794, and like that diary entry it is concerned with tranquillity. Biran introduces tranquillity as a gloss on the Stoic ideal of *constantia* or 'constancy' (*la constance*). Tranquillity, suggests Biran, has been ignored by modern philosophy, which values displays of passion as the sign of heroism. But, replies Biran, did not Cicero show, using the 'weapons of the Stoics', that true courage lies in moderation rather than ostentation? 'True courage', he writes, 'is nothing but that affection of the soul which supports and suffers evils, obedient – without fear and without murmuring – to the supreme law of necessity.' Yet Biran is uneasy about the way in which Cicero and the Stoics present the tranquil Sage as someone who is entirely unmoved by passion. 'If I were to add anything to the opinion of Cicero', remarks Biran, 'I would say that if by passion we understand, as a general rule, any extraordinary movement of the soul which directs the will firmly to a particular object, it would be true to say that man [*sic*] achieves nothing great without passion.' Rather than present passion as that which philosophical training overcomes, Biran chooses to see it as that which philosophical training transforms. Such transformation takes place through the cultivation of good habits: 'Thus it is education that decides the good or bad quality of the passions.' What this means is that effort again becomes essential for philosophy, for no less than heroic courage Biran's tranquillity demands hard work. As he reflects, 'if, when it comes to principles in which we take only a feeble interest, such as those of the abstract sciences, it is so difficult for us to change our ideas, how much more painful must it be to destroy the sentiments which to us have been rendered natural by habit.' 'The worthiest use of philosophy', he thus concludes, 'is to help us in this painful work (*pénible travail*).' Moreover, because education is mediated through society, the best milieu for the philosopher is not the desert but society. 'While [people] erred', Biran muses, addressing Philosophy, 'you founded their cities, you gathered them into society.'[84]

Is the Sage in Biran's portrait a Stoic or a Christian? Neither answer, I think, is satisfactory. Evidently, Biran's intention when gently modifying the Stoic position of Cicero is not to come down on one side of an ideological divide. In any case, the very position which, in 'Portrait of the Sage', is identified as a kind of Stoicism is, in Biran's diary entry from 27 May 1794, identified as profoundly Augustinian: 'O good Fénelon, come and comfort me!'[85] The importance of Cicero and Fénelon is the ideal they symbolize. This ideal is tranquillity, and it is tranquillity – rather than the schools and faiths to which it has been associated – that chiefly occupies Biran's mind.

What, then, is at stake for spiritual exercise in tranquillity? We may summarize the answer in the following way: spiritual exercise shows tranquillity to be caught up in a world of effort. Effort impinges itself on tranquillity, whether it be in Augustine's flight from distraction or in the solitary walker's desire for the quiet of the desert. Thus effort challenges repose, putting pressure on what would otherwise become an escapist fantasy of sweet nothingness. Reciprocally, tranquillity challenges effort. In the 'Portrait of the Sage' what Biran likes about tranquillity is the way it renders the work of philosophy inconspicuous. Philosophy demands no special schools or retreats away from society; she is society. Similarly, the Sage does not advertise their labour; they remain moderate even while suffering. In other words, tranquillity transforms the quality of effort from something that is necessary to proclaim to something it is hardly worth speaking of. Such silence is possible because the virtuous person performs efforts constantly but does not advertise the fact, nor are they, at all times, aware of their labour. In Biran's account of the 'state of rapture' which overtook him on 27 May 1794 it is likewise a question of understanding effort in a way that does not involve heroism or overt displays of strength. There it was passivity and spontaneity which Biran used to convey what, in the 'Portrait of the Sage', he describes as the Sage's constancy. The transformation which tranquillity brings to bear on effort is related to the transformation which, in Augustine's *Confessions*, love or desire effects on movement. In the *Confessions* it was a question of finding the mode in which movement could be imagined apart from volitional effort.

This movement Augustine called 'love' because in relation to it a person moves without intending to move. For the one who meditates and prays, the aim is the same: to make the effort in a manner that is spontaneous rather than self-willed. In both cases, the spiritualist and the Augustinian, the critique which effort brings to repose is answered by taking seriously the evidence of experience, in which effort is undeniable, but in which effort is not reducible, at all time, to volition. Both writers achieve this close engagement with effort through their style of philosophising. Literary introspection, of which Augustine's *Confessions* and Biran's *journal intime* are examples, may feign spontaneity, but it cannot disavow the effort taken to present and compose the self without risking also rendering spontaneity itself a fiction.[86] From the perspective of tranquillity, it is the facts of spirit which show the empiricism of exercise.

I began by sketching spiritual exercise through the eyes of a tradition which took an adverse view of the conventional opinion that philosophy should be equated with effort. With its roots in non-conformist Quietism, spiritualist philosophy questioned the ethic of struggle and effort which has dominated modern thought. Through figures like Fénelon and Rousseau it continued Augustine's mysticism of repose and questioned the Stoic elevation of effort. In the final analysis, however, the evidence of Biran's 'state of rapture' suggests that it is not necessary that philosophy choose between training for effort and training for repose, no more than it is necessary that philosophy choose between Stoicism and Christianity or between ethics and metaphysics. If by ethics we mean action, and by metaphysics the purpose and principal of any action, it is difficult to see how an exercise that aims at happiness could ever successfully separate the two. Where such separations occur, where effort is seen as the end of spirit, or spirit as the absence of any effort, spiritual exercise emerges as an unhappy contradiction. Biran's philosophy thus stands at a turning point in the history of spiritual exercise. In the spiritualist thought that follows from *biranisme*, ancient conceptions of moral therapy are investigated anew: the ideals of spiritual exercise in light of the varied experiences of exercising spiritually. What this experience is and how such investigations are formed we will see in the following chapters.

2

The spiritual life: Maine de Biran

The alternative philosophy of spiritual exercise proposed in this book originates in the tradition of French thought known as 'spiritualism'. Spiritualism takes its inspiration from Maine de Biran (1766–1824), in whose work the association between philosophy and spiritual exercise is striking. We know, for instance, that Biran received his secondary education in the 1780s from the Brothers of Christian Doctrine, a religious order whose philosophical outlook was shaped by the ideal of meditation. The Brothers of Christian Doctrine contributed to an intellectual milieu already exercised by what critics have since called 'literary introspection', or the 'conscious investigation of a mind by itself'.[1] Major figures of the age, such as Étienne Bonnot de Condillac and Jean-Jacques Rousseau, chose to present philosophy as the examination of consciousness, as a careful study of the *vie intérieur* or 'interior life'. Biran is no exception. He belongs to the family of philosophers whom Charles Augustine Sainte-Beauve once named *métaphysiciens et méditatifs intérieurs*, 'introspective metaphysicians and meditators'.[2] Summing up his life's oeuvre in the *Nouveaux essais d'anthropologie* (New essays in anthropology) (*c.* 1823–4) Biran writes: 'From a sustained and persistent attention to myself, fixed for so long on interior phenomena (*les phénomènes intérieurs*), there has resulted a great number of psychological ideas, observations and studies.'[3] And already in 1802, when introducing his first published essay, *The Influence of Habit on the Faculty of Thinking*, Biran had explained that his work was 'the study of my inner self', noting that 'I was seeking at that time particularly to attain a greater degree of self-knowledge: I seemed to be writing only for myself.'[4]

Of course, the desire to attain 'a greater degree of self-knowledge' is not particular to spiritual exercise; it goes back to the very beginnings of philosophy, to Socrates and to the Delphic oracle. But the desire to write 'only for myself' is a theme of which the literature of spiritual exercise gives an especially developed example. It is not easy to picture a genre in which self-sufficiency is more important. 'Do not go out into the marketplace, return to yourself,' writes Augustine in *De vera religione* (Of true religion), 'truth dwells in the inner man [sic]'.[5] At the same time, it is equally hard to imagine an ideal of introspection which is more earnestly invested in the renunciation of self-sufficiency. In the Augustinian tradition of spiritual prayer, the purpose of meditation is the abandonment of the self to God, and tension between self-sufficiency and self-renunciation is a common theme in the literature of spiritual exercise. Such tensions go back, ultimately, to the tension between effort and grace which is the principal concern of Augustine's own spiritual writing, for while self-examination is effort that prepares for grace, self-renunciation is the desisting from effort by which grace is received. Here too Biran's work is typical. Constantly it returns to the idea that the examined self is the self whose efforts at self-examination, paradoxically, have been given over to a higher power. In his *journal intime* Biran describes 'the spiritual life' (*la vie spirituelle*) in this way, as the 'absorption in God through the loss of the feeling of self (*moi*)'.[6] Similar tensions are found among Biran's contemporaries. Everywhere we meet with the same confrontation of opposites: autonomy and dependency, self-examination and self-renunciation, effort and grace. In fact, Biran's ideal of philosophy as a spiritual exercise whereby effort would be transformed into grace is inherent in the contradictory presentations of introspection that we find among French thinkers in the eighteenth century, including those Biran read before writing his first essays.

I

Most eighteenth-century notions of philosophy were invested in ideals of spiritual exercise in the sense of introspection. What captivated French philosophers about introspection was its independence from established systems of thought; here was a way of doing philosophy that required no special book learning – philosophy untouched by the schools. Introspection offered a means of knowledge that seemed, or so they supposed, to be free of the confused ideas and errors of judgement attributed to classical metaphysics. Metaphysics, of course, remained a source of interest. But the speculative nature of its claims merely confirmed the identification of philosophy with a practice distinct from discussions of substance and essence. Such views agreed very well with René Descartes' notion that philosophy was – or ought to be – meditation on the mind by itself. This does not mean, however, that Biran's contemporaries were in agreement regarding the nature of meditation. We shall see that Descartes seems to combine at least two distinct ideals of meditation. As a result, eighteenth-century accounts of philosophy present deeply conflicted ideas of its method, with ancient anxieties regarding the limits of introspection making their way into the new descriptions of meditation.[7]

At one extreme, among the more popular notions, is the image of introspection as a great effort performed by the meditator without any outside help. Gary Hatfield, discussing the early modern origins of this image, connects it to Descartes' tendency to stress the 'autonomy of the meditator'.[8] One recalls the opening of Descartes' *Meditations* (1641), where the author describes the necessity of distrusting everything he has learnt and relying only on what he can discover by means of his own inner eye.[9] Descartes' ideal, which recalls the religious retreat and draws on his intimate knowledge of the Ignatian tradition, became a governing one in eighteenth-century philosophy. According to Condillac in *Treatise on the Sensations* (1754), 'we perceive nothing but what is in ourselves.'[10] Verifiable knowledge for Condillac thus begins and ends with autonomous introspection, with what the mind can observe regarding itself – by itself. Self-examination requires an environment free from those distractions which might turn attention away from the self. So Condillac, like Descartes, pictures the philosopher as a retreatant, as a man 'left to himself' and 'cut off from society'.[11] Condillac, a great stylist, describes the philosopher-retreatant in what has since become the principal thought-experiment of eighteenth-century epistemology: an originally inanimate statue which, endowed with nothing but the primitive organs of sense, generates consciousness and a 'feeling of self' through its reaction to sense-impressions. The ideal of autonomy is central to this whole thought-experiment. When, towards the end of the treatise, the statue eventually speaks, its first object of 'amazement' is its own self:

> What am I? What was I? ... Amazed at myself I reflect more carefully ... I direct my attention from one object to another, and gathering together into the notion I form of each, the ideas and relations I notice in them, I then reflect upon them ... I only perceive myself. I only enjoy myself ... I see myself, I touch myself, I am conscious of myself, but I do not know what I am.[12]

Every observation in the statue's meditation on itself affirms the central image: there is no knowledge except self-knowledge, no perception except self-perception, no touch except auto-affection and so on. Finally, to know the self is not to know what the self is but pay attention to the awareness of self. All is determined by what the meditator can know without going outside themselves.

In this image of introspection the effort of the meditator is significant. Condillac's thought-experiment is an experiment in spiritual vigilance; the 'I' which the statue discovers and explores is a result, entirely, of the attention it gives to sensations, feelings, perceptions. Again one recalls Descartes, and his repeated warnings of how difficult meditation will prove: 'I would not urge anyone to read this book,' Descartes instructs,

> except those who are able and willing to meditate seriously with me, to withdraw their minds from the senses, and from all preconceived opinions. Such readers, as I well know, are few and far between.[13]

Like Descartes' meditator, the statue reflecting on its own self relies wholly on its own effort and depends on no outside help. At several points in the *Treatise* Condillac also explains the nature of this effort, which, like Descartes, he calls 'attention'. Attention comes in two forms, passive and active. Passive attention is attention caused by sensations impressing the organism from outside; active attention is caused by a desire arising from within the organism. It is the latter type of attention that interests Condillac. This attention originates with the self and reinforces the autonomy of the meditator: 'Recollecting, comparing, judging, discerning, imagining, wondering, having abstract ideas, and ideas of number and duration, knowing general and particular truths, are only different modes of attention.'[14] Active attention stands not only for a philosopher's careful meditation on what lies 'in ourselves', but for the nature of consciousness as such. Cut off from society and freed of distractions it is easy to see that the statue has knowledge only of objects to which attention has been given. Conversely, when attention is not exercised the result is a lack of knowledge: 'as for the objects which do not interest [the statue],' explains Condillac, 'they are part of the confused mass of which it has no knowledge.'[15] It is thus as an autonomous effort that meditation, for Condillac, validates the comparison between philosophy and the spiritual retreat.[16]

The idea of the autonomous meditator was a regular theme in eighteenth-century thought, and there are several reasons for its persistence. Evidently it reinforced a popular image of the philosophical recluse. Treatises like those by Condillac required the author to secure a certain degree of leisure and retirement in order to be written at all. Even during the eighteenth century, to be a philosopher was a calling that retained features of the monastic *vita contemplativa*. Fashions among writers too aided in the popularization of philosophy as the temporary elimination of distraction, as a form of cognitive, if not spiritual, retreat. During the early modern period, when meditation began to emerge as a central concept in philosophical discourse, philosophers turned – or returned, as David Marno has shown – to spiritual exercise understood as 'undistracted attention'. Now old ideas of prayer as attention directed to the inner life offered seventeenth-century philosophers their most useful structuring concept. During this time, to do philosophy in any form was to invoke the model of the retreat – the mind freeing itself from the concerns of everyday life and turning its attention wholly to the object of study, its own self.[17] But the ideal of undistracted attention also sustained an old image of philosophy as intellectual labour. Comparable views, combining meditation as retreat with meditation as effort, can be seen in French philosophy during the eighteenth century. Among philosophers the ideal of meditation has never been as significant as it was then, nor has it been presented in more formidable terms. The popularity of Condillac's philosophy coincided with the beginnings of psychology and the work of Pierre Cabanis, Charles Bonnet and Antoine Destutt de Tracy, to mention but a few of the most significant thinkers writing on the nature of consciousness. When we read these writers, it is not easy to tease apart the ideal of meditation from the exacting style of psychological introspection. Both reinforce one another and contribute to the significance of this new introspective method. A good example is Bonnet's celebrated description of his own work as meditation in the *Essai analytique sur les facultés de l'âme* (Analytical Essay on the Faculties of the Soul), which first appeared in 1755, only a year after *Treatise on the Sensations*. The essay contains a preface clearly indebted to Condillac. Here philosophy is pictured by Bonnet as a cognitive retreat. In Bonnet's well-known phrase, 'My brain has become a retreat for me, where I have tasted pleasures that have charmed my afflictions.'[18] Thus Bonnet elevates the 'books of meditation', which have

> a special character and are easy to recognise: they shine with their own light. Because they resemble none but themselves, already they are interesting by virtue of their originality. The air of invention, freedom and life which they characterise, fixes all eyes on them. We are surprised not to have found in it that which we have seen almost everywhere else; to have discovered new sources of Truths; and even more to feel that one learns to think. It is a new sense which is developing in the reader, and which they are astonished to acquire.[19]

But above all, Bonnet follows Condillac in identifying meditation as an autonomous activity. 'I had no other guide in my meditations,' he explains, 'than the principles that I myself had made.'[20] Moreover, for Bonnet effort is the *sine qua non* of such meditation, an undertaking not for the merely curious. Looking within, relying on nothing but one's own principles, is hard work:

It seems the mind (*l'esprit*) is made to look more outside than within itself ...
It cannot concentrate for a long time on the same object. It wants to see much,
quickly and easily. It is repelled by a dissection, frightened by an analysis.[21]

The eighteenth century was enthralled by the notion that philosophy could be – indeed should be – a form of spiritual exercise and *hard work*, and it is not necessary to mark further the convergence between the psychologist's disparagement of those too repelled by meditation to undertake the 'cognitive retreat' to the 'brain', and Descartes' conviction that only those willing to submit to the ardour of self-examination would benefit from reading the *Meditations*. Marno has traced the ideal of difficult and undistracted attention to Ignatius' *Spiritual Exercises* (1522–4), where effort seems to rival the significance of divine grace.[22] Indeed, what is striking in the use of meditation by Descartes, and later by Condillac and the psychologists, is the absence of anything like grace. The same preponderance of effort is observed by Hatfield in his analysis of Descartes' *Meditations*. 'Descartes,' writes Hatfield, 'never makes the search after truth dependent upon the grace of God.'[23] Instead, Cartesian meditations praise the self-sufficiency of the meditator, their intellectual determination and their quest for 'objective truths in the intellect'.[24] Historians of philosophy have thus suggested 'effort', particularly effort directed to the self, as a striking feature of French thought from Condillac onwards.[25] Such vigilance derives from the tradition of spiritual exercise, even as it develops and transforms it.

But philosophers of the eighteenth century did not always imagine the meditator as an autonomous figure. Were the philosopher to doubt their efforts, or entertain different presuppositions regarding the abilities of the human mind, introspection could be seen as the very opposite of a self-sufficient increase in self-knowledge. Philosophers then made use of another image familiar from the literature of spiritual exercise, the image of the meditator overwhelmed by God. 'And being hence admonished to return to myself,' writes Augustine in the *Confessions*, 'with the eye of my soul (such as it was) I discovered over the same eye of my soul, over my mind, the unchangeable light of the Lord.'[26] Above the inner light that had until then aided introspection, Augustine discovers the dazzling light of God. How inconsequential seemed the efforts of the inner light compared with such overwhelming illumination! This image of introspection too is evident in Descartes' *Meditations*, where it competes with the ideal of autonomous effort. 'I should like to pause here,' writes Descartes at the end of the third meditation, 'and spend some time in the contemplation of God; to reflect on his [sic] attributes and to gaze with wonder and adoration on the beauty of this immense light, so far as the eye of my darkened intellect can bear it.'[27] During this style of retreat, introspection becomes the site of cognitive confusion, inner conflict and self-doubt; it awakens uncertainty regarding the efforts of the mind to pay attention and see clearly, and so reveals the limitations of self-observation. It is associated with the renunciation of self and appeals to divine grace that one finds in the Augustinian tradition of spiritual exercise. As Marno explains so well, 'Augustine is aware of the spiritual ideal of undistracted prayer but ultimately rejects it in favour of a fundamentally ambivalent experience of attending that instead of implying gnostic perfection reveals the need for divine grace.'[28]

A good example of this way of relating to meditation – as an arresting of effort – appears in a well-known section of Rousseau's *Émile, or On Education* (1762), 'A Savoyard Vicar's Profession of Faith'. It is a passage that Biran probably had in mind when writing his first essays.[29] Here the Savoyard Vicar, a fictional character, gives his profession of faith in the form of a meditation on the self. The meditation begins, like the meditations of Condillac, with an autonomous figure successful in their efforts to discern themselves. The Vicar finds certain confirmation of the self in the 'force of ... mind': 'let this or that name be given to this force of my mind ... let it be called *attention, meditation, reflection,* or whatever one wishes. It is still true that it is in me and not in things, that is it I alone who produce it.'[30] So far the Vicar conforms to the image of meditation as an autonomous activity. But then the Vicar turns his attention to God. The result is different. 'The more I think about [infinite essence],' he explains to Émile, the young protagonist, 'the more I am confused.'[31] Like Augustine or Descartes dazzled by God, the Vicar is overwhelmed by the experience of a more-than-human presence. When he now returns attention to the self the certainty he had first experienced is replaced by confusion. Far from confirming the ability of mind, meditation produces a conflicted image of human nature:

> In meditating on the nature of man [sic], I conceived I discovered in it two distinct principles; one of which raised him to the study of eternal truths, to the love of justice and moral beauty, and to the regions of the intellectual world whose contemplation is the wise man's delight; while the other took him basely into himself, subjected him to the empire of the senses and to the passions which are their ministers, and by means of these hindered all that the sentiment of the former inspired in him. In sensing myself carried away and caught up in the combat of these two contrary motions, I said to myself: 'No, man is not one. I want and I do not want; I sense myself enslaved and free at the same time. I see the good. I love it, and I do the bad. I am active when I listen to reason, passive when my passions carry me away'.[32]

Rousseau's Vicar meditates, but meditation does not lead immediately – or even evidently – to the intellectual pleasures promised. Condillac and the psychologists saw meditation as a method which, though difficult, effortful and rare, was nonetheless possible by anyone ready to free the mind from distractions. The Vicar is more cautious. With the body a constant distraction, instead of intellectual pleasures fulfilled he comes to view meditation as the disappointment of such pleasure. As one commentator puts it, on Rousseau's model reason is not self-sufficient but 'annihilated before God'.[33] The meditator is revealed to be no longer autonomous but dependent on a presence beyond their comprehension. Though grace is not invoked explicitly by Rousseau in this passage (indeed, the Savoyard Vicar – like Descartes – is careful not to ask anything of God), the arrival of grace is implicit in the finitude of the meditator who can achieve nothing by their own efforts. With the self obscured by meditation, the absolute value of introspection itself is questioned.[34]

What we have here is an image of meditation that is different to the one adopted by Condillac, Bonnet and the psychologists. Both images begin with the observation of self. Both are variations on introspection. But Rousseau's Vicar gazes further afield. For him, the purpose of meditation does not end with the self; it begins with it. So while he does not doubt the power of attention – the 'mind's ability' – he does doubt the power of attention to grasp what it seeks. The two images have been linked to competing views of human nature. Are there limits to what the mind can do – to its 'efforts' – or is the mind a limitless power? In theological terms, are human beings creatures dependent on their creator, or are they autonomous, like God? For Hatfield and Marno, these distinct views of human nature resolve, in turn, into competing traditions of spiritual exercise. While effort is positive and mostly praised in the Ignatian tradition – to which I count Condillac, Bonnet and the psychologists – it is deplored and generally questioned in the Augustinian tradition – of which Rousseau is a late example. But to differentiate between distinct traditions is perhaps to exaggerate the claim of either position. Descartes combines elements of both, as does Rousseau – as does, we shall see, Biran and the spiritualist philosophers. Nonetheless, the more overtly the Augustinian the approach to spiritual exercise, the more it seems that effort is not only worried but itself an object of enquiry. As countless readers of Augustine have found, it is in the tradition of introspection descending from his work that we arrive at something like a dialectic of self-examination, of the meditator simultaneously constituting themselves through their efforts of curiosity and becoming dissembled by wonder.[35]

What is at stake in this dialectic of introspection? To picture introspection as an autonomous activity is to praise the ideal of undistracted attention. But the word 'attention' is not free of its own distractions. Frequently attentiveness is invoked to describe an ideal state. At such moments the ideal it suggests is one of autonomy, vigilance and activity. Yet it is not possible to be always attentive, no more than it is possible to be constantly awake. A sense of the impossible nature of undistracted attention creeps into every philosopher's encouragement to pay attention. Then it is a question of warning against the difficulty of attention and deploring the scarcity of earnest meditators; hence a more pessimistic view of meditation emerges from an otherwise optimistic portrayal of the cognitive retreat. For this reason, in eighteenth-century philosophy the ideal is conveyed together with a degree of rebuke, a chastisement of the culture which has made undistracted attention so difficult to attain. Facility is held in suspicion. This point is emphasized by Bonnet: 'It seems the mind … cannot concentrate for a long time on the same object. It wants to see much, quickly and easily. It is repelled by a dissection, frightened by an analysis.'[36] In the context of French Catholicism, the rejection of facility revives Jansenist ideas of the fallen state of human nature, of its incapacity to reach the truth.[37]

But to picture meditation as the overwhelming of the self by God is to imagine it as another expression of fallen nature. This unstable vision communicates the demand to abandon the self to God: cease from effort, accept the limitations of the mind and invoke grace. In the context of the cognitive retreat, this model has the meditator discover not their autonomy, but their dependency. Meditation on the self alone is satisfying, rewarding labour; meditation that seeks God is frustrating effort that destabilizes the self. It discovers an irreducible inability that limits the activity of the mind and makes it dependent on exterior powers, at the same time as it urges rest from the mind's efforts. Moreover, it welcomes, rather than repudiates, facility in the sense of easiness and repose. It invites attention to be experienced as a state rather than as an activity.[38] Perhaps the inner struggle image is a more realistic view of human nature. Certainly it is old and complex. St Paul writes about the Christian torn between two laws: the law of the 'inmost self' and the law of the limbs.[39] This image of the *homo duplex*, the 'twofold man', was popular and figured widely in eighteenth-century thought. Rousseau's Vicar takes recourse to it in his meditations, Biran uses it frequently, and no less a luminary than Georges-Louis Leclerc (Comte de Buffon) used it to explain human nature.[40] Little wonder that many thinkers of the era were drawn to an Augustinian understanding of meditation.

What is striking about these contrasting ideas of philosophy is not, of course, their relative accuracy as descriptions of meditation. The meditator was never perfectly autonomous nor entirely dependent. In meditation the autonomy and dependency of the self are both aspects of one practice, and autonomy and dependency are each as necessary to meditation as the other. Moreover, both converge on the deepest level. Following Marno and others, I have linked them to contrasting views of spiritual exercise: the one Ignatian, the other Augustinian: the one stressing autonomy, the other dependency; the one praising mental effort, the other invoking grace. But the basic idea of spiritual exercise remains the same in both cases. Ultimately it originates in a shared question, a debate regarding the relationship between effort and grace, autonomy and dependency. Such concerns are spiritual as well as philosophical, making claims on the basic orientation of human nature. Among the uses of meditation that one finds in eighteenth-century philosophy there is scope for either view, and many thinkers draw freely on both ideas as appropriate representations of philosophy.

All this suggests that during the period immediately preceding the appearance of Biran, French philosophy in general and introspection in particular were closely associated with the ideal of spiritual exercise of one kind or another. Yet for a long time critics and historians have tended to view introspection as a thoroughly secular genre. In his seminal study, *French Introspectives: From Montaigne to Gide* (1937), P. Mansell Jones made a strong case for identifying the era's 'purely intellectual pursuit of self-comprehension' with a secular mode of discourse.[41] Jones detected that after the early modern period meditation became increasingly interested in the self and increasingly disinterested in the outside world – society, God, the good. To Jones it seemed that introspection's attention to the meditator was quite distinct from the attention to God that one found in religious meditation. As introspection became the 'disinterested investigation of a mind by itself' it became less religious.[42] Finally, he puts it this way: 'The secular ... must be our field ... because "secular", or as we shall call it "literary" introspection is, or appears to be, if not a gratuitous act, less consciously motivated, at least, than the religious variety.'[43] Michel Foucault, in a seminar on 'Technologies of the Self', also reflected on the gap that seemed to separate literary introspection from religious meditation. The eighteenth century, he suggested, constituted a 'decisive break' with the tradition of Christian spiritual exercise.[44] Or rather, the 'human sciences' used the devices of spiritual exercise for new ends. Christian spiritual exercise stressed the importance of confession, inner struggle and self-renunciation. The eighteenth century employed these 'techniques of verbalization' for a different purpose. The new context, Foucault explains, was one of increased individualism. 'Reinserted' in this new context, techniques once used to question the individual's autonomy were now used to affirm the self-sufficiency of the meditator and buttress the certainty of self-knowledge: 'without renunciation of the self but to constitute, positively, a new self'.[45]

But if some critics and historians detected differences between eighteenth-century ideas of introspection and spiritual exercise, others have marked the similarities. To begin with, few would deny the religious roots of Rousseau's style of meditation. It has been compared to Augustine's *Confessions* and to 'metaphysical meditations' more broadly.[46] Charly Coleman has shown how the religiously charged themes in Rousseau's work – such as self-renunciation and abandonment to God – emerge directly from an earlier tradition of spiritual exercise with Augustinian roots. Self-renunciation, passivity before God and abnegation of the *moi* were at the core of Jeanne Guyon's popular (and controversial) *A Short and Easy Method of Prayer* (1685) and the work of François Fénelon whom she inspired, and Fénelon in particular was widely read during the eighteenth century. The ideal of abandonment to God offered, Coleman argues, an alternative to the 'self-possessed Enlightenment subject'.[47] Eighteenth-century introspection, at least in the Augustinian variety that is of particular interest to us here, then appears on the opposite side of secularity: 'I call this countercurrent of the secularising process,' suggests Coleman, 'resacralisation'.[48] But even when the subject of meditation is 'self-possessed' and ostensibly secular, introspection may be shown to have religious roots. Coleman links secularization, with its emphasis on the individual, to Cartesianism and post-Tridentine Catholic reformism. So too did Marno and the historians of spiritual exercise, tracing the autonomous meditator to Ignatius of Loyola. No less than their forebears in the seventeenth century, eighteenth-century thinkers – whether 'secular' or 'religious' – were concerned with philosophy as *spiritual exercise*.[49] If Enlightenment introspection, then, paved the way for secularity, it also perpetuated religious ways of life, and achieved both by combining and recombining different aspects of the spiritual exercise tradition.[50] This fact has become central in our contemporary image of philosophy as a practice of self-transformation – and of the philosopher as exercitant. It was always there in the practice of introspection. But during the eighteenth-century introspection was a religious ideal that became allied to positions suspicious of religion, while remaining a spiritual project at the heart of philosophical practice. Nowhere is this more evident than in the essays on the spiritual life Biran wrote after the zenith of the Enlightenment.

II

When the object of desire is inaccessible to the external senses and distant by its nature from all the impulses of an organic or animal sensibility, the priority of an influence that is affective – sympathetic – can evidently belong only to the imagination which should, in principle, be directed, fixed and sustained by the aid of voluntary signs on the ideal to which it is attached. In thus exalting itself little by little through an assiduous contemplation the movement of the imagination passes to the sensitive part of the human organism (that is, the one closest to the soul) which responds most directly to emotions of any kind.

The continuity or the frequency of the same desire – of the same sensible tendency towards an ideal appropriate to the need or to the present state of the soul – fixes, so to say, its whole life in an interior centre, the unique home of the soul's purest, most elevated sentiments. All active or passive faculties, all ideas, are suspended, as are the functions or natural movements of the animal organism. The *moi* no longer lives, no longer exists for itself: it seems to be *one* with the ideal, the object of *desire* which has preceded and brought about this *absorption*; and in reverting to itself, in remembering its transports, its ecstatic pleasures, it believes itself to be united, identified with the very source of being, of life and of the happiness of the *soul*. Such is this superior order of the faculties ... which the Neoplatonists have described better according to intimate experiences and could never explain in their systematic reflections ... In both cases, too, the personality disappears, the *moi* is absorbed and lost: here in the world of bodies where its nature is degraded, there in the world of spirits which is its superior pole, its proper tendency, its most sublime direction.[51]

This passage appears towards the end of Biran's final and unfinished work, the *Nouveaux essais d'anthropologie* (New Essays in Anthropology) (*c.* 1823–4), after the author has discussed the nature of the inner life. It is an apology for introspection and remarkable in its attempt to reconcile what we have just been discussing as two distinct attitudes towards this style of philosophizing: the autonomous and the dependent, the style of effort and the style of grace. Yet despite an investment in the autonomy of the meditator there transpires a real sense of her ultimate dependency. The perdition of self and the union with spirit, hence the contrast between an initial 'assiduous' effort and a final state beyond 'active and passive faculties', is a principal feature of meditation when used by *biranisme* and spiritualist philosophy. Certainly, a loss of self and a consequent receiving of grace were always characteristic of spiritual exercise. But the usual context of spiritual exercise was the soul's passivity in relation to God. With Biran, however, a vitalist ontology enters into spiritual exercise. Unusually among French philosophers Biran was an admirer of Leibniz and well read in the latter's theory of spiritual substance, a theory Biran sometimes referred to as 'spiritualism'. Like Leibniz, Biran tended to identify spirit with an innate life-force. In this philosophy life preceded any distinctions, in the organism, between activity and passivity and so the self that disappeared into it might be said to return to an original state of pure energy. For Biran, self was an aspect of this spirit, and its passivity in relation to God was at the same time its divinization. Though Biran does not spell out the difference, we feel the influence of eighteenth-century vitalism on the *Nouveaux essais*.[52]

It is this tension between autonomy and dependency that explains, to a great extent, the convergence between Augustinian mysticism and spiritualist philosophy. Many spiritualists invoke, at the centre of their philosophy, the efforts of the *moi* to realize itself in relation to spirit, while at the same time insisting on the effacement of self in spirit. In Jules Lachelier's famous definition of spiritualism, the philosophy that takes its bearings from Biran and was popularized by Félix Ravaisson '[believes] that the unconscious thought which operates in Nature is the same as the thought which becomes conscious in us'.[53] What lends to spiritualism its special character is a close relationship between the philosophical and the mystical; empirical methods are used to describe the incommunicable experiences of the inner life. This emphasizes the feeling of novelty at introspection. For even though it is easy to detect Augustine in Biran's meditator, whose personality is absorbed in spirit during contemplation, it is still the case that Biran's text is a psychological essay, a study in 'anthropology'. Does this mean that spiritual exercise has become, finally, a respectable philosophical method? Evidently Biran wants us to think that his philosophy has facilitated this achievement, but also that philosophy had always begun with the attempt to commune with the divine through meditation. We sense it in the genealogy Biran gives to contemplation: 'Such is this superior order of the faculties ... which the Neoplatonists have described better according to intimate experiences and could never explain in their systematic reflections.'[54]

But what sort of exercise is Biran's 'assiduous contemplation'? Like meditation according to the Ignatian ideal, it is the study of the mind by itself: the imagination fixing its desire for a long time on the interior centre of the soul. The reader may associate it, initially, with the autonomous meditator one finds in Condillac and the psychologists. Or if this is not the whole picture, then evidently 'assiduous contemplation' is meant to conjure up a prodigious effort of undistracted attention. Had not Biran stated as much in the introduction to the *Nouveaux essais*?: 'A sustained and persistent attention to myself, fixed for so long on internal phenomena, have resulted in a great number of psychological ideas, observations and studies.'55 And in the *avant-propos* Biran does not hesitate to emphasize that the knowledge gathered by the philosopher is 'certain and evident' to the self that possesses it. For this reason, he writes,

> there are (as I have been convinced by experience) these ideas or *facts* that are certain and obvious to those who possess them and incommunicable to others who, naturally, are placed quite outside the point of view from which alone it would be appropriate to grasp them. That is why, also, the subject of this book will appear abstract, obscure and repugnant to most readers and similarly to philosophers who begin from points of view most remote from mine and are accustomed to combine their ideas on an entirely different plane.
>
> What I dare to ask of all, what I have the right to expect from their justice, is not to hasten to judge from without that which is judged only from within and refers only to the inner truth. A reflective consciousness dictated this work essentially in good faith by the nature of their subject. Neither imagination nor wit nor a scientific mind will suffice. Only the reflective consciousness of every man [sic] of good faith, curious to know himself, can answer the call made to him by my book.[56]

How are we to understand Biran's image of introspection? Many commentators have suggested that the *moi* is key to Biran's whole philosophy. We know that he inherited his conception of the self from Antoine Destutt de Tracy, a follower of Condillac who argued, against Descartes, that the self originated as a 'feeling of effort' born from the will's resistance to external stimuli. Hence Biran favoured the formula *je veux, donc je suis*, 'I will, therefore I am', to Descartes' *je pense, donc je suis*, 'I think, therefore I am'. We know also that Biran's notion of effort goes back, via Leibniz, to an ancient tradition of vitalism that emphasizes the *vis insita,* the innate force of organic life.[57] Biran repeats these themes during the discussion of the inner life in the *Nouveaux essais*. Here the 'manifestation of the *moi* is precisely the highest point of energy of the will or of effort battling against a resistance'.[58] 'What is this feeling of the *moi*', Biran asks, rhetorically, in the introduction: 'is it an abstraction of our mind or is it to the contrary the fact of existence, the first and only reality which it is given us to know or grasp immediately without venturing outside of ourselves?'[59] The *moi* of Biran's meditator is in many ways the same as the self of Tracy, Leibniz and the vitalist tradition; it is the self of effort and vital power. But at the same time it is not difficult to observe the qualifications Biran places around the *moi*. They are there in the unexpected and striking gloss which Biran makes on the experience of spiritual ecstasy. He says it is different from what we experience when directing the will deliberately towards an object: 'All active or passive faculties, all ideas, are suspended, as are the functions or natural movements of the animal organism.'[60] In a single sentence Biran exposes the experiential paradox that gives the lie to so many philosophies of introspection. Introspection is usually envisioned as a heightened state of consciousness, as a more intense state of awareness. But is this an accurate description of what it feels like to be absorbed by an object? Is it not more akin to a loss of consciousness, as when we become so absorbed in what we are doing that we forget about everything except the object of desire? So Biran describes contemplation as the experience of having a body without being aware of the fact. In such a state there can be no feeling of self: 'In both cases the personality disappears, the *moi* is absorbed and lost: here in the world of bodies where its nature is degraded, there in the world of spirits which is its superior pole, its proper tendency, its most sublime direction.'[61] (Simone Weil will come to a similar conclusion.) To understand how deeply Biran was invested in this image of meditation as the renunciation of self and the loss of effort we have only to take a closer look at the anthropology with which Biran frames the *Nouveaux essais*.

The first hint of a dependent self appears in the introduction to the *Nouveaux essais*. Here Biran creates a kind of heuristic device for understanding human nature, analysing it according to 'three lives': animal, human and spiritual. The first relates to everything the body does on its own without the influence of the *moi*, the second to whatever the *moi* feels, wills and achieves, the third – 'the most important of all' – to what is known 'outside the senses'; everything, Biran says, which 'philosophy has believed until now to be abandoned to the speculations of mysticism'.[62] Biran did not find time to complete the portion of the *Nouveaux essais* devoted to the 'spiritual life', but even so the introduction is clear on its main feature. The principle of the spiritual life is dependency, in the sense of grace. Where the self is concerned, spirit is the end: purpose and final resting place. 'Every faculty relative to the spiritual life,' writes Biran,

> constitutes the spirit of man [sic] in a state of pure receptivity by an influence *superior* to itself, but not foreign to its most elevated nature, an influence which, in manifesting itself to [the spirit's] interior gaze, at the same time manifests it to itself in its depths and in its relationship to an ideal order of infinity, an ideal of beauty, of intellectual and moral perfection which can only be glimpsed or perceived momentarily as the end (*but*) of its labours; the conclusion of its education in this fleeting and phenomenal world, the simple figure of *reality*, of the immutability of life, of the immortality of happiness which, for the man who

will have fulfilled his *task*, must accompany the ineffable feeling when all that is mortal in him will be *absorbed by life*.[63]

Like the eternal Sabbath in Augustine's *Confessions*, Biran's 'world of spirits' is a place of repose where the self no longer labours but exists in a state of 'pure receptivity'. The obvious comparison between receptivity and grace is not explicit here but is acknowledged elsewhere. In his *journal intime*, after describing once more the 'feeling ... of the soul's repose after and not before effort', Biran adds: 'Thus is explained the great saying that faith does not come by works, that *love* gives everything (*donne tout*)'.[64]

The spiritual life illustrates the dependency of the self and the limitations of human effort when faced with the infinite. In the fragments of an unfinished section on the 'life of the spirit' Biran elaborates on the difference between the spiritual and the human life. Once again he identifies the human life with the *moi* and its efforts, while the spiritual life is associated with the end of effort, a time when 'in the midst of darkness only light shines, the shadows retire, a pure calm succeeds the storm, a sweet peace is felt where previously a frightful war raged'.[65] He now also explains the origin of the 'frightful war' that is absorbed in spirit. The war is caused by a struggle between the *moi* and the body as the *moi* resists the passions and resists its 'animal nature'.[66] Again Biran uses this commonplace image to illustrate the dependency of the self. On the one hand the self is dependent on the body which absorbs human life with its passions, on the other hand it is dependent on spirit which absorbs the *moi* with sublime and elevated ideals. 'Human life' is the 'intermediary state' where

> the being preserves their personality with their freedom to act: this is *conscium, compus sui*, which is the state proper to *man*, where he [sic] exercises all the faculties of his nature, where he develops all this moral force in battling against the disorderly appetites of his animal nature, in resisting passions ... Above and below this state there is no more battle, no more effort or resistance, as a result there is no more *moi;* but now it is becoming *divine*, now *animal*.[67]

Like the self discovered by Rousseau's Savoyard Vicar, Biran's *moi* is conflicted and precarious, persisting through its own efforts while bordered on either side by more-than-human powers that overwhelm and absorb it – animal and spirit respectively. Entering either of the animal or spiritual states distinct from human life requires self-examination and effort but also the renunciation of self and the abandonment of effort.

III

Biran leaves little doubt about the difference between his idea of contemplation and more popular notions of spiritual exercise. The modern reader comes to the *Nouveaux essais* through Biran's *journal intime* or personal journal, which contains many reflections on the three lives and moreover connects them to Biran's own inner life. At one point in his journal Biran makes a revealing comparison between the 'human life' and Stoicism. 'Everything which is most sublime in Stoic morality,' he writes, 'is nothing but human virtue, the power of the human *moi*, having nothing but itself for its support.'[68] The context for this judgement is a passage where Biran comments on John 1.17: ' The law indeed was given through Moses; grace and truth came through Jesus Christ.' We are invited to imagine Stoicism as a 'law of Moses', as a morality separate from the ethical teachings of the New Testament. For Biran the former is characterized by autonomy and the opposite of dependency; here is a way of life independent ('having nothing but itself as its support') of the 'grace and truth' attributed to Christ. The contrast between dependency and autonomy, between recognition of grace and exertion of human power, is reinforced in the passage immediately preceding, where Biran describes the 'man [sic] born from blood … who is conducted by … a will constitutive of the human person or of the *moi*; who makes the centre of everything and the origin of everything in themselves rather than the origin of themselves in God.'[69] Critics have noted how hostile are Biran's comments towards Stoicism during the composition of the *Nouveaux essais* – how Stoicism is contrasted with Christianity, and Stoic morality with the 'life of the spirit'.[70] But in characterizing the human life in general as Stoic Biran also foregrounds and so elevates the significance of Stoicism. He gives to Stoicism the whole relevance of the *moi*. It would have been easier to dismiss Stoicism altogether. True, Stoicism is now, as the 'human life', second best to the spiritual life. But Stoicism also lays claim to what is 'sublime' in human effort. To convey the full impact of mystical absorption, then, the preceding state – in which the *moi* exerts its efforts and achieves self-consciousness – must be fully drawn. In this way Biran projects a sense of the significance of human effort, of the *moi*, through which every person wishing to engage in mystical contemplation must first pass. As a contrast but also a challenge to the 'spiritual life' nothing could be more effective than Stoicism.

Biran's critical appreciation of Stoicism is not confined to discussions of the spiritual life. It is found everywhere in the *journal intime*. If we sometimes forget that Biran does not take a wholly negative view of Stoicism it is because the contrast with Christian mysticism often is very sharply presented. In his final years Biran looked less kindly than ever on Stoicism, which as a younger man he had admired and praised, at times lavishly. 'It is necessary that the will presides over all that we are: such is Stoicism', we find in an entry from 23 June 1816: 'No other system is as consistent with our nature.'[71] But years of illness brought with it dissatisfaction with Stoic exercises, and with the power of the will to bring about happiness. Yet even so enough is left of his earlier admiration to contradict any simple opposition between Stoicism and Christianity.[72]

Aside from the comparison with the 'human life', the most striking reminder of Biran's residual admiration for Stoicism are his comments on Fénelon which appear with increasing frequency in the final volumes of his *journal intime*. These comments defend Fénelon, whose position was controversial for suggesting that effort might contravene the necessity of grace and promise holiness to anyone who practised spiritual prayer. Fénelon often contrasted his own position with that of the Stoics, and it is doubtless from Fénelon that Biran learns to critique Stoicism. At first Biran's attitude to Stoic exercises had been optimistic, since the Stoics offered techniques for achieving tranquillity of mind. Biran, we remember, suffered from chronic pain and was ever in search of ways in which to achieve calm and end the struggle with his body. Hence the interest in Stoicism, praise of Stoic morality and the many references to Marcus Aurelius scattered through the *journal intime*.[73] But Biran also contrasts Stoicism with Christianity. And in his 'Lettres au P. Lamy, Bénédictin, sur la grace et la prédestination' (Letters to Father Lamy, Benedictine, on grace and predestination) Fénelon had proposed that while the Stoics had the right idea about happiness – it was a form of tranquillity – they overestimated the ability of the mind to achieve happiness. For tranquillity, argued Fénelon, was not a matter of willpower. Tranquillity – in the sense of repose – was the absence of effort, including the efforts of the will to achieve tranquillity. Fénelon thus compares tranquillity to grace, 'absolutely undeliberate, involuntary, and received in the soul in a purely passive manner'.[74] In Fénelon's philosophy, while spiritual exercise and prayer may prepare the soul to receive grace, it is not exercise that in the end elicits grace. Biran makes this the core of his critique of Stoicism. Grace, not willpower, gives a more realistic understanding of the experiential paradox that determines any programme of spiritual progress. On 9 February 1819, he puts it like this: 'according to the Stoics we are able to do all this by ourselves; according to the Christians we are not able to do anything except with or through grace'.[75]

It is not difficult to see why Biran continues to appreciate Stoic techniques, nor is it difficult to see why he prefers, in the end, Fénelon's understanding of spiritual exercise as prayer. An adult life of chronic pain had taught Biran that tranquillity was either impossible or else its possibility lay in an effort different to the ordinary kind: an effort more negative than positive, more involuntary than voluntary – more like waiting than willing. So we find Biran suggesting, in a succession of entries composed in 1823, the following criterion for spiritual exercise: it should transform the inner person and be practicable by anyone, regardless of their physical or mental state:

> [E]xperience proves that to *act, meditate, pray* are always the necessary conditions for the manifestation and development of the life of the spirit. It does not matter whether the person, considered as an organism, is sad, dejected, discouraged, lazy, or happy, confident, full of a feeling of power and vital energy.[76]

Effort or willpower, with which Biran, in his final years, summarizes Stoic morality, does not meet his criteria for spiritual exercise because power demands strength and excludes those who are suffering, weak or otherwise unable to exercise their will in the requisite fashion. 'Christianity is more an exercise of the soul's sensibility, or of *love,* than it is a use of personal *power* or of reason,' he writes, adding that 'Stoicism, to the contrary, is a pure exercise of power, of reason: it is wholly pride, implacability.'[77] As a method for attaining happiness Stoicism seems, to Biran, less erroneous than it is impracticable. Those able to exercise willpower are already happy and so have no need for the method, while whose who do have need for the method lack power and so are not able to make the effort required to practise the method. Biran argues that when a person is weakened by illness or suffering in some way they cannot move themselves towards happiness. But they can still be moved, and they can still desire happiness, for to desire, Biran says, is not to move at will but to be moved by love towards an object of attraction. In such cases weakness can even have its benefits, Biran argues, because it gives the lie to the hubris implicit in moral therapy. No one is truly independent or self-sufficient. 'Neither the most elevated sensibility, nor that which is lowest,' writes Biran, 'possesses its own sustenance: it awaits it always from without or from above: hence the need for *prayer* – all desire is a prayer.'[78] It is for this reason that Biran follows Fénelon and favours prayer over Stoic exercises as the most practicable method for attaining happiness.[79]

In Biran's anthropology both Stoicism and Christianity correspond to a distinct idea of spiritual exercise. Like any philosophy which uses meditation as its method and ideal, 'Stoicism' exalts the meditator, their autonomy, mental effort and the power of the *moi* to know itself. It denies transcendence. It is the 'human life', declaring that happiness is the result of human effort, that virtue is up to us. 'Christianity' represents the contrasting image. Initially the *moi* is satisfied by its efforts to resist the passions. It rejoices in the 'sublime' heights to which its efforts have conveyed it. But then the *moi* discovers that the body is still there, that the efforts to conquer the body are not over. There will always be disquiet, inner conflict, weakness. So the *moi* begins to desire that which it cannot grasp by its own efforts: repose, calm, peace. To aid it in this desire, the *moi* invokes divine grace: it prays. This is the 'life of the spirit'. It denies totalizing immanence and looks beyond the self. In Biran's expression, it 'awaits' what it desires but cannot achieve. Like the manuals of spiritual prayer, the life of the spirit declares the limitations of the *moi*, the finitude of effort and the rapture of repose.

As the purpose of meditation, the spiritual life conducts the *moi* towards ecstasy, not by annihilating its efforts, but by transforming them. Meditation begins with hard work, undistracted attention and ascetic self-discipline. Repeatedly, the reader is made aware of the initial investment of effort required: '[I]n this sublime tendency,' writes Biran, 'and in the most active employment of the means which can bring about states of ecstasy (such as meditation or attention fixed for a long time on the same subject, especially in spoken prayer, determined first by the most energetic intention, etc.).'[80] Until ecstasy is reached, we are reminded of the labour that preceded it. The experience of ecstasy, moreover, has its analogue in the human life. When Biran explains the spiritual life in his *journal intime,* he recognizes how easily it might be confused with nihilism: 'The absorption in God through the loss of the feeling of *moi* – and the identification of this *moi* with its real, absolute and unique object – is not the absorption of the soul's substance or of the absolute *force* which thinks and wills.'[81]

As the self is absorbed by life, so thought and will are returned to 'absolute *force*'. Although Biran makes the life of the spirit a model of spiritual passivity (receptive, patient and calm), he does not overlook the exertive aspect of life. This experiential paradox is disclosed in the relationship between the three lives. At the same time as Biran insists on their difference, he also emphasizes their logical coincidence: 'These living forces or *these lives*,' he writes in the foreword to the *Nouveaux essais,* 'which the interior experience learns to distinguish and which the intimate feeling does not allow to confound are *three* and not only *one*, though logically there is only one man [sic] and psychologically only one unique *moi*.'[82]

Biran's anthropology represents the rejection of the old ideal, evident in the philosophy of the *moi*, that man is the measure of all things. In the human life, according to the fragmentary narrative in the *Nouveaux essais*, effort achieves sublimity but at the same time becomes aware of its limits. It exists *sublimis*; to reach beyond these limits are without its power, hence the necessity for grace. Nonetheless, human effort is not rebuked, nor does grace demand pure passivity. The interest of Biran's spiritual exercise, finally, is the result not of choosing between autonomy and dependency, effort and grace, but of insisting on the necessity of both states. Such is the experiential paradox of spiritual exercise that, in Biran's spiritualism, reaches its most intense articulation. In this spiritualism effort prepares for but does not elicit grace, and so both may be said to derive from the same source – from an incommunicable, ecstatic life that is the perennial object of spiritual exercise. In the elevation of the spiritual life Biran sustains an ancient and religious ideal of philosophy as the path of mystical contemplation and the ecstatic absorption of self.

IV

Even so, it is still necessary to contend with our first observation: that in the *Nouveaux essais* Biran amplifies the *moi*, human effort and the labour of contemplation. To conclude that Biran rejects the ideal of human effort in favour of grace does not ring true with the impact made by his philosophy. One remembers that the *Nouveaux essais*, no less than the spiritual life, are the result of many years of attention fixed on the self. Biran does not dismiss the efforts of the human life. They are necessary wherever there is desire for truth. Here the *moi* is the centre of attention and power. The wonder of the *moi*, its mystery and appearance as the first fact of experience – all this we can relate back to the psychology of Condillac and his followers. More than anything the form of the *Nouveaux essais* lends itself to a psychological interpretation of the *moi*, like the observations made by Condillac's statue. How then can one negotiate a mysticism of spirit with a philosophy of the *moi*?

It should be said that many critics are not of the opinion that the *Nouveaux essais* embrace anything like a positive view of the human life, or, to be more precise, of effort.[83] Maybe this is because Biran, like many philosophers in the Augustinian tradition of spiritual exercise, emphasizes the inner conflict and anxiety which is the cause of effort. Thus we do not see, immediately, what is 'sublime' about the human life. And yet to argue that the human life is not important is to neglect what Biran does with the *moi*. The *moi* is the site of feeling, thought, freedom and virtue, and throughout the *Nouveaux essais* it is accorded extraordinary influence over the body. We see the will influencing physical objects as well as objects of the imagination. Its powers border on the supernatural. During the discussion of the inner life Biran even uses the power of the will to explain such occult and apparently magical phenomena as magnetic healing:

> By virtue of this (at least) partial power of the will over the production of images [i.e. the imagination], such an individual – who reunites a certain force of the imagination with a quite mobile interior organisation – may become master, to a certain point, of certain organic functions, foreign in their nature to every direct and *immediate* influence of the will.[84]

That it is the self – the *moi* – which effects change in the organism is a point to which I shall return. At present it is important to see only that the *moi* does possess a remarkable power to make things happen outside itself. Of course that power is not direct or 'immediate', Biran is clear on this. The popular understanding of magic, he reminds, is not accurate. At the same time, he warns against 'a too-absolute scepticism' where magic is concerned.[85] The example he uses is habit. Often, merely to desire, repeatedly and for a long period, a change in one's body can bring about some aspect of that change. Say that I desire improved health and visit a magnetizer twice a week for a year in order to improve my well-being. The habit alone may help me to continue in a resolve to follow new diets and exercise regimes. In this way the *moi* may influence the body indirectly through what Biran calls 'mediate effects' or 'organic sympathy'.[86] True, the 'mastery' Biran here attributes to the mind is not absolute, being effective only 'to a certain point'. It ends where suggestion terminates. But all the same it is a form of mastery. One thinks of Descartes in the *Discourse on Method* (1637), dreaming of a way for humans to become, through their own efforts, masters and possessors of nature.[87]

The efforts of the *moi* link the human to the spiritual life, the life of grace. The tension between human and spirit is symbolic of the paradox which grounds Biran's anthropology. One critic, Georges Le Roy, for this reason argued that effort and grace and the two lives connected to them are the key to the theme of Biran's entire philosophy.[88] In the *Nouveaux essais* there is little mistaking the spiritual quality of the *moi*. It is no coincidence that Biran's explanation of magnetism resembles so closely his explanation of prayer. The two phenomena correspond to the two kinds of absorption distinguished by the author. In the case of prayer, the imagination is fixed on something beyond itself. So the self will be 'lost' in the more-than-human, 'the world of spirits'. Magnetism, by comparison and contrast, corresponds to the animal life, which like the spiritual life exceeds the reach of the *moi*. Here the imagination is fixed on something bodily. So as it focuses on the object of desire the self will be 'lost' in the body and become animal: 'as a result there is no more *moi*, but now it is becoming *divine*, now *animal*.'[89] Incorporeal though it is, and turned beyond the human, contemplation is yet difficult to distinguish from ordinary suggestion and magic. Here magic mirrors meditation, as effort does abandonment. 'From all this, it follows,' writes Biran, 'that the lowest degree of abasement, like the highest point of elevation, can apply, equally, to two states of the soul where it loses its personality equally.'[90]

If this is so, how are we to understand 'assiduous contemplation', the first step towards spiritual repose and ecstasy, as a challenge to the ideal of human effort? Why does not Biran make the reader feel more strongly the difference between what the *moi* achieves by its own, quasi-magical means, and what it achieves by prayer, by losing itself in the 'world of spirits'? The answer may be found by comparing the *Nouveaux essais* to Biran's very first published work, *The Influence of Habit on the Faculty of Thinking* (1802).

There are several reasons why one might see the *Influence of Habit* as a companion to the *Nouveaux essais*. During his lifetime it remained the author's only published monograph and set the tone for the reception of Biran's philosophy and the development of spiritualism. To many readers Biran was – and still is – remembered as the author of an important essay on habit.[91] But there are other reasons also. Each essay pays homage to introspection. Each begins as a meditation on the self, explaining that the insights to follow are the result of the author's careful study of himself. For this reason, each gives special weight to the image of philosophy as the result of spiritual retreat. In the *Influence of Habit* Biran describes the circumstances which brought him to write the essay:

> When I began this Memoir I did not think that it was destined to see the light of day: without aspiring to literary glory, I wished only to occupy the leisure of my retirement and to use for the study of my inner self the time that the particular circumstances in which I was placed, added to poor health, did not permit me to utilise in any other way.[92]

Later, as Biran lists the rewards of introspection, he praises it with the following description:

> This method, with which thought always knows whence it comes and where it is, advances slowly, but with certainty, without ever forgetting or losing sight

of itself; can stop at will or continue its progress; passes from darkness to light through well-controlled gradations, is led in short without being hurried along, enlightened without being dazzled.[93]

Like the absorption into spirit that awaits the meditator in the *Nouveaux essais* this is, effectively, another path to illumination. If we read carefully we discern an anticipation of that later piece. In his notes to the *Nouveaux essais* he had written: 'Thus only light shines on the realm of shadows, the shadows retire, a pure calm succeeds the storm.'[94]

It would not be difficult, however, to argue that the differences far outweigh the similarities between the two essays, for while the *Influence of Habit* praises introspection the account it gives seems to be centred wholly on effort. There is no mention of spirit and no hint of grace. In fact, the entire essay is an eulogy to mental effort and a relentless attack on the negative influence of actions that become habitual and unreflective – an attack, in other words, on precisely that state after effort that Biran praises in the *Nouveaux essais*. 'Increasing facility corresponds to the weakening of the *effort*; and if this effort should become nil, there would be no more consciousness of movement, no more volition,' he writes in *The Influence of Habit*.[95] In this book, as in the philosophy of Condillac, Bonnet and the psychologists, virtue is vigilance and facility the great temptation. 'Thus is born and strengthened habitual belief, blind faith! obstinate faith!' exclaims Biran when disparaging anything that would make mental effort easy: 'which, to the shame of the human spirit, exerts a much more general influence than the authority of reason and all the splendour of evidence!'[96] Because facility is enabled by habit, habit is to blame for the errors of reason. Habit 'excludes [the] attention in order often to substitute for it a blind mechanism'.[97] It 'circumscribes' the individual in 'a circle of operations which are always repeated in the same manner', leaving them to execute actions 'without thinking of them, distractedly and as if in a sort of somnambulism'.[98] Only the special effort of attention can repair the damage. '[The] individual will, therefore,' writes Biran, 'begin by giving particular attention to the exercise of each of his [sic] senses, for it is only from this source that enlightenment can come to him.'[99] It is an effort that demands 'determination' and 'deliberation':

> [T]he individual must be determined to do deliberately all that he [sic] previously did through habit; he must go back to the source of his signs, unreel their functions, re-establish them by an act of his will, associate them firmly through a series of (deliberate) repetitions with all the sense impressions, all the products of thought, all that he perceives, all that he feels in himself and outside of himself.[100]

The pessimistic tone carries over into Biran's account of the active effort with which the determined individual is rewarded for their undistracted attention. If passivity is a near-universal temptation, if the easy is always preferable to the difficult, then how realistic is attention? 'How should one *reflect* on [the *moi's*] habits, the most intimate, the most profound of all?' asks Biran in the opening of his essay.[101] The answer: only by means of an effort so great it seems almost impossible. 'The first step of reflection is in everything the most difficult,' he writes, 'it belongs only to the genius to take it.' But even 'for the great man who has the power to wonder' introspection is difficult, for genius too is obscured by habit. Biran continues:

> As soon as the great man [*sic*] who has the power to wonder, looks outside of himself the veil of habit falls, he finds himself in the presence of nature, questions her freely, and receives her answers; but if he seeks to concentrate his gaze on himself, he remains still in the presence of habit, which continues to veil the composition.[102]

Yet Biran does not stop at the negative influence of passivity on thought. Habit may dull reflection, but it may also facilitate reflection, as repetition facilitates the performance of any activity. Thus habit 'may alternately serve [the philosopher] and harm him [*sic*]'.[103] When it serves the philosopher, habit has a beneficial influence on the faculty of thinking. Then facility is positive, for it makes reflection more accurate. Indeed, the activity of paying attention to the self, of reflecting on its habits, is itself a practice that needs to be repeated many times; the effort of attention needs to become second nature and easy before it can enlighten the mind. So the method which Biran recommends as the path to enlightenment is itself, if not easy from the outset, then certainly easy by practice. It is a habit. As Biran acknowledges, there are 'good memory habits' as well bad ones, and the aim of philosophy is not to reject habit altogether but to transform bad habits into good ones:

> To exercise by appropriate means all the powers, but gradually and without ever overworking them, to make a habit, a necessity of representing ideas clearly and of connecting them with their signs; to keep ourselves from being led by words and purely mechanical forms; such are the first conditions which a method must fulfil in order to attain the end proposed.[104]

Here there is nothing in what Biran recommends that would reject habit outright. To the contrary: the philosopher must 'make a habit'. Consequently, there is nothing that would elevate effort unreservedly, for habit makes actions easy to perform and almost effortless. The 'exercise' advised is to be done according to the 'appropriate means' – 'gradually and without ever overworking'. Even at this early stage in Biran's career, the end and *ending* of effort are significant factors. These factors increase in significance as Biran's thought matures. Eventually they become associated in his mind with grace, for grace too, as the French captures so well, is a kind of easiness and gracility.

The difference between effort and easiness, finally, is the difference between effort and grace, or between the Ignatian and the Augustinian ideals of spiritual exercise. Thus the difference between the *Nouveaux essais* and the *Influence of Habit* is not that one rejects and the other accepts effort, the *moi*, and mental vigilance. Like his older self, the author who writes the *Influence of Habit* is aiming at the enlightenment of the inner life. What is more, the form which this enlightenment takes in the *Nouveaux essais* is not, at bottom, different from the form it takes in the essay on habit. There it was a question of passing from effort into a state of grace beyond either activity or passivity, here it is a question of proceeding from the difficult to the easy effort. For Biran introspection – meditation, prayer, attention, contemplation (Biran gives introspection many names) – begins with a great effort because to concentrate the gaze on oneself is to break old patterns of thought that have left the self in darkness. In the typology I have been using to interpret spiritual exercise, one could say that introspection begins in an Ignatian mode. Then introspection *seems* like a difficult effort. But once the old habit is broken and reflection becomes the norm then reflection too becomes a habit. Now introspection *feels* like an easy effort, or no effort at all. This is the Augustinian mode, though it is a state that is more often pictured than achieved. So we might describe it, with Biran in the *Nouveaux essais,* as an absorption of effort by that which exceeds it in every way. What this overwhelming presence is Biran does not say. 'Life', 'spirit', 'light', 'love' 'grace' – these are commonplaces of mystical vocabulary that lend themselves to being quoted rather than understood, and to being experienced rather than analysed. Biran's recognition of the basically incommunicable nature of what he is attempting to describe redeems his introspective method from psychology in the narrow sense. And yet he does not err in the opposite direction. That he is suspicious of mysticism as a genre is evidenced by his choice to refer to the spiritual life as a theory of human nature: anthropology. In the end he does not agree with any spiritual exercise that would reject the analytic examination of consciousness and the efforts of the *moi*. As if wary of extreme Quietism he equivocates on the nature of the spiritual life and insists on its logical coincidence with the *moi*. The experiential paradox of the spiritual life has the effect of tempering the rejection of effort with which it began. Biran's spiritualism is a philosophy of neither effort nor grace but of parity between them.

V

I started off by saying that there is in Biran's work a striking association between spiritualism and spiritual exercise that provides an alternative account of the philosophy of spiritual exercise, of philosophy *as* spiritual exercise. This association is genealogical. It connects Biran's introspective style to an ambiguity in the eighteenth-century image of philosophy as introspection. Is it appropriate to picture introspection as the activity of an autonomous self or should one see it as the patient attitude of a dependent *moi*? As effort or grace? Biran's spiritualism gives proof of both ways of thinking about meditation. The *moi*, like the meditator, is both affirmed and absorbed during contemplation. As attention is fixed for a long time on the inner life the effort that sustains introspection changes in quality from strain to relaxation, drawing spiritual progress as a dialectic of effort and repose. The essay on habit, Biran's first published piece, pioneers this dialectic: it discovers a qualitative difference between the effort which initially characterizes introspection, and the easiness with which introspection ends. Over the course of Biran's lifetime, this terrain is mapped in more detail. In the *Nouveaux essais*, Biran's last work, the dialectic is dramatized as spiritual transformation. The reader is conveyed from effort, struggle and war to repose, calm and peace, from self-possessed autonomy to ecstatic dependency. Finally, we are allowed an image, but only an image, of the spiritual life *after* spiritual exercise.

Such is the alternative account of the spiritual life to which every subsequent chapter in this book will refer. Simply understood, it is a dialectic of effort and grace, action and passivity. But how fitting is it to claim so paradoxical an image for Biran? Does not the *Nouveaux essais* end up elevating the life of the spirit over the human life? And what of that first life, the life of the body? Is it altogether superseded? The answer which Biran's anthropology suggests is that neither life should be – indeed could be – considered in isolation. Insofar as the *Nouveaux essais* praises the Augustinian ideal of grace it draws on Biran's sense that there is a universal life from which effort emerges and to which it will one day return. Were a reconciliation between effort and grace possible it would be because in the human life physical and spiritual are aspects of the same reality. In *The Relationship between the Physical and the Moral in Man* (1812), a piece that bears significant resemblance to the *Nouveaux essais*, Biran had made his most passionate anticipation of the theme. Here Biran discusses 'two lives': the life of the body and the life of the soul. 'It is another fact of internal observation,' he writes, 'that the health of the soul influences that of the *body* at least as much as the latter does the former'.[105] To consider both lives at once is the task of philosophy, which combines the physical and moral sciences, uniting 'all their theoretical insights and all the data of a double observation, *internal* and *external*'.[106] The result of this, as Biran calls it, 'moral therapy', is a state of rapture. 'Do you believe', he asks,

> that raptures such as those of Pythagoras, or of an Archimedes, on first catching sight of a truth so ardently sought after, are not quite conducive to establishing, between the life of the soul and that of the body, that precious solidarity that conveys to one the energy and the sort of immortality belonging to the other?[107]

It is widely recognized that Biran's image of the two lives and of moral therapy anticipates the anthropology of the *Nouveaux essais*. Body and soul, mortality and immorality, are but aspects of one life. Philosophy, Biran writes, is to see the twofold as a dialectic: 'double observation'. 'The human person,' Biran loved to quote, 'is single in vitality, twofold in humanity' (*homo simplex in vitalitate duplex in humanitate*).[108] This is philosophy's therapy: to cure dualism with double vision, and so end the inner conflict which causes human beings so much misery. Such therapy ends in ecstasy. Effort and truth converge. Life knits everything together. It is with this method that Biran goes on to approach spiritual exercise in the *Nouveaux essais*.

Biran's image of the spiritual life trades on ancient ideals in which philosophy is seen as a path to illumination. And yet there is something new in his image that arrests the reader and accounts for the influence exerted by Biran's work on later thinkers. There is no one explanation for the suasion of *biranisme*, but the philosophical milieu of the time seems to have made the ancient vision more believable. The discovery that meditation was a valid philosophical method – indeed, that meditation itself validated the truths of philosophy – gave new impetus to the ideal of introspection. Even though most eighteenth-century philosophers chose to imagine meditation as the undistracted study of the mind by itself – as self-sufficient effort – and even though Biran rejects much in this picture, his spiritualism nonetheless elevates the ideal of meditation in some form. Beginning with the *Influence of Habit* and culminating in the *Nouveaux essais*, the belief that philosophy should be conceived as meditation shapes Biran's whole philosophy. Certainly, in these two essays we move from a psychology that seems mostly secular to one that is qualified by religious mysticism, and yet in both essays the method remains unchanged. Like the concentrated gaze of the meditator in the essay on habit, contemplation in the *Nouveaux essais* is a form of attention, practised assiduously over many years and directed towards the inner life. And though Biran grows more suspicious regarding the value, ultimately, of attention considered as an effort, his conviction that meditation begins with such effort does not change. The fascination of Biran's spiritualism emerges from the simplicity of the method with which he grounds the path to enlightenment and ecstasy.[109]

But there is also an association between Biran's spiritualism and spiritual exercise that looks to the future of French philosophy. Biran's style of philosophizing sketches in advance the prominence given to the tension between effort and facility. As in the work of Henri Bergson whom Biran influenced greatly, philosophy begins with a great effort of attention. The individual breaks free of old habits and looks at the world with attention. Errors, writes Bergson,

> did not come from things themselves but from an automatic transfer to speculation of habits contracted in action. What a careless attitude of the intellect had done, an effort on the part of the intellect could undo. And for the human mind that would be a liberation.[110]

But in Biran's spiritualism effort is not absolute. Philosophy is an effort the purpose of which one day is to become easy, a habit. Simone Weil, the philosopher in whose work, as we shall see, Biran's approach reasserts itself most strikingly, even goes so far as to reject wholly the idea that attention is an effort. 'When we become tired,' she explains,

> attention is scarcely possible any more, unless we have already had a good deal of practice. It is better to stop working altogether, to seek some relaxation, and then a little later to return to the task; we have to press on and loosen alternately, just as we breathe in and out.[111]

Ideally, philosophy should be easy and attention effortless, like breathing or walking. It should be levity, not gravity; grace, not effort. So practice is necessary; it is good to make of philosophy a habit – as long as it does not become inattentive. And this observation becomes central to human nature as such, as Biran remarks in the *Influence of Habit*: 'Why, after having attached wings to thought, does not habit permit it to direct its own flight, instead of holding it obstinately fixed in the same direction?'[112] In Biran's spiritualism philosophical effort is not an ideal state, any more than muscular tension is (for a thinker like Weil) an ideal state of the body. But in a life where so much that is easy is unreflective, effort provides resistance to the norm. And yet the dream of every exercitant is to perform their discipline spontaneously and without deliberation. Here, as in Biran's spiritual life, a person is returned to an existence undivided by reflection – to life. As Gilles Deleuze once remarked, in the *Nouveaux essais* Biran 'discovered, beneath the transcendence of effort (*l'effort*), an absolute, immanent life'.[113]

The paradox of habit is what allows the reader to consider soberly the reality of philosophy as spiritual exercise. Like habit, the spiritual life is difficult and easy at the same time but not in the same way. Assiduous contemplation rewards the meditator with ecstasy. This cannot be denied even when Biran makes us see how effort offers only an optimal environment for rapture to take hold of the philosopher. In this context philosophy is similar to the experience the retreatant following Ignatius' *Spiritual Exercises* (1522–4) might recognize. But in the world of spirits there is only life; no distinction between activity and passivity, hence no effort as such. The feeling of being alive is the first datum, the primal gift. What in spiritualism is connected to this first life coincides with grace as gift and becomes synonymous with it. A coincidence of grace and life absorbs effort and transforms it. Here too the experience of philosophy resembles a religious exercise, but now it is the spiritual absorption of the self as described by Augustine, Fénelon and Rousseau. Thus we do not need to interpret Biran's spiritualism as either secular or religious, any more than we need to observe the division when it comes to introspection as such, for both sides of the division are in essence spiritual and concerned with the spiritual life. It suffices to distinguish between two contrasting aspects of the spiritual life, of two modalities qualifying the method of ecstasy. In the *Nouveaux essais* they are dramatized in the relationship of effort to grace, which mirrors the relationship between effort and easiness in the essay on habit. Just as, in the example of the good habit, attention persists, although transformed from a difficult to an easy effort, so in spirit effort persists, although transformed from deliberation to desire. To act and to be acted upon are no longer distinctions that matter; only love matters. Even as effort is absorbed by life there is feeling, thought and desire. Biran returns to this point many times in his notes:

> The *feeling* of virtue which triumphs over inclination, the feeling of becoming satisfied, is in effect the feeling of *divinity* for those who do not know it or for whom the light of a positive religion has not yet shone. This is how we must understand this incontestable truth, which is by means of *feeling* alone, *love*, through which the soul finds itself elevated to God, provided that we listen well, that it is a feeling which is in no way passive, neither spontaneous, nor prevents action.[114]

And from here to spirit. Biran entertains no fanciful notions of spirit annihilating activity in order to give way for an absolute passivity. But the resemblance between grace and passivity can also be understood in critical terms. If the human life tends towards hubris, if the meditator ascribes every discovery to their own efforts, then rest, repose and peace offer means of resisting another commonplace of the status quo.

These summary notes supply us with enough material to draw up the method of spiritual exercise as laid out by Biran. It begins with a person curious to know themselves, learning to cultivate the habit of paying attention to their inner life, and reaching, finally, a state of rapture in which every effort of attention, even the fundamental experience of effort itself, is transformed into a state of ecstatic repose. But the meditator does not leave this world; the life of the spirit is one aspect of the human life, as the life of the body is one aspect of the *moi*. So there is now a promise of implementing the experience of ecstatic repose in the life of effort. It goes without saying that what has been acquired is not a new self but a new way of looking at the self – and at the world. The ideal of spiritual exercise is neither effort nor repose but a method of observation that is a coincidence of both and the paradox of their simultaneity: the effort that is easy, the ease which is intense desire. Yet Biran, though he develops the image of philosophy as introspection with remarkable conviction, makes of it nothing more than a propaedeutic. Introspection is a provisional first step towards spiritual ecstasy, and Biran insists on the inability of self-examination to elicit rapture unaided. Like human effort, introspection is circumscribed and finite. Rapture takes hold where effort ends; logically, effort demands grace. 'Biranian thought has nothing to do with introspection,' observes Michel Henry, 'with the "interior life" in the sense of the classical examination of consciousness.'[115] The exercitant finds that where the *moi* is concerned, the terrain is more dizzying than the examination of consciousness could allow. For all the talk of attention directed towards the *moi*, Biran's spiritualism does not answer directly the call of the Delphic oracle. We remember that at the sublime height of self-knowledge there is spirit which absorbs the self, spirit into which the *moi* is lost. It is almost as if, to the exercitant, the *moi* itself existed as a (finite) perspective on infinity, not as an independent realm to be explored. The self makes an effort to reach spirit, but in the end it is the lure of spirit which draws the self within reach of rapture. In every exercise, effort is determined by the pull and tug of life, spiritual exercise by spirit's exercise.

For us, the most striking result of studying Biran's method is to discover his insistence on the finitude of effort. Rapture coincides with certain passive and receptive ways of looking at the world. We will see that Biran's method is very like what we find in studies of the inner life among later thinkers in the spiritualist tradition and beyond. Admittedly very few are able to pursue the experiential paradox to the same extent as the *Nouveaux essais*. In this book I propose that Weil comes closest to continuing the spirit (if not the letter) of Biran's philosophy, but her example is by no means free from difficulties. Spiritualist philosophy accesses spirit by using attention – spiritual exercise – to break through a world of easy habits, but frequently it struggles to recognize the easy nature of attention when cultivated as a habit and way of life. Even so it is the same paradox that is assumed. Biran's two principles of effort and grace anticipate Weil's dialectic of gravity and grace, where spiritual levity contrasts with the heaviness of muscular exertion. It is an Augustinian ideal shaped and mediated through close contact with Stoicism. Mostly, however, Biran's philosophy anticipates the way philosophy would become, in the twentieth century in particular, oriented around inner work, mental effort and self-examination. Precisely because he gives introspection and meditation such significant roles, he also makes it very difficult to recognize the provisional nature of the effort with which they begin. Biran is thus both herald and warning to the philosophy of spiritual exercise.

3

Grace: Félix Ravaisson

In the previous chapter I traced a new philosophy of spiritual exercise through Maine de Biran's spiritualism, noting its critical use of Augustinian introspection to destabilize the self-sufficiency of the meditator and so introduce, into the heart of philosophical method, the necessity of recognizing something like 'grace': the desires, raptures and involuntary ecstasies which happen to the philosopher independently of any effort on her part and throws her into a state of receptivity and passive surrender. But I also indicated that Biran's own interpretation of grace – ever in tension with the effort which prepares for it – was precarious. This chapter will show how, by studying the fate of grace in the work of Biran's most significant follower, the philosopher and art historian Félix Ravaisson (1813–1900). We will see how Ravaisson acts as a threshold figure in the philosophy of spiritual exercise we are considering here: at once the last great outpost of Augustinian mysticism – writing obsessively about grace, surrender and unconscious desire – and a child of Empire committed to modern ideals of heroism, of effort and the apotheosis of human achievement. For although Biran had imagined the spiritual life as the purpose of philosophical practice, and though his contemporaries had all thought of philosophy as a form of meditation modelled on the spiritual retreat, it would take several decades for a spiritual ideal to crystallize fully in France. When it did, the style was different. By 1867, the year Ravaisson's famous report on *La philosophie en France au XIXe siècle* (Philosophy in France in the Nineteenth Century) was published, Biran's mysticism had been translated from its original context to become a national ideal, a question of defining the collective 'spirit' as much as – if not more than – the individual's spiritual progress. In the famous words of the final sentence of Ravaisson's report, 'If the genius of France has not changed',

> nothing will be more natural for her than the triumph of the elevated doctrine – which teaches that matter is but the last degree and, as it were, the shadow of

existence – over systems that reduce everything to material elements and to a blind mechanism; which teaches that true existence, of which everything else is but an imperfect sketch, is that of spirit; … that, beneath the disorder and antagonisms that agitate the surface where phenomena occur, at bottom, in the essential and eternal verity, everything is grace, love and harmony.[1]

'Grace, love and harmony' – the imagery is Biranian, but the confidence with which it is painted is new. Intrepid and not infrequently 'oracular', Ravaisson prescribed where Biran described. Less interested than was Biran in the *how* of the interior life, he aimed to articulate its *why*, its nature and reason.[2] It is impossible to exaggerate the importance of this difference in approach. As Raymond Lenoir wrote in 1919: '[Ravaisson] wanted to stay in the school of life. But he learned from philosophers that a personal experience can receive a dialectical development. He tried to transform the philosophy of life into a science of being.'[3] Under Ravaisson, spiritualism was widely regarded as a reinvention of metaphysics and appeared to have left behind for good the introspective approach favoured by Biran.

But the emphasis on 'appearance' is important. Ravaisson's turn to metaphysics did not cause a radical break with Biran's ideas (which in any case were not lacking in metaphysical concerns). For while the influx of German idealism now encouraged a more abstract perspective on spirit, in France spiritualism never lost touch with the Augustinian roots that had shaped the philosophizing of an earlier generation. Time and again Ravaisson refers to spiritualism as a philosophy of 'the heart': of intuition, deepest feeling and intimate experience. So thoroughgoing was this element that it caused Ravaisson to remark how his 'views seemed, rightly or wrongly, to have a mystical air hardly made to please'.[4] And certainly mysticism won Ravaisson many enemies, though it also won him numerous allies. For while mysticism was concerned with speculative realities not easily accessible to reflection, nonetheless it was grounded in concrete experiences of ecstasy and illumination – we have to remember that mysticism in this context always meant a tradition of interior prayer and spiritual exercise, such as the one Biran had read in the *Spiritual Letters* of François Fénelon and imitated in his own journal. Thus mysticism for Ravaisson provided a response to that worry over the 'dry formalism' of metaphysics, a worry which Andrea Bellantone has pointed to as the chief preoccupation of the young Ravaisson: 'how to do metaphysics without falling into a sterile and abstract exercise?'[5] Far from being an embarrassment to Ravaisson's metaphysics, it seems that mysticism – the philosophy of spiritual exercise – helped to secure its continued popularity and success. Tracing the emergence of Ravaisson's metaphysics from its sources in the Augustinian tradition will be the purpose of this chapter. But though the setting of the chapter is historical, concerned with debates specific to the nineteenth century, the questions addressed here are ones that have since remained central to the philosophy of spiritual exercise: namely, how to translate (if at all) the incommunicable experiences of spiritual existence to the propositions of a spiritual philosophy? Here, it is as a 'spiritual philosophy' that we will be tracing the philosophy of spiritual exercise.

As it is today, the 'mysticism' at stake for the metaphysics of Ravaisson will not be found, however, in any one fixed definition of the term. In the 1860s the context for interpreting the spiritual life was not the same as it had been during the seventeenth century, the golden age of mystical literature in France, or even as it had been at the time of Biran's death in 1824. With the fall of the second republic and establishment of the second empire in 1852 came a fresh enthusiasm for heroism and manly virtue, and a concomitant disinterest in those Quietist values with which Biran, following Fénelon, had associated the spiritual life: repose, tranquillity, calm. 'Keen to live dangerously and to act, man [sic] discovers unsuspected forces within him. He exalts energy and *virtù*,' summarizes Lenoir, writing about the period in which Ravaisson's philosophy emerged.[6] Meanwhile a cluster of scientific hypotheses – principally, of vitalism, evolution and the struggle for survival – encouraged philosophers to view effort as the locus of mystery and awe. It was the high point of Romanticism. Even Ravaisson, who was as suspicious of vitalism as he was of the arguments of Charles Darwin, was committed to a view of reality that perceived the ultimate principal of life to be pure energy. We will see that in Ravaisson's spiritualism, mystic communion takes place wholly within the sphere of spiritual 'action' (*l'action*), and spiritualism itself is known as the 'heroic philosophy'. Thus Ravaisson responded with enthusiasm to the idea of spiritual action wherever it appeared, not least in the philosophy of Stoicism, that other ideal of the spiritual life which was thought, traditionally, to exalt effort and power. In turn, perhaps this promise had always been there in the Augustinian tradition; in the evocation of spiritual tranquillity following a long battle – of grace drawn as if to celebrate the very heroic effort it was set to challenge and resist.[7]

Accepting the foundational role of mysticism for spiritualist thought as it developed in France in the nineteenth century, then, does not mean contradicting established facts about the history of the period. The Augustinianism that appears here is both continuous and discontinuous with the tradition on which Biran drew. As a result, spiritualism itself is both in agreement and in tension with Biran's philosophy of the spiritual life. Already before Ravaisson enters the scene spiritualism had suppressed its old association with the Quietist ideas that appear in Biran's late work, a move made possible by the work of Victor Cousin, Biran's first editor. Under Cousin's early leadership 'spiritualism' even attempted, and failed, to suppress the association with mysticism and spiritual exercise *tout court*, preoccupied instead with the challenge of defining spiritual existence in rationalist terms. The result was a contest within the spiritualist school between rationalism and mysticism, expressing in new terms the old contest between effort and grace, for where 'rationalism' represented what human reason could achieve through her own efforts, 'mysticism' symbolized the opposite: an intuitive knowledge accessed passively and in contradiction to effort. This contest between rationalism and mysticism is expressed most clearly in the preface Cousin wrote for his 1834 edition of a then-unpublished essay by Biran, *Nouvelles considérations sur les rapports du physique et du moral de l'homme* (New Considerations of the Relationship between the Physical and the Moral in Man). Cousin's preface was a seminal piece, for it elevated Biran to wide renown, but it also attempted to exorcize from Biran's philosophy its grounding in spiritual exercise and Augustinian ideals. As such it influenced profoundly Ravaisson's generation even as Ravaisson will be seen to react strongly against it, and in its argumentation prepared the way for later appropriations of spiritual exercise by philosophical methods like phenomenology. Only when Cousin's role in the reception of Biran is understood can we make sense of Ravaisson's contribution and of the often polemic nature of his Augustinianism.

I

Victor Cousin's preface to Biran's *Nouvelles considérations* concludes with equivocal praise of the author's philosophy, which, though 'true in itself', Cousin judges to be 'profound, but narrow'.[8] One has the sense that Cousin approached Biran's written work in the same sanguine manner he approached the philosopher himself. On 15 January 1821 Cousin, a young and charismatic professor at the Sorbonne, met to discuss philosophy with the elderly Biran at the latter's Paris residence. Biran's journal records the details of the meeting, which ended in disagreement. 'Professor C., who recognises no other revelation than that of reason,' remarks Biran, 'denies the actual influence of an intelligent force superior to our soul.'[9] Biran then goes on to contrast Cousin's view with that of François Fénelon, and with Fénelon's idea that revelation is received through an 'abnegation' of reason whereby the *moi* abandons itself to God and assumes an attitude of passivity.[10] A similar reference to Fénelon completes the manuscript of Biran's *Nouvelles considérations,* written in 1820, a year before the meeting with Cousin. Here Biran explains that there is, above the faculties of understanding, a 'creative faculty' which, while not being entirely passive, nonetheless has 'nothing properly active' about it.[11] What Biran has in mind is intuition, which he compares to an 'interior revelation' and distinguishes from reason. It is, he writes, like the knowledge given to Socrates by his *daimon,* or the grace which 'operates in us and animates us'. And again Biran cites Fénelon as his authority on the topic, quoting passages from two short essays of spiritual direction, 'The Miracle of Self-Denial' and 'The Interior Voice of the Spirit':

> God's second miracle is to work in our hearts as he [*sic*] pleases, after he has illuminated our understanding (*notre esprit*): he is not satisfied with simply revealing his own charms. Rather, by his grace, he makes us love him by producing his love in our hearts. It is not (adds this philosopher of the heart) the outward law of the gospel alone that God shows us by the light of reason and faith. It is his spirit within us who speaks, touches, operates in, and moves us to action. So it is the spirit who does in us and with us whatever we do that is good, just as it is our soul that gives life to the body and regulates all its movements.[12]

What Fénelon describes here is the experience of being moved to action, that is, of acting without volition: of passive activity. Fénelon uses the classical imagery of 'spirit' to explain the non-human agency that compels such involuntary activity to take place; Biran thinks of it in philosophical terms as 'intuition', or the knowledge which a person discovers without knowing how. But Cousin is not convinced, and when, in 1834, he sits down to write his preface to Biran's *Nouvelles considérations,* he is keen to clarify the disagreement with his deceased friend. If reason is given by God, why, Cousin asks, should knowledge of God lie beyond its active abilities? So in his preface to the *Nouvelles considérations* Cousin repeats what, no doubt, he had said to Biran in person: no real philosophy could ever countenance an appeal to grace. 'Biran', he writes, 'takes refuge in a kind of mysticism ... he addresses himself to divine intervention, to a revelation not accidental but universal, by means of which God unites himself to man [*sic*] and teaches him the truth ... [Thus] the author of a wholly personal and subjective theory, ends, almost, by appealing to grace.'[13]

But how to make sense of this deplorable 'appeal to grace' – of the fascination with mysticism, Fénelon and the literature of spiritual exercise – in a philosopher whom Cousin otherwise admired? After all, Cousin's preface, despite its guarded tone, is also full of praise for Biran. It ends by proclaiming Biran, 'the most original ... of my teachers' and 'the foremost French metaphysician of my time'.[14] 'Metaphysics' is the key word here: Cousin wants philosophy to be free of mysticism, and yet on this point it seems the history of French thought disappoints, since not only Biran but also René Descartes had invoked grace and of course had written his *Meditations* (1641) in the tradition of Augustinian mysticism. A comparison between Biran and Descartes thus occupies a central part of Cousin's preface. Like Descartes, Cousin says, Biran was a spiritualist philosopher, that is, one who rejected materialism and thought mind irreducible to the body.[15] And like Descartes, Biran approached God through the analysis of thought. These were methods of which Cousin approved. Indeed, much of the preface is devoted to lauding Biran as the inheritor of Cartesian spiritualism and as the restorer of metaphysics. Biran is 'the first in France to have rehabilitated the glory of Descartes', says Cousin. Biran even improves on Descartes, for where Descartes separated spirit too much from body, Biran returns spirit – in his analysis of the *moi* and the 'feeling of effort' – to lived experience.[16] In Biran's philosophy one finds, according to Cousin, 'spiritualism restored in philosophy on the same plane as experience':

> but it is not an extravagant spiritualism without relation to the world which we inhabit. For the spirit which we are – the *moi* – is given to us in the relation which it forms with the first term, but of which the second term is a sensation, and a sensation which is located in such or such a point of the body. Thus, spirit is given to us together with its contrary, the outside together with the inside, nature at the same time as man [*sic*].[17]

Even so, Cousin does not think that either Biran or Descartes succeeded in remaining faithful to their discoveries; discoveries which, he argues, ought to have celebrated – not depreciated – the achievements of reason. The downfall of both Descartes and Biran, argues Cousin, begins with the way in which they 'resort to divine intervention', invoke intuition and introduce the concept of grace and passive knowing into metaphysics; with the way in which they draw on the tradition of spiritual exercise. Thus neither philosopher, in Cousin's opinion, is truly spiritualist. True spiritualism is concerned above all with human freedom, and mysticism appears to destroy freedom when it introduces, over and above active, self-determining reason, a passive faculty of inspiration or intuition. Such endorsements of passivity, writes Cousin, spell 'the slippery slope which leads all of spiritualism to mysticism'.[18] In detailing the sins of mysticism Cousin becomes so enthusiastic that he seems to subscribe wholeheartedly to the logic of the simple *cogito*. 'Not only do I feel, but I know that I feel; not only do I will, but I know that I will,' he writes, against Biran, 'and it is precisely that knowing which is consciousness.'[19] Without such consciousness, how could Biran ever hope to attain knowledge of God? It seems mysticism has weakened Biran's power of discernment. 'One is far from the feeling of muscular effort in this conclusion', judges Cousin, for, 'exhausted in his work, he no longer had enough power or light to seek and discern [reason].'[20]

For Cousin self-consciousness is the essence of spirit. This is Cartesianism in the narrow sense. Below or above the *sui generis* fact of the *cogito* there is nothing. From such a perspective it makes little sense to speak, as Biran does in the conclusion to the *Nouvelles considérations,* of what does not belong to self-consciousness: of the *unconscious*, of the less than active reflection – in short, of the sort of experience that spiritual exercise is supposed to reveal to the philosopher. Hence the depreciation of Biran in the eyes of Cousin, for whom metaphysics must be kept separate from mysticism in the Biranian sense. So, when elsewhere Cousin proclaims spiritualism as his own philosophy, Biran is erased from its history. In 1853, as Cousin composes another famous preface, this time to the first edition of his celebrated *Lectures on the True, the Beautiful, and the Good,* spiritualism is a tradition whose modern appearance begins simply with Descartes. Biran is no longer mentioned among its more recent restorers. 'Our true doctrine, our true flag, is spiritualism,' writes Cousin, 'that philosophy as solid as generous ... which Descartes put under the severe form of modern genius.'[21] And Cousin's readers are told to use the power of reason to aid and defend this 'noble philosophy', despising anything that might tempt strong minds to succumb to 'the senses and the imagination', the same faculties which, in these lectures, are associated with mysticism. As Cousin writes there, mysticism 'attacks liberty itself':

> The ideal of virtue is no longer the courageous perseverance of the good man [*sic*], who, in struggling against temptation and suffering makes life holy; it is no longer the free and enlightened devotion of a loving soul; *it is the entire and blind abandonment of ourselves,* of our will, of our being, in a barren contemplation of thought, in a prayer without utterance, and almost without consciousness.[22]

Cousin's descriptions of mysticism here are significant. Every phrase matters, for 'abandonment', 'contemplation', 'prayer without utterance, and almost without consciousness' are all characteristics of Fénelon's spiritual direction and the mysticism of repose. Cousin rejects this tradition, contrasting it as death to the life of 'courageous perseverance'. Such is Cousin's judgement of mysticism. He does not approve of what happens to the efforts of reason in the philosophies of

Descartes and Biran. He laments the weakness which brings both philosophers to invoke divine grace and place their metaphysical meditations within the orbit of prayer and passive supplication. His interpretation of virtue is self-assertive and martial by comparison. It leaves little place for anything that would allow a relaxing of effort: abandonment, prayer, contemplation. At the same time, the origin of Cousin's own method is contemplation, the careful analysis of thought on which Cousin elsewhere bases his own interpretation of spiritualism. Although he opposes the more-than-human faculty of intuition to which meditation seems inexorably to lead, he cannot find an alternative method with which to replace it. Even so it is not difficult to see what Cousin desired by resisting the mystical in spiritualism. Cousin was trying to harmonize his appreciation for meditation with what he believed about the power of reason. This was a sober spiritualism in which he thought to establish all the speculative expanse of introspection on rigorous grounds. As Cousin puts it in his *Lectures*, 'The unity of modern philosophy … resides in its method, that is to say, in the analysis of thought – a method superior in its own results, for it contains in itself the means of repairing the errors that escape it, of indefinitely adding more riches to riches already acquired.'[23]

Cousin stands at the intersection between two quite different approaches to spiritual exercise, the one scientific – meditation as a tool for analysing the data of consciousness – the other religious – meditation as a means of preparing the soul for encounters with divine presence. As such it is a position not dissimilar to that occupied, less than a century later, by Edmund Husserl's phenomenology, which Paul Ricœur once described as a 'spiritual discipline (*ascèse*)'.[24] The difference, of course, is that Cousin resists mysticism while Husserl's phenomenology, though not itself overtly mystical, nonetheless has lent itself easily to mystical interpretations. In the phenomenology of Jean-Luc Marion, for instance, as in the spiritualism of Biran, there is that which can be analysed through reflection; and then there is the 'excess' of the given, which defies reflection and completes it as intuition.[25] On a deeper level these two approaches to spiritual exercise correspond to the two ideals originally distinguished in the context of Biran's work. These ideals have been referred to earlier as Ignatian and Augustinian respectively, the one tending to Stoicism, the other to one or more variations of Quietism, the theology of interior prayer with which Fénelon was associated. Cousin may be seen to be articulating, however imperfectly, his preference for the former of the two, both of them contained within Cartesian thought: on the one hand a wholly rational ascent to God achieved by mental effort alone; on the other hand, an interior revelation of God received by grace through the faculty of intuition. There are passages in the *Lectures* where Cousin recognizes something of this distinction, and its implications, which will continue to draw spiritualism into the orbit of Stoicism. Attempting to convince his audience of the wondrous powers of mental effort, Cousin writes: 'Our reason, enlightened by true science, can perceive this light of spirits; reason rightly led can go to God, and there is no need, in order to reach him [sic], of a particular and mysterious faculty.'[26] Precisely how reason might attain the divine by its own efforts Cousin does not say, and the line between philosophical optimism and pride becomes vague. But to Cousin, the rationalist philosopher unpersuaded by Fénelon, even the pride of the Stoics is to be preferred to the sloth of the Quietists:

> The best Quietism can, at most, be only a halt in the course, a truce in the strife, or rather another manner of combating. It is not by flight that battles are gained; in order to gain them it is necessary to come to an engagement, so much the more as duty consists in combating still more than in conquering. Of the two opposite extremes – Stoicism and Quietism – the first, taken all in all, is preferable to the second; for if it does not always elevate man [sic] to God, it maintains, at least, human personality, liberty, conscience, whilst Quietism, in abolishing these, abolishes the entire man, oblivious of life and duties, inertness, sloth, death of the soul, - such are the fruits of that love of God, which is lost in the sterile contemplation of its object provided it does not cause still greater aberrations![27]

For those attentive to Cousin, this was spiritual exercise! Far from being repelled by the presumptions of effort, Cousin is attracted repeatedly to its promise of vigour and liberty. Spiritual exercise is for him a question of exercise in the sense of fitness: the mind alert and conscious, the body struggling to resist temptation, 'combating still more than conquering'. In an important sense it is the struggle itself which for Cousin constitutes spirit. Its operative metaphor is martial, its dominating metaphor the constancy of a Stoic.[28] To describe spiritual exercise in these terms was to undo the paradox of the two ideals contained within Descartes' original spiritualism, not to mention in that of Biran. Doubtless such solutions tempt any philosophy of the spiritual life, and it is a solution to which the Ignatian or Stoic ideal, when emphasized for its own sake, is particularly impelled. Six years after the appearance of Cousin's preface to Biran, its challenge to spiritualism was accepted by the philosopher whose ideas would become the principal rival to Cousin's spiritualism: Ravaisson.

II

Ravaisson received his initial philosophical training in the national curriculum devised by Cousin, and, while he is most famous for securing the demise of the latter's influence, he nonetheless inherited a recognizably Cousinian approach to the discipline. Cousin's lasting legacy to French higher education had been to react against the *idéologues,* followers of Condillac, by encouraging a return to the history of philosophy and a revival of metaphysics. Ravaisson followed Cousin in both these respects, writing his first large-scale work on Aristotle's *Metaphysics* and always combining talk of spiritualism with discussions of ancient philosophy.[29] And yet it is usually Ravaisson's name, not Cousin's, which is associated with spiritualism in a founding capacity. The reasons are to be found in mysticism. Where Cousin made the rejection of mysticism part of his definition of spiritualism, Ravaisson did the opposite, proposing a mystical experience as the beginning and end of any philosophical endeavour: and this, in an age when Romanticism was securing the significance of imagination, intuition and feeling, would prove to make all the difference for the future of the movement.[30]

To recognize the full impact, then, of Ravaisson's position it is first necessary to be clear about the relationship between spiritualism and mysticism in this period. For though Ravaisson used the adjective 'mystic' to describe what he thought of as spiritualism, the term was not without contention, as shown by the example of Cousin. The staunch resistance to mysticism in the seventeenth and eighteenth centuries was well known.[31] Mystical writers, such as Fénelon, were accused not only of indulging in extravagant prose; they were also charged with committing acts of civil disobedience and immorality. Presented as retreats, their literature provided refuge from the outside world and, it was thought, a vantage point from which to deviate from secular as well as ecclesiastical norms. To many, 'mystic' was a term of abuse, and was used as such in the polemic against Fénelon. There was, thus, nothing new in Cousin's opprobrium; he was expressing a commonplace suspicion of mysticism, borrowed from earlier theological debates. His celebrated *Lectures on the True, the Beautiful, and the Good*, originally delivered in 1815–21 while Ravaisson was still a young child, are frank on this point. Here Cousin pours scorn on Fénelon, and expends an entire lecture expounding the vices of Quietism: 'Quietism lulls to sleep the activity of man [*sic*],' he says, 'extinguishes his intelligence, substitutes indolent and irregular contemplation for the seeking of truth and the fulfilment of duty.'[32] And: 'Ecstasy, far from elevating man [*sic*] to God, abases him below man; for it effaces in his thought, by taking away its conditions, which is consciousness.'[33] These are not new ideas.[34] But there is certainly a novelty in the way Cousin separates spiritual figures from spiritualism, and mysticism from a philosophy of the spiritual life. Today, when philosophy is so often distanced from its religious roots, it is perhaps not easy to recognize the full impact of Cousin's early attempt to separate the two. But as Michel de Certeau has shown, in France spiritualism and mysticism were once very closely allied. Indeed, in the seventeenth century they meant much the same thing, with 'mystic', the younger of the two terms, appearing in frequent hendiadys with 'spiritual'.[35] To refer to a text as 'spiritual and mystic' was to designate a style of vivid prose, centred on the individual and addressed to private readers (Fénelon's letters of spiritual direction – or Biran's journals, are both good examples of this genre). It was also to assume, at least implicitly, that there was such a thing as a spiritual existence distinct from quotidian life to which all should and could aspire through special exercises or methods.[36] And the reality is that many, if not most, of the thinkers identified as 'spiritualist' by nineteenth-century philosophers were also attracted to both sets of ideas – not least of whom Descartes, as Cousin readily admitted. This was true also within – one should say especially within – Cousin's own circle. The very same year, 1834, that saw the appearance of Cousin's preface to Biran, saw too the publication of an *Essai sur l'histoire de la philosophie en France au XIXe siècle* (Essay on the History of Philosophy in France in the Nineteenth Century) by Jean-Philibert Damiron, a friend and colleague of Cousin. Damiron's *Essai*, while paying respectful homage to Cousin, then unquestionably the leading French philosopher of the day, allows more scope to discussing the relevance of mysticism. Surely, he reflects, philosophy begins not with abstract ideas but with 'religion, the inspirations of feeling, the conceptions of poetry, in a word', concludes Damiron, 'of mysticism – and the most natural mysticism ... which serves to institute and guide minds'.[37] Yet if spiritualism refuses anything but the analysis of thought, how could it hope to see beyond what was evident to the senses alone? It seemed that spiritualism, by rejecting mysticism while proclaiming an allegiance to spiritual existence, was contradicting itself. What is remarkable is that Cousin ever hoped to sustain a vision of the spiritual life that was not only hopelessly illogical, but hopelessly anti-historical.

But the problem was how to appreciate the tradition of spiritual exercise without committing one's whole philosophy, inadvertently, to the extremes with which it was then associated: Quietism. Very few wished to revive the debates of the eighteenth century. At the same time, the intellectual milieu was changing dramatically. I am referring in particular to Romantic reactions against the rationalist world-view to which Cousin, albeit with reservations, still adhered; to a new regard for feeling and sentiment on the one hand, and an enthusiasm for the occult and supernatural on the other. Together these currents steered spiritualist philosophers on a course favourable to mysticism, and prepared for a new appraisal of spiritual existence in the light of Augustinian ideals. To analyse the French context exhaustively demands a study of its own. But a sense for how the changing times effected a revival of Augustinian spirituality is possible if we look briefly at the defence of mysticism in three pieces by Ravaisson: 'Contemporary Philosophy' (1840), *La philosophie en France au XIXe siècle* (Philosophy in France in the Nineteenth Century) (1867) and *Philosophical Testament* (1901).

The first, 'Contemporary Philosophy', argues the case against Cousin and champions a new philosophy inspired by Biran. By the time it was published, in 1840, Ravaisson had already articulated his own position in the essay *Of Habit* (1838), a work likewise indebted to Biran. Ravaisson was a persuasive exponent of Biran's philosophy, which he gives a poetical-metaphysical gloss that remains unique in the history of spiritualism. Like Cousin, Ravaisson saw the possible trouble with Biran's philosophy, in the place where grace seemed to annul effort. But the discovery does not cause Ravaisson to separate the two terms from each other; instead, he wants to maintain a grasp on both effort and grace, using the doubleness of grace – the way (like habit) it emerges from yet does not depend on effort – to problematize any simple equivalence between grace and passivity, and avoiding the narrow rationalism of Cousin by emphasizing the need for something like paradox when it comes to understanding the operation of grace. In fact, the whole denouement of Ravaisson's argument in 'Contemporary Philosophy' is very like the ending of Biran's *Nouvelles considérations,* where Biran cites Fénelon on the necessary passivity of the intellect where matters of grace are concerned. But with Cousin's accusations against Biran's mysticism still fresh in the public mind, Ravaisson must work harder than did Biran to show why a philosophy of grace does not lead irrevocably to Quietism. As a result, Ravaisson's understanding of grace delves deeper than does Biran's mostly unqualified sense of the term – deeper, retrieving more of the sophisticated dialectic that one actually finds in the work of Augustine and Fénelon, but also exploring further than did Biran the nature of effort itself.[38]

Even so, there is no doubting Ravaisson's fidelity to Biran. In all the spiritualist corpus it is difficult to find a more impassioned defence of the Augustinian ideal than 'Contemporary Philosophy'. Though the piece was published originally as a review article of a recent publication, rarely has it been read in this capacity. The reason can be found by turning to the final pages of the article: here there is no longer any mention of the work supposedly under scrutiny; there is only Ravaisson philosophizing, delivering his own vision of reality, a vision that moves seamlessly from Biran's philosophy to a mysticism of divine love, grace and universal harmony that is characteristically Augustinian, and distinct from the thought-world of Cousin. Hence its status as a turning point for spiritualism.³⁹ In the 1840s Cousin was still very much at the height of his influence, and 'Contemporary Philosophy' not only presents what it hopes will be an alternative to Cousin's spiritualism, but describes also the present state of the movement under Cousin.

Once more intuition – the mystic's mode of knowledge – plays a principal role. Nothing could be more different to the rationalism of Cousin than the case against him mounted by Ravaisson towards the end of the article. This is the precise wording of the judgement: '[Cousin] seeks to abandon intellectual intuition while conserving the absolute.'⁴⁰ And the full meaning is: despite insisting that there is but a single mode of knowing (reason), Cousin retains as the purpose of reason that which exceeds its ordinary capacities. It was a criticism that Ravaisson was not alone in voicing to the public. Friedrich Schelling had originated it in a piece recently translated by Ravaisson, which Ravaisson now cites: 'Is [Cousin's understanding of reason], Schelling asks, the mysterious result of a kind of occult quality of intelligence?'⁴¹ There was thus very little, Ravaisson argues, to Cousin's judgement of Biran. 'It seems to me', he writes, that Cousin 'distorts and annuls [Biran's philosophy] by the restrictions he imposes on it'.⁴² Ravaisson even claims that Cousin did not fully understand Biran's doctrine of effort to which he professed fidelity, for Cousin forfeits what is intuitive about the immediate apperception of the *moi* by placing above it ratiocinating intellect. No, Cousin will have no part to play in the 'new course' Ravaisson now prophecies for philosophy. Instead, the future will be guided by Biran, and those philosophers who have followed his lead in '[transporting] psychology from an abstract phenomenology into the living centre of personality'.⁴³ Reflecting on Cousin in the history of French thought, Jacques Derrida described this moment as one where Cousin's attempt to escape mysticism by the 'naturalization' of philosophy ends, ironically, by mystifying what reason seeks to clarify.⁴⁴ In any case, Cousin's desire to lay mysticism to rest had served only to breathe new life into the very discourse he so despised and feared: spiritual exercise according to Fénelon.

In choosing to ally himself with Biran – and in breaking openly with Cousin – Ravaisson must now contend with the unavoidable problems posed by mysticism: Quietist spirituality. At stake in this discussion is the role of passivity. What did Biran mean when he said that intuition was passive, whereas reflection was active? More importantly, were the two concepts necessarily exclusive? 'Contemporary Philosophy' ends with a dialectic of passivity and activity that introduces what François Laruelle describes as a 'radical immanence' distinct from the dualities that characterize Biran's metaphysics.[45] Thus Biran's thesis of passivity is never accepted literally. Granted, Ravaisson says, Biran did claim that '[w]e do not know ourselves except as free activity, and consequently we will never know what we are in the passive ground of our being'.[46] And it is possible, Ravaisson concedes, that Biran really intended passivity in an absolute sense to signify 'an abyss without measure, an impenetrable night'.[47] Such had been Cousin's understanding of the Biranian experience of 'grace'. But Ravaisson does not favour this interpretation. Starting from the reasonable assumption that grace does not destroy but perfects effort, Ravaisson argues instead for a paradox or continuity between the two terms. 'Effort supposes, as Maine de Biran himself recognised,' writes Ravaisson, 'an anterior tendency that, in its development, provokes resistance.' This, he continues, 'is an original activity, prior to effort':

> In order for the will to be determined by the abstract idea of its object a real presence must already secretly move us. Before the good is a *motif* in the soul it is already, as by a prevenient grace, a *motive*, but as a motive that does not differ from the soul itself. Before acting by *thought*, it acts by *being* and in *being*, and this is all there is that is real in the will.[48]

The will chooses, but it chooses based on desire, and desire is not subject to conscious volition, being more like a given state than a chosen act. Desire itself is never anything but good (Ravaisson is describing something deeper than taste and appetite). Hence Ravaisson calls desire 'prevenient grace', meaning grace already present or given, as opposed to grace which arrives unexpectedly, though both forms of grace refer to a phenomenon beyond the control of the will. This would have qualified it to be described as 'passive' in the eyes of Biran, since the person is passive in relation to grace; Ravaisson avoids the term, but the sense is the same: to describe a state in which effort has the quality of easiness and spontaneity, rather than conscious exertion.

The treatment of grace here in the conclusion to 'Contemporary Philosophy' recalls a famous passage at the end of Ravaisson's *Of Habit*:

> In this way the profound words of a profound theologian might be confirmed: 'Nature is prevenient grace'. It is God within us, God hidden solely by being so far within us in this intimate source of ourselves, to whose depths we do not descend.[49]

'Prevenient grace' was a key idea in the theology of Fénelon, whose *A Demonstration of the Existence of God, Deduced from the Knowledge of Nature* (1712) Ravaisson cites as his source for the striking expression 'Nature is prevenient grace'. Actually, the exact phrase does not appear in the *Demonstration*, which speaks instead of finding God in nature. Writes Fénelon, 'What do I see in the whole survey of nature? God. God everywhere, God ever present and still only God.'[50] But Ravaisson's paraphrase captures well what Fénelon elsewhere describes as the secret presence of grace in creation, the desire that motivates pre-reflectively every movement of body and mind. 'I believe with St Augustine,' explains Fénelon in the same volume, 'that God gives each man [sic] a first seed of intimate and secret grace which mixes imperceptibly with reason and prepares man to pass from reason to faith,' and continues: 'God mixes the beginning of the supernatural gift with the remains of good nature, so that the man who holds them together … carries within himself a mystery of grace of which he is profoundly ignorant.'[51] Hence Ravaisson's description of grace, in 'Contemporary Philosophy', as 'a real presence [that] must already secretly move us', as 'a motive that does not differ from the soul itself', etc. For Fénelon, 'prevenient grace' described the pure love of the heart with which the soul co-operated spontaneously, independently yet not separately from reason. In this way he followed Augustine in asserting at once the irresistible nature of grace and the ineluctable freedom of will and reason.[52] In *Of Habit* and 'Contemporary Philosophy' Ravaisson uses the phrase similarly to avoid opposing rational effort directly with grace: what theology calls prevenient grace philosophers call anterior tendency or formal cause; hence what is 'given' is not quantitative (rational effort) but qualitative (desire or purpose). Grace could thus be a means of finding for mysticism a middle way between mental effort and spiritual passivity, a means of thinking about the immediacy of spiritual knowledge without destroying reflective consciousness. A philosophy of spiritual exercise close to Biran, indeed in some ways closer to Fénelon and Augustine than was Biran's, makes itself felt. Still, the overall interpretation remains Biranian.

Like Biran, moreover, Ravaisson is swept away by the equivocal experience of grace. Where grace is concerned my experience is one of passivity, for I did not will grace; and yet I am not inactive, for I am impelled by love. This reality, says Ravaisson in 'Contemporary Philosophy', is less like inactivity and more like being moved; it is like desire and love, 'no longer a mode' but 'the substance of the soul.'[53] Applying this principle to the will and to reason, Ravaisson rejects the idea, evident in Cousin's spiritualism – with its implications of moral and intellectual hubris – that effort could determine itself, in favour of a more modest approach. 'Love is no longer, like the Will, the abstract act of a *principle* intent on pursuing the *end* … it is the complete reality, the perception, the consummation of the Principle, united to its end, identified with it.'[54] Ravaisson thus disagrees with the reduction of life to vital force or effort; such effort is never without a source, and it is the source which must explain what is left unexplained by effort. But as so often in Ravaisson's philosophy, he rejects, too, the opposite approach. 'The passive substrate of phenomena is only an abstraction formed by the imagination,' he concludes, 'and there is true reality only in the inner activity of Mind.'[55] Though he is advocating a mystical spiritualism distinct from vitalism, Ravaisson is not endorsing a Quietist way of life. The whole point is to show that in light of inner experience such definitions are all inadequate:

> Perhaps a full and adequate understanding of this is possible only in God. Perhaps in this sense the reflection seeking it is to the soul 'what the asymptote is to the curve, which it attains only in the infinite' ... [W]ho cannot find in his heart the obscure but infallible awareness of this?[56]

In effect, Ravaisson is forging a link between the old spiritualism of Fénelon and Biran, with its pessimistic attitude towards mental effort, and the new spiritualism of Cousin, with its rationalist faith in the powers of the mind and its cult of vitality. In this context it is not surprising to see Ravaisson discrediting the language of passivity. The very apposition of 'grace' with 'the inner activity of Mind' anticipates the modern conception of philosophy as mental self-exercise. At the same time, the distinction between effort, a conscious volition, and grace, an unconscious activity, puts pressure on any simple alliance between spirit and mind in the modern sense. In other words, the notion of 'passivity' which Ravaisson rejects embodies a purely hypothetical mysticism. It separates spirit from spiritual existence. But it does not exclude from mysticism the experience of intuition: of the immediate, the spontaneous and the involuntary. For while passivity to Ravaisson is an abstraction, the involuntary is not; and it is *as* the involuntary – as love, desire, 'prevenient grace' – that what Ravaisson calls 'activity' and 'mind' in fact first appears to the *moi*: 'In order to desire', he reflects, 'it is necessary that, *unknowingly*, we take pleasure in it in advance and that we place ourselves in the object of our desire.'[57] Insofar, however, as Ravaisson's is a solution to the problem posed by Cousin's rejection of mysticism, it is one that comes with no easy answers; it returns the reader inexorably to the internal tensions of Biran's position. At the heart of things there is, indeed, 'original activity', 'eternal love', an immortal, vibrant life; and yet this activity itself is not effort. Here is certain mystery, but its certainty is also its incomprehensibility. This is the stake of every claim by philosophers to articulate faithfully the life of the spirit, but it is also, as Paul Ricœur learnt from Ravaisson, the experiential paradox that grounds perception of the world as such.[58]

Put differently, Ravaisson's conception of the spiritual life is presented as a progressive Augustinianism. We might see it as an ideal of the spiritual life where grace, though distinct from effort, still stands to effort in a positive relationship. Despite his preference for paradox, equivocation and the middle term, Ravaisson always worked hard to convince critics that spiritualism was a philosophy concerned positively with *action*. In 1867, now for several years Inspector General of Higher Education and on the way to becoming the most influential philosopher in France, Ravaisson is still telling readers that French philosophy shows encouraging signs of 'what might be called a spiritualist realism or positivism, whose generating principle is the consciousness that spirit takes in itself of an existence of which it recognizes that every other existence derives and depends, and which is none other than its action'.[59] The passage appears in the second of the three texts under consideration here, Ravaisson's influential *Philosophie en France*. It is the first full-scale attempt by a French philosopher to articulate an alternative to Cousin's spiritualism, published the very year of Cousin's death, in 1867. Though the study cannot be summarized as Biranian in the precise sense, there is a significant way in which it is in agreement with Biran's philosophy, for Ravaisson's is a philosophy of the spiritual life and of grace. Of course, there is no more mention here of grace being a kind of passivity – Cousin's relentless attacks on Quietism had dissuaded any philosopher from allying themselves, as Biran had done, too closely to the genre of spiritual exercise and mystical introspection. But if one understood the heart of the spiritual life to be the co-extensiveness of two spheres, a way of thinking with the apparent contradiction between grace and effort, then grace was not restricted to the language of repose and passivity. Ravaisson was attempting to aid the tradition by giving it a new identity, one that would be more in tune with the age's appreciation for effort, even as it eschewed a philosophy centred wholly around vitality and human achievement. Despite his indebtedness to Biran's spirituality of repose, Ravaisson has the inspiration to set aside the habit of portraying grace from the perspective of the passive recipient and instead narrate its appearance from the animated aspect of that which gives:

> In almost all the ancient East, and since time immemorial, it was an ordinary symbol of divinity that this mysterious, winged being, the colour of fire, who consumed itself continually, annihilated itself to be reborn from its ashes ... According to Christian dogma ... God descended by means of his son, and descended thus without descending, into death, for life to be born, a life entirely divine. 'God became man [*sic*] so that we should become God'. The spirit, abasing itself, became flesh; flesh will become spirit. Liberality, the source of justice itself,

is the characteristic virtue of great souls: the supreme name of the Christian God is grace, gift, liberality; extreme liberality by which, liberally indeed, God gives himself, creates his creature from his own being, nourishing her from his being, making her resemble God and making her as divine as himself. 'You are gods'.

These thoughts are those towards which, if we are not mistaken, our modern systems gravitate ... Truth shows itself to us wherever we live it, from the earliest times, in very nearly every country. Only, today truth shows itself, perhaps, more stark and more whole. We understand better, it seems, what the ancients meant when they said, 'Eros was the first and is still the most powerful of the gods'; or else, 'God is charity'.[60]

A modern reader might find the report's tone mystic in the extreme, but it is difficult not to notice in it a novel sensitivity to the effort involved in grace, a recognition of charity in action that only infrequently appears in Biran's spiritualism. Self-sacrifice, abasement – these are all images that occupy central roles in Biran's mysticism, as they do in the work of Fénelon from whom Biran borrows most of his mystical vocabulary. But where Fénelon, like Ravaisson here, will often gloss self-sacrifice as a mode of giving, Biran chooses instead to show it as a mode of passivity – so, abnegation is necessary in order for the soul to *receive* grace. By contrast, in the report of 1867, abasement is necessary in order to *give* liberally. Here Ravaisson in fact is closer to Fénelon than was Biran. Of the abandonment or abnegation of the self evidenced by the 'holy mystics' Fénelon writes, in *Maxims of the Saints* (1697), that it is an operative mode, whereby the 'selfless soul gives herself totally and without reservation to God'.[61] Ravaisson's imagery can be traced, ultimately, to this idea, which Fénelon inherits from Augustinian spirituality. As he states elsewhere, Ravaisson prefers giving to receiving.[62] Hence the peculiarity of his language of grace, the way it is distinct from grace in the nominative sense, as a gift received, or as a passive state of the soul, that so dominates in Biran's accounts of contemplation. At the same time, Ravaisson's description of grace as the 'virtue of great souls', is closer, in many ways, to Cousin's emphasis on duty, deed and courage than it is to the thought-world of Biran. And yet in the report Ravaisson repeatedly goes out of his way to distance himself from Cousin, to whom he delivers several memorable asides, the most generous of which is to summarize Cousin's position as a species of 'demi-spiritualism'.[63] 'Victor Cousin is not appreciated in this account' one reviewer remarked, acerbically, commenting on the publication of *Philosophie en France*.[64] The new tone achieved by Ravaisson is made possible, I suspect, by a shift in viewpoint regarding the effort involved in the spiritual life. For the fact that what Ravaisson describes as charitable action implies forms of voluntary suffering and death means that the effort in question still retains a link with passivity. Though it is easy to see a continuity with the spiritualism of Cousin, not many would have identified, immediately, the Cousinian element in Ravaisson's spiritualism. In truth, *Philosophie en France* represents a deliberate reinvention of Biran's mysticism that we will see concluded only in Simone Weil's philosophy of spiritual exercise. Ravaisson anticipates a typically Weilian paradox: love that is effortless but at the same time a superlative achievement, passive and yet active: 'the greatest of all efforts, perhaps, but a negative effort'.⁶⁵ As it happens, the concluding image of *Philosophie en France* is precisely this equivalence between grace and greatness, here figured as 'heroism':

> From earliest times our forefathers [*sic*] believed profoundly in immortality, a belief which is based on consciousness of the infinite, of the divine in us. Thence came, said the ancients, their indomitable value. They were given this praise of possessing to a supreme degree (with courage, the mark of magnanimity, which consists in giving, if necessary, one's own life) eloquence or the gift of persuasion ... Now, that one above all knows how to persuade who knows how to love, who is great enough to give themselves, to sacrifice themselves: 'Be great, and love will follow you'. Thus Christianity was nowhere better or more readily received than with our forefathers. Is not Christianity summarised in the dogma – which is found in the best of all ancient wisdom, the constant thought of our ancestors – that love alone is the author and master of all? From this same thought, from this thought of love and of devotion which is the foundation of heroism, was born among us, in the middle ages, chivalry.⁶⁶

Like Weil's understanding which it anticipates, Ravaisson's image of love is intensely paradoxical. To love is to give, but the greatest gift ends the giver's life and seems to negate love. So while the description of love as heroic virtue suggests that great deeds are the criterion of value for the spiritual life, this is not what Ravaisson means. Or more accurately, while charity is measured in magnanimity, its greatness derives from subtlety rather than show: 'eloquence or the gift of persuasion'. Greatness is quality, not quantity; a way of doing something, rather than an estimation of things done. Hence the praiseworthy hero, in this passage, does not care for personal glory but is content to operate incognito through gentle words and imperceptible persuasion. It is a very good representation of what Ravaisson had in mind when he said, in 'Contemporary Philosophy', that grace, while an activity, is not an effort. The metaphor now preferred by Ravaisson expands the concept from doctrine to myth: grace is no longer an abstract notion but a figure with its own genealogy and origins, traceable to pre-Christian 'forefathers'.

Above all, Ravaisson's genealogy of grace points to one forefather in particular: Hercules, the hero *par excellence* whose endurance was admired by many ancient writers, most famously by the Stoics. Ravaisson's *Philosophical Testament* (1901), edited and published posthumously shortly after his death in 1900, addresses the connection. We read here a glowing appraisal of the Stoic hero and of Stoic philosophy. Beginning where *Philosophie en France* left off, Ravaisson identifies the hero with the 'Stoic saying' that a person 'was born … not for themselves, but for the whole world'.[67] 'This was exemplified', explains Ravaisson, 'above all by the son of Jupiter, Hercules, who was as valiant as he was compassionate, always generous to the oppressed, and finished his glorious career by climbing to Olympia'.[68] In addition, the Stoic hero imitated the gods, 'the giver of goods' and thus embodied grace in their show of charity, generosity and hospitality, acts which in turn encouraged 'the belief in divine beneficence'.[69] It is this philosophy of compassion and hospitality, writes Ravaisson, which is 'the spiritual or spiritualist philosophy'.[70] Stoicism: such is, for Ravaisson, spiritualist philosophy. In a long note appended to the *Philosophical Testament*, Ravaisson explains how a spiritual philosophy was intimated also by Stoic cosmology more broadly. The Stoics believed the world to be the result of an alternating tension and relaxation – *tonos* and *anesis* – of a divine creative fire. Ravaisson interprets the doctrine to indicate an idea similar to his own theory of prevenient grace or, as he puts it in this note, 'pre-existent love'. Life, he explains, emerges as the result of a divine desire spontaneously 'dispersing' itself and bringing itself back together again. Needless to say, Ravaisson sees a similarity between this doctrine and the mystical image of grace as abandonment, a movement of 'abasement and then recovery, or resurrection', which figured already in *Philosophie en France*. It is the imagery we recognize from Fénelon and the literature of spiritual direction. Here it becomes a 'Stoic and Christian theory'.[71]

The idea of tension and relaxation is central to this whole essay, which is devoted to finding different images with which to convey the mystical principle of abandonment as revealed, so Ravaisson believes, by both Stoicism and Christianity. Thus, in evolution, grace is the fact that 'everything comes from principles or causes that create by giving themselves'; in organic life, grace is the 'pulse' of diastole and systole, '*sursum* and *deorsum,* otherwise called awakening and sleep, life and death'; among moving bodies (a subject which fascinated Ravaisson, who was also a keen painter and art historian), grace is the beauty peculiar to each, which Leonardo da Vinci said could be captured in a serpentine line or undulation tracing the curves of organic form.[72] In this way grace is neither pure effort nor absolute passivity, but the middle term; the point where activity becomes effortless, and effort becomes spontaneous. In Ravaisson's notes from this period, the image of tension and relaxation is used to illustrate explicitly the idea of a principle that creates by sacrificing itself:

> Philosophy is revelation through the Heart, its need for immolation. Two principles: male and female, red and azure, earth and Heaven, hardness and softness, egoism and abandon, *tonos* and *anesis*.[73]

The 'need for immolation' mentioned here stands for classic images of passivity. It recalls Fénelon's idea of abandonment and self-annihilation, while 'revelation through the Heart' implies the faculty of intuition. But they are offset by concepts of tension and effort: the male, the red, earth, hardness, egoism, *tonos* and so on. It is this Stoically inflected Augustinian ideal which Ravaisson uses to redefine the philosophy of the spiritual life, just as Cousin compared his own position favourably to Stoicism earlier in the century.

Yet although the similarities between Ravaisson and Cousin are evident, so too are the differences. *Philosophical Testament* does not endorse Stoicism fully, not even in the jesting manner of Cousin. When it comes to morality, writes Ravaisson, the Stoics had the right idea, but odd notions of how to go about the good life. They understood, he says, that morality was the 'art of life', the art, that is, of fashioning life beautifully, according to the principles of beauty. But this is as far as Ravaisson's praise will go. For the Stoics 'excluded compassion as a weakness' and considered 'every passion [a] weakness and sickness'.[74] To the Stoic, only the action that was rational and voluntary was good. But what was the hero's generosity without compassion, spontaneity and the ability to follow the heart? The difference between the Stoic and the spiritual art of life, then, becomes the difference between rationalism and mysticism, calculation and feeling, reason and revelation:

> How should we achieve this state of constant generosity? Even more than for the fine arts, it is true for the art of life that we do not reach this goal by ... the dryness of precepts, but by imitation. It is not so much a question of communicating a good theory to the understanding as one of giving a good impulsion to the affections, to sensibility, to the will, which operates by the contagious force of reality and life.[75]

By identifying Stoicism with an extreme form of rationalism Ravaisson repeats a commonplace criticism. Stoicism, a philosophy that aims to free the philosopher from the thrall of passion, cannot speak to the heart. Thus it takes leave of everything the heart stands for: life, movement, plasticity, change – in a word, 'reality'. Naturally the argument has the benefit of contrasting Stoicism with spiritualism, the philosophy, Ravaisson wants us to understand, of lived experience. But is the heart wholly separate from reason? It is here that Ravaisson gets to the paradoxy of the spiritual ideal. 'In a beautiful thing', he writes, citing Leonardo da Vinci, 'everything appears to have been a breeze, *col fiato*. It is completely different from what appears to have been made with effort, *con stento*.'[76] And yet not entirely different. For just as heroism, grace is an activity. But just like grace, heroism is spontaneous. So one might liken the effort of grace or heroism to the effort of habit and instinct, which is to say, to an effort that is paradoxically effortless, 'outside of our power': 'How can we explain,' he asks, 'that there exists in us a science so vast, so profound, often so sure as are instincts and habits in general, but which, however, would be outside of our power?' The answer: we cannot. Only intuition, and the evidence of the inner life gives proof: 'We can only [explain] this to a very small extent, but it is nonetheless certified by an irrefutable experience.'[77] But even for this sort of insight reason is required along with intuition; the Stoic with the mystic, Hercules with Christ.

The *Philosophical Testament* concludes with a list of those who recognized the significance of intuition: Paul, Augustine, Blaise Pascal, even Descartes, who 'believed that he owed the highest truths he found to divine inspiration.'[78] And Ravaisson ends by staking the claims of spiritualism on a real distinction between reason and intuition: 'The heroic philosophy does not build the world with mathematical and logical unities, and from the abstractions understanding detaches from reality; it attains, by the heart, the lively living reality, the moving soul, spirit of fire and light.'[79] Thus ends Ravaisson's last word on spiritualism. Although no longer concerned with Cousin directly, it is a final defence of mysticism – of the spiritual philosophy which is also a philosophy of the spiritual life – in light of rationalist persuasions.

III

By the time Ravaisson's *Philosophical Testament* appeared posthumously in 1901 the integration of an older, mystical, spiritualism with the requirements of its newest form was well established. Here were all the ideals of spiritual exercise which had shaped Biran's methodology, but presented in a new form, as metaphysics rather than as an exploration of the inner life. True, it was not always easy to discern the Augustinian commitments in Ravaisson's philosophy, which as a rule shied away from introspection, or in his invocation – however critical – of Stoicism. Even for a philosophy indebted to Biran (by now famous for his admiration of Stoicism) it was unusual to see the Christic and stoical so closely intermingled. And yet the underlying ideal of Ravaisson's spiritual philosophy remained Augustinian in character, visible in the fact that none of the commonplace criticisms of Stoicism really applied in those striking instances where Stoic doctrine was praised by Ravaisson. Insofar as Stoic ideas were now part of a spiritual philosophy, they were not identical to those espoused by Cousin: Ravaisson's 'Stoicism' was mystical in essence and a spiritual exercise in all but name. Nonetheless, the situation was a curious one, and in 1876 Charles Rénouvier, Ravaisson's contemporary, said as much. In his short polemic 'D'une forme moderne du stoïcisme' (Concerning a modern form of Stoicism), Rénouvier's basic position is much the same as Ravaisson's, but his hostility to Stoicism is considerably more pronounced. The article ends by denouncing roundly the 'new Stoicism' in France. 'The cult,' he writes, ' ... is the great political – one might even say religious – malady of the freethinkers of the nineteenth century.'[80] How could modern philosophy compare itself to a school with such deep flaws? It was a question that cut to the quick of spiritualism, for it exposed once more the divided nature of the ideal of spiritual exercise on which it was founded. Only now, in place of what we have been calling the Ignatian tendency of the spiritual ideal, there was Stoicism. This posed new problems, or rather cast old problems in new moulds. For while it would be possible to reconcile the claims of an Ignatian with an Augustinian position (both recognized parts of the same religious tradition), it was more difficult to see how a pagan ethic could be united with a religious mysticism derived from Christianity.

Scholarship of past decades has done much to illumine what is at stake here: the relationship between an enthusiasm for Stoic philosophy and the slow revival of Augustinian ideas that reach an epitome in Ravaisson's spiritual philosophy. To begin with, though a kind of Augustinianism has long been considered the principal characteristic of French thought,[81] it never did constitute a monolithic tradition untouched by internal tensions. William J. Bouwsma's important work on European humanism, for instance, has demonstrated how, in the early modern period, Stoicism in particular formed with Augustinianism 'an ideal polarity' within 'a larger movement'.[82] In this ideal polarity one saw Stoic ideas both rejected freely and freely adopted, depending on the nature of the confrontation. The two ideals could even be seen 'to complement each other as law is complemented by grace, or the earthly by the heavenly city',[83] with the same figures cited 'on both sides' of the debate.[84] And long after the early modern period Stoicism continued to be a device by means of which Augustinian values could be tested and scrutinized. For this reason, we should not be surprised that interest in Stoicism flourished at the moment when Augustinianism enjoyed increased popularity, or that an interest in the philosophy of spiritual exercise should coincide with enthusiasm for the Stoics' 'art of living'. One might even say that a rise in Augustinianism was as important to the age's fascination with Stoicism as was its *Schwärmerei* for Greek culture. At any rate, for Ravaisson as for Biran, it was impossible to claim the Augustinian position without confronting its Stoic interlocutor, in the same way that any invocation of grace would also evoke the real presence of effort.

For although Stoic values came into conflict with parts of Augustinian spirituality, meaning that it was not easy to see how any prayer for grace could be acceptable to a Stoic, those same values allowed philosophers to avoid the pitfalls associated with the extreme ends of Augustinianism. Here we must include not only Quietism but also Jansenism and the 'tragic' worldview of popular writers like Pascal and Jean Racine. Their pessimism regarding human effort and antipathy towards Stoicism, once so fashionable during the early modern period, were all subject to interrogation during the nineteenth century. It no longer sufficed to see the spiritual life wholly in opposition to the Stoic ideal, as a disdaining of effort and withdrawal from the world; the spiritual life was also – and always had been – the business of speaking plainly on behalf of truth in the midst of everyday life. And it seemed the old manuals of spiritual direction simply were not capable of conveying these new aspirations and hopes. 'We should also remark,' writes Ravaisson, regarding the intellectual milieu of previous centuries, 'that the Gospels do not prescribe the wild solitude … which Pascal was taken by.'[85] At the same time, Ravaisson's own philosophy was encouraging readers to return to a wholly Augustinian and intensely personal understanding of the spiritual ideal, to see it in light of the 'primitive revelation that is the heart', as Ravaisson puts it in the *Philosophical Testament*.[86]

During this time the significance of Stoicism was emphasized further by revived interest in some of its ancient doctrines. This was not a new phenomenon. In France a venerable tradition of Neostoicism stretched back to at least the sixteenth century and had continued uninterrupted through to the age of revolution. But in the nineteenth century, as writers turned their attention from Hellenistic philosophy to the older classicism of Plato and Aristotle, appraisals of Stoicism were not infrequently inflected with a condescension and prejudice that had not been present to the same extent in earlier accounts.[87] Along with Epicurean hedonism, Stoicism was seen as the decadent product of a failing Roman Empire, and no match for the Christianity that soon replaced it. To present a marked contrast between classical authors and Hellenist philosophies was thus a familiar trope in any history of philosophy written during this period. Rénouvier – who authored the polemic against 'modern' Stoics I cited above – employs it in the second volume of his *Manuel de philosophie ancienne* (Manual of Ancient Philosophy) (1844), when he observes a 'weakening of speculation' affecting Stoic philosophy in the Roman Empire: 'From the time when the conquest of Greece was accomplished', he argues, 'the Greeks themselves lost much of their speculative ability.'[88]

Though it is usual to conclude that this contrast between Greek and Hellenistic philosophy was intended in a triumphalist way, condemning Stoicism wholesale, there were many who took a more nuanced approach. As Michel Spanneut has shown, the lively interest taken in Stoicism by nineteenth-century thinkers was neither wholly prejudiced nor entirely unscrupulous. Most philosophers writing about the history of Stoicism were genuinely fascinated, for instance, by the ideas of the early or Greek Stoa. Regardless of whether a philosopher rejected later so-called Roman Stoicism (most of them did), they were still able to write enthusiastic appraisals of Stoic doctrine. By turning to Zeno and Chrysippus rather than Epictetus, for instance, it was possible once more to see in Stoicism a philosophy worthy to contend with. This older Stoic, it was thought, was closer to Heraclitus than to Seneca, and had much more in common with a religious mystic than with a moral athlete. Rather than striving to control her passions and endure every kind of misfortune with equanimity, this Stoic attempts to live as citizen of a divine cosmos; she venerates the spark of divinity present in all beings, loves her fellow person and desires ultimate union with God.[89]

To this distinct interpretation of Stoicism Ravaisson's spiritualism contributed in several important ways. One striking doctrine of the early Stoa was the idea, which we have encountered once already, that the world was held together by a cosmic force or 'tension'.[90] While Ravaisson rejected the extreme interpretation of this doctrine – that the world was reducible to vital forces, an interpretation that was known, in the nineteenth century, as vitalism or animism – he agreed that matter was not the passive, inert stuff imagined by mechanistic science. Movement, not inertia, was the principle of life: this was a central, if not the central, claim of his philosophy, and it was one that Ravaisson now linked to ancient Stoicism. With these different ideas converging there emerged all the prerequisites for a spiritual vindication of Stoicism, as Ravaisson showed in his *Philosophical Testament*.

But there was also the old Augustinian suspicion of Stoic morality. Given the roots of spiritualism in Christian religion, such suspicions were bound to intensify, as indeed they did. Until the end of the 1870s, when scholarly interest in Roman Stoicism revived in earnest, judgements of Stoicism as a whole were largely negative, even as Greek Stoicism, under Ravaisson's interpretation, was proving increasingly a source of fascination.[91] The classical example of this double attitude becomes clear in Ravaisson's influential *Essay on Stoicism*. First published in 1857, *On Stoicism* anticipates the arguments in the *Philosophical Testament* and is largely an elaboration of the sections on Stoicism found in a much earlier piece, the second volume of Ravaisson's 1845 *Essai sur la Métaphysique d'Aristote* (*Essay on Aristotle's* Metaphysics). There Ravaisson had presented Stoicism as an exciting but ultimately failed attempt to develop what Ravaisson takes to be the central insight of Aristotle's philosophy: activity (*energeia*).[92] *On Stoicism* presents the ancient school in much the same way, while emphasising its positive sides and giving attention to Stoicism as an art of life. The purpose, after all, is to present a sympathetic view of Stoicism. Mostly the impression is made possible by focussing on the early Stoa, but even Roman Stoicism receives, in places, a surprisingly generous appraisal by Ravaisson. On the subject of Stoic exercises, for instance, Ravaisson suggests that grace is not entirely foreign to the Stoic, who is able, albeit indirectly, to pray: '[I]t seems,' writes Ravaisson, 'that sometimes the Stoics recognised the incapacity of man [*sic*] to arrive at perfection without the help of God. "Ask God", said Epictetus, "for help and assistance"'. After which Ravaisson can ask: 'Who does not hear in these words Christianity itself?'[93]

But it is the doctrines of early Stoicism that really interest Ravaisson, above all the idea of *tonos*:

> Heraclitus said: 'the harmony of the world is back-stretched, like the bow or lyre'. It was an ordinary thing for the ancients both to show, by the example of the lyre or bow that always remain taut, that nothing can subsist without an alternative succession of work and rest ... The words of Heraclitus came to be, moreover, the summary of an entire system of physics and cosmology. He explained nature, as did the Stoics after him, by a fire that is alternately enflamed and extinguished. It is very likely that, before the Stoics, he also had had the idea of explaining, by alternating tension and relaxation, the two alternative and contrary states of fire. It is possible to relate another sentence of the same philosopher to the same idea: that Jupiter made the world while playing. The world, according to Heraclitus, was the result of the partial extinction of divine fire; extinction, as we have just seen, was seemingly for him, as it was for the Stoics, relaxation succeeding tension. Hence, what is commonly considered, and rightly so, as having to alternate, in human life, with work, *ponos*, *spoude*, so that relaxation alternates with tension, was not pure and simple repose, but play, *paidia*, *jocus*.[94]

It goes without saying that the 'alternating tension and relaxation' described here is the same image that Ravaisson will later use to explain the nature of grace. These ancient Stoics inherit from Heraclitus a view of the world that is, to Ravaisson's mind, as inherently spiritualist and religious as that of Aristotle; even, perhaps, more in tune, on this point at least, with the religious viewpoint than was Aristotle's philosophy. For while Aristotle had understood rightly that the origin of all things must be quite distinct from inertia, *On Stoicism* reveals nonetheless a lingering uneasiness about identifying God, as Aristotle had done, with an abstract concept like 'actuality'. It is as if, by describing the divine life as one of 'tension' rather than actuality, the Stoics steer clear of the abstract speculations associated with that term, as well as that more problematic abstraction, passivity – a concept even Aristotle had proposed as a thought experiment and which now came freighted also with Quietist spirituality. Every reason, then, to look for another metaphor with which to convey the all-important discovery of divine life and energy at the heart of reality. And what, to Ravaisson at least, seemed the advantage of 'tension' is clear from this passage: like actuality, tension is comprehended in relation to its opposite, but unlike actuality the opposite of tension is not the dreaded abstraction of passivity; it is not, as Ravaisson puts it, 'pure and simple repose' but 'play' – 'play' is how Ravaisson glosses the Stoic concept of *anesis* or 'relaxation'. It is a significant move. We recall how Ravaisson would attempt, in the *Philosophical Testament*, to imagine grace as an *effortless* activity by comparing it to spontaneity, beauty, undulation and so forth. 'Play' captures well the same theme. Moreover, it ties grace still more firmly to Stoic thinking by slipping in *ponos*, 'labour', as the extended sense of *tonos*. As work is to rest, so tension is to relaxation, creativity to creation. In the *Philosophical Testament* it will be grace which creates the world through its spontaneous self-giving activity; in the essay *On Stoicism*, play performs the same function.

Of course any regard for Stoicism, however measured, could not bracket indefinitely the Christian polemic against the ancient school, and *On Stoicism* anticipates also the reasons, developed in the *Philosophical Testament*, for rejecting Stoicism. Again the motivations rest with the idea of *tonos*, which, it is suggested, the Stoics recognized but also misinterpreted. To the Stoics, concludes Ravaisson, '[o]utside of this principle [of *tonos*]', above and below it, 'there is nothing true or good'.[95] According to Ravaisson, it was the Stoics' well-known proclivity to elevate *ponos*, 'labour', as their criterion of value which caused *tonos* to be understood in terms of brute force or effort. Thus *tonos* was divided from *anesis*, a division represented historically by the split between Stoicism and Epicureanism. 'One of the first and the most renowned Stoics, Cleanthes, characterises the philosophy of pleasure by the idea of relaxation, *anesis*', writes Ravaisson, explaining that 'Stoicism is founded on the diametrically opposed idea of effort or tension, *tonos*':[96]

> From another perspective, just when Aristipuus of Cyrene was making of pleasure the sovereign good and goal of life, the Cynics – while proposing as an ideal for man [sic] the laborious life of Hercules, crowned in his apotheosis – established that the condition of any god, and perhaps the good itself, is the opposite of pleasure, namely pain or work, *ponos;* and the goal of pain, says Diogenes, is the *eutonia* of the soul, *eutonia*: the correct and adequate tension.[97]

On such a view, says Ravaisson, where effort is valued above all else, it is easy to see how Stoicism would become known as an elitist morality 'made only for men'.[98] Such Stoicism disdains as a vice physical weakness; the Stoic's wisdom, Ravaisson goes on, 'will prefer to be extinguished ... than to be associated with an ill or deformed body'.[99] In light of this, one might expect Ravaisson to praise instead the Epicurean alternative, but the Epicureans seem to Ravaisson an even worse extreme. According to Ravaisson, hedonism is summarized in 'these two entirely negative precepts ... to bear and to abstain'.[100] Even when exposing the limits to an art of life based solely on effort, Ravaisson never wavers from his commitment to demonstrating the moral and metaphysical inadequacy of passivity. Here, of course, Ravaisson's own fascination with heroism and indeed with the figure of Hercules, which would become so prominent in the *Philosophical Testament*, is evident. Never mind that Ravaisson thinks about heroism, morality and the art of life in ways that are distinctly Christological, inflecting all these categories with Fénelonian images of self-sacrifice and abandonment: when set against his repudiation of passivity, the Augustinian foundation of Ravaisson's spiritual philosophy becomes significantly less obvious, and the Stoic element more apparent than ever.

Thus, although Ravaisson is distancing his own position, ultimately, from Stoicism, he certainly invites readers to confuse the two. As Mark Sinclair points out, Ravaisson seems 'to write the essay as if testing an interesting hypothesis'.[101] On the whole, the most striking aspect of *On Stoicism* is not its commonplace Christian triumphalism but Ravaisson's evident – however qualified – enthusiasm for the ancient school. Aside from anything else, the overlap between Ravaisson's ideas and those he purports to find in early Stoicism are too obvious not to invite comparisons.[102] In fact, as we shall see in the next chapter, several prominent philosophers did make such comparisons. Stoicism possesses, wrote Émile

Bréhier in his influential *Historie de la philosophie* (History of philosophy) (1928), 'that particular character which brings it closer to spiritualism'.[103] What made the comparison so attractive was the way it seemed to reconcile, in a novel way, the two distinct positions found within nineteenth-century spiritualism. We may call these positions mysticism and rationalism, corresponding to the ideal polarity of Augustinianism and Stoicism respectively, a polarity going back ultimately to the experiential paradox that spiritual exercise gives to philosophical method. At the same time that Biran's spiritualism, with its invocation of grace and critique of Stoic ideals, seemed to condone a suspicion of human reason, Cousin's work was giving evidence to the contrary: spiritualism, the philosophy of spiritual action and human freedom, was more like Stoicism than it was like Augustinianism. As a result, Cousin had called into question the whole self-identity of spiritualism as a *spiritual* discourse, deracinating it from a long tradition of reflection on the interior life and obscuring the continuity between philosophical method and spiritual exercise that had existed in Biran's work. According to Cousin, true spiritualism was incompatible with spiritual exercise; philosophy must choose between reason or intuition, Stoicism or Quietism – it could not accommodate both. Descartes and Biran, in his view, were simply wrong when they 'invoked grace' and attempted to make sense of reason in light of revelation. There was no reconciling the life of effort with the life of grace.

But at the same time it was difficult, even for a thinker like Cousin, to bracket indefinitely the mystical or properly spiritual element from spiritualism; in defining spiritualism as rationalism Cousin had also narrowed the meaning of both terms. Ravaisson's *On Stoicism* responds to this problem, albeit indirectly, and through the medium of intellectual history. For clearly the Stoicism under consideration is not only a sketch of the ancient school evocatively drawn; it is an image of the present moment, a device for re-evaluating the ideals of modern thought. We see this in the way *On Stoicism* seems to encompass both sides of the ideal polarity apparent within spiritualism, professing a philosophy of effort but also – this was Ravaisson's 'discovery' – a philosophy of grace. Thus Ravaisson neither praises nor rejects definitively Stoic philosophy, with all the repercussions such a move would have for spiritualism; instead, he suggests ways in which Stoicism, as an art of life, both anticipates and deviates from the requirements of the spiritual philosophy he wants to promote. A child of revolution and empire, Ravaisson is attracted irresistibly, as was Cousin, to the self-determination and heroism associated with the Stoic philosopher; but, a mystic in the tradition of Fénelon and Augustine, he is wary of placing all his trust in human achievement. Where he differs from Biran, however, is in refusing the latter's easy dissociation of Stoicism from the spiritual life. *On Stoicism* suggests that there are several places – the doctrine of 'tension and relaxation', Epictetus' prayer to God, etc. – that anticipate mysticism. So, unwilling to reject wholly the image of the Stoic philosopher, he still wants, like Biran before him, to say that while effort may shape the spiritual life effort does not determine it. What determines the movement of spirit precedes effort: this is love, desire, a life according to the Augustinian ideal – but an ideal that now becomes less easy to disentangle from Stoicism than even Biran had imagined. Hence Ravaisson comes to a conclusion very close to the one Simone Weil will defend so strikingly half a century later: when seen in a certain light, the Stoic life becomes a Christian life.

The need to effect a similar convergence between the Stoic and the Augustinian, the rational and the mystic – the life of effort and the life of grace – continued to exercise Ravaisson throughout his writing career. The clearest example of this may be found in a late essay 'On Pascal's Philosophy' composed ten years or so before the *Philosophical Testament*, in 1887. Here Ravaisson brings together all the topics just discussed and organizes them according to a penetrating dialectic. The essay takes the Augustinian ideal, now reinvented as spiritualism, and transposes it onto Pascal's philosophy. The choice of Pascal is obvious and yet presents peculiar difficulties to the philosopher committed to a sympathetic image of Stoicism. As a thinker who invokes the heart, Pascal is the Augustinian *par excellence*, and a natural starting point for anyone wanting to situate their work in this tradition; but Pascal was also an extreme example of the ideal: he disdains Stoicism, moves in Jansenist circles, and tends towards Quietism in his insistence on the spiritual annihilation of the self. How then was a modern reader able to appreciate Pascal's mysticism?

Ravaisson's approach is to acknowledge the limitations of Pascal's own position whilst defending the coherence of what he takes to be its basically Augustinian thesis. Rightly, he says, Pascal shunned as the 'supreme temptation' that part of Stoicism which promised to make of humanity a god.[104] And he praises Pascal for following Paul and Augustine in recognizing the dangers of self-deification. Human reason cannot reach God unaided: it needs help, it needs grace. Thus Pascal recognizes, alongside human reason, an 'intuitive mind' (*l'esprit de finesse*): the realm of 'the heart'. To act according to the heart is to attune oneself to feeling as well as to reason; it is to act spontaneously, to forget self-interest and allow the will to be guided by charity and love for others. This is what Ravaisson calls the 'spiritual ideal' to which, he says, Pascal's philosophy aims.[105]

But in Ravaisson's opinion Pascal ventures too far in the opposite direction from Stoicism when he insists that the self should be not merely hidden from view but suppressed, even annulled.[106] This, thinks Ravaisson, is to fall short of the spiritual ideal otherwise evident in Pascal's philosophy. Ravaisson suggests that part of the problem may be connected to an overly literal interpretation of the Gospel passages on spiritual poverty. Where Pascal treats them as injunctions validating acts of extreme asceticism and self-denial, Ravaisson questions such an interpretation. 'Jesus Christ did not say in an absolute way,' responds Ravaisson, ' "Happy is the pauper!" He said: "Happy is he [sic] who is poor through spirit".'[107] And so we arrive at the discussion referred to earlier, where Ravaisson distances himself from Pascal's presentation of mysticism as a literal renunciation of the world:

> We should also remark that the Gospels do not prescribe the wild solitude into which the Oriental [sic] fakir plunges, and which Pascal was taken by. Christ says in them, by comparing himself to the precursor who had lived in the desert on woodland honey and grasshoppers, that, as for himself, he is an eater and drinker ... that he does not, in other words, disdain taking his place at the table of human beings; and it is after an evening meal, surrounded by men whose lives are mixed up in his own, closest to him the one he loves more than the others, that after the singing of a hymn, *hymno dicto*, he founds the supreme ritual, consummation of the antique mysteries, in which the divinity is communicated to all.[108]

By pointing out that Christ did not endorse extreme self-denial – at least not in the athletic sense implied by Pascal – Ravaisson distances the philosophy of the spiritual life (his own position) from asceticism. This is not entirely unlike Cousin's separation of spiritualism from mysticism, and an intrepid piece of argumentation. But it is one that Ravaisson thinks necessary, if the spiritual practice to which the spiritual ideal is connected intimately is to be something other than moral therapy. As he goes on to say, if the spiritual ideal is 'dependent on such and such a particular form of existence',[109] then by definition it is no longer spiritual, that is, in excess of material circumstance. The spiritual ideal, as we saw with Biran, is universal, and to be universal, an ideal must be more like a style or method than a particularised set of regimens. Here the motivation behind Ravaisson's earlier worry about passivity, and his concomitant appreciation for Stoicism, becomes easier to see. While a life of self-deification and exaggerated belief in human effort implies its own contradictions and inevitable misery, so too does the life of abject self-denial proposed by Pascal. In fact, there is an irony about Pascal's whole rejection of Stoicism which Ravaisson's reading brings to light. For while Pascal rejects the Stoic for elevating effort above grace, Pascal too ends up elevating effort in his attraction to ascetic practices. The result is that Pascal's philosophy begins to look very much like the Stoicism it seeks to disparage.[110] Ravaisson wonders whether Pascal would have arrived at such an understanding of ancient philosophies had he been 'better informed about their history'.[111] No doubt Ravaisson means the comment to promote his own work in the history of philosophy, which he hopes will set the record straight on the relevance of Stoicism for any spiritual ideal.

Having interrogated Pascal's spiritual philosophy, and found it wanting, Ravaisson returns to that part of Pascal's thinking which initially he had defended and praised: the 'intuitive mind'. A correct understanding of intuition is for Ravaisson the key to Pascal's whole idea of the spiritual life, and most of the essay is dedicated to illustrating and expanding its meaning. The concept is misunderstood, writes Ravaisson, if we think of it in terms of a purely passive faculty opposed to reason. 'It is not that the mind does not do it,' he says, citing the *Pensées*, 'but it does it tacitly, naturally and without any art.'[112] The intuitive mind is for Ravaisson the middle term between passivity and effort, and in describing it thus he lends to it all the characteristics which elsewhere he attributes to grace: effortlessness, 'suppleness and flexibility', abandon. True, Pascal never himself made the connection between intuition and grace, but to Ravaisson the conclusion is self-evident: 'to define the mind capable of understanding it, [Pascal] would have noticed that one of its essential characteristic is the capacity to undulate in every direction without effort.'[113] To Ravaisson, any recuperation of the spiritual ideal in Pascal's philosophy will for this reason proceed via intuition, and at the end of the essay Ravaisson turns to the concept when tackling that part of Pascal's philosophy concerned, most obviously and notoriously, with spiritual exercise: the so-called wager. The wager, by this point, has been looming over Ravaisson's essay from the outset; it is there in the negative opinion, which Ravaisson addresses in the opening paragraph, that Pascal was a thinker who '[sacrificed] reason for faith'.[114] Such is the common interpretation of the wager: because faith is incomprehensible to reason it is better to act as if one believed (in the hope that faith might come) than to try and arrive at faith by means of reason alone. Ravaisson disagrees: this view assumes that faith and reason are mutually exclusive, a claim nowhere supported by Pascal, for whom intuition does not contradict reason but stands to it in a relation of paradoxy: intuition is of the mind and yet not mindful of itself ('it is not that the mind does not do it, but it does it tacitly, naturally and without any art'). The meaning of the wager, Ravaisson thinks, is to be found in Pascal's sense of intuition. The person neither tries to believe nor tries to reason their way to belief but instead relaxes the mental effort to believe – which is not the same as assuming the total mental inactivity that the wager is thought to imply. It is when the effort to believe is relaxed, says Ravaisson, that space is allowed for belief to develop in the artless way ascribed by Pascal to intuition and by Ravaisson to grace: 'quite naturally', as Ravaisson puts it.[115] Of course, relaxing the effort to believe is no guarantee of receiving belief, which remains an unsolicited gift; but it prepares for the eventuality of grace in the only way that is really within human power, with all the limitations to reason such a statement entails: 'Just as reasoning, when it has accomplished what it can accomplish,' writes Ravaisson, 'just as the practice humiliating the recalcitrant personality can still only prepare for the revelation by the heart, so too in Christianity everything, even sacrifice, is merely preparation, figuration of a unique truth, which is the gift that God makes of himself in the heart through charity.'[116]

Right here Ravaisson's attraction to Pascal is stated clearly. 'Practice ... can still only prepare for the revelation by the heart': effort prepares for, but does not solicit, grace, in the same way that for Augustine the will aims for the beloved but does not itself create the desire that moves it. It is Augustinianism in generative tension with Stoicism. To accept a narrow Augustinianism, such as the one Ravaisson intuits in Pascal's severe asceticism, it would have been necessary to reject any positive relationship with effort and dismiss the continuity between grace and nature. But to recognize the ultimately provisional nature of effort and recognize the primacy of what Ravaisson calls the 'preparedness' for grace – a state whose relationship to activity is ambiguous at best – is to acknowledge precisely the passivity that causes Ravaisson such worry. The basis of this attitude is drawn wholly from an understanding of the spiritual life as one of cultivating receptivity to grace, and the imagery of 'abandon' with which Ravaisson chooses to describe grace derives ultimately from Fénelon. At the same time, Ravaisson is not of Fénelon's school in the same way as was Biran. Ravaisson, we recall, prefers giving to receiving, action to passivity. Thus grace remains for him less unexpected gift than a primary datum: prevenient, already-given. Every effort of human reason to receive grace will in light of this fact be not so much a vain struggle as simply a misapprehension: grace being already given, to receive grace is not to earn grace as a reward for good deeds nor is it to hope for what is impossible; it is to recognize oneself already in a relationship of dependence with a more-than-human presence. Hence Ravaisson, in distinction from an earlier tradition, attributes abandonment to activity rather than passivity: with grace present in nature as spontaneous and uncontrolled desire every attempt to become like grace will involve effort, paradoxically, undoing and abandoning itself, becoming as spontaneous and effortless as it is possible for any effort to be. But while this certainly retrieves some of the quality intended by the notion of passivity in the spiritual tradition, it still commits itself to an uncomfortable silencing of the concept itself. Any association with Quietism sullies the spiritual life, as it tarnishes the metaphysics which, ultimately, the spiritual life underwrites. In this way Ravaisson's irresolution regarding Stoicism is comparable to his hesitancy over Augustinianism.

Is it then still appropriate to include Ravaisson within the Augustinian tradition, as I have proposed here? For what are we to make of a spiritual philosophy so obviously in favour of the old tradition of spiritual exercise in some respects and so reticent about it in others? For while Ravaisson proclaims Augustinian ideals he no longer writes in the style associated with Augustinian introspection. At the end of his life Biran could describe his philosophy as the result of meditation and prolonged attention to self. Ravaisson does not, because he could not. And yet we have seen how his whole polemic against Cousin and against contemporary philosophy centred around the project of re-orienting metaphysics to the incommunicable ecstasies of the interior life: the philosophy of the heart. Ever since the publication of Ravaisson's *Philosophie en France*, in 1867, commentators have tried to make sense of Ravaisson's version of spiritualism and his relation to the whole tradition of the 'interior life' inherited from Biran, but with little clarity achieved. It simply is not possible to ignore either Ravaisson's obvious attraction to pagan alternatives (Stoicism) or the disdainful tone with which he sometimes dismisses spiritual writers such as Pascal. For this reason, one influential interpretation, suggested by Dominique Janicaud, has been to leave aside completely the Augustinian inheritance and focus instead on the role played by Greek philosophy in the development of Ravaisson's thought. After all, as Janicaud rightly points out, discussions of Greek philosophy occupy the bulk of Ravaisson's work, and mentions of Fénelon are relatively few and far between. Thus, '[w]hile the direct ancestors, more or less, of our nineteenth-century spiritualists are to be sought in the seventeenth century, with the "spirituals" – with Pascal, Bossuet, Fénelon – it is, even more profoundly, the inheritance of Greek metaphysics we have to recognise'.[117] While such an approach draws attention to the important work Ravaisson did for the reception of Greek philosophy in the nineteenth century, when it comes to understanding the origins of spiritualism and the whole spiritual ideal that shapes French thought in this period it has several disadvantages, as should be evident, I hope, from the foregoing discussion. For by drawing attention away from Fénelon and the 'spirituals' in the history of spiritualism, one also draws attention away from what those writers represented: namely, a mystical,

Augustinian tradition of interior prayer and spiritual exercise. The result is a return to a position reminiscent of Cousin rather than Biran, where metaphysics is separated as far as possible from the spiritual ideals to which spiritualism aspires. Moreover, by juxtaposing metaphysics with religion ('spiritual' writers like Fénelon) it is implied that the two are somehow distinct, or if they are not then Greek metaphysics suffices to communicate whatever is valuable in Christian mysticism. And indeed, Janicaud praises Ravaisson's spiritualism for precisely this, its ability to present the study of the 'interior life' as metaphysics rather than spiritual exercise, separating philosophical method from religious sensibility. Thus spiritualist philosophers are those, according to Janicaud, who 'seek a renewal of metaphysics and a direct route to the absolute in an ever more profound method of the interior life'.[118] Again, a reminder of Cousin's attempt to separate spiritualism from its religious roots and understand the spiritual life as a rational enquiry into the data of consciousness.[119]

It is noticeable how distinct is Ravaisson's own attitude to philosophy from that proposed by Janicaud, or indeed by Cousin. What Ravaisson strived for, or so at least he argued, was to show a metaphysical concept apparent from the spiritual life – grace – implicit in philosophies where it was not otherwise an obvious theme. As Denise Leduc-Fayette has shown, Ravaisson thus considered Christ as the key to Greek metaphysics – not the other way around.[120] Readers familiar with Weil will recognize this approach, which is closer to pre-modern attitudes than to modern and contemporary opinions. James Frazer, for instance, argued that it was Greek philosophy (or, more accurately, Greek culture) which held the keys to Christian religion. Pierre Hadot similarly would claim that the secret to Christian spirituality were to be found in Greek philosophy. Janicaud's position is closely allied to this tradition, as are many current philosophies of spiritual exercise. But Ravaisson's readings of Stoicism which we saw just now cannot easily be assimilated to such approaches. The finally Augustinian, mystic appearance of his Stoicism is no mere concession to Christian dogmatism masking an 'actual' interest in Greek philosophy. It emerges from a conviction that Greek philosophy and Christian religion comport with one another, that metaphysics and mysticism cannot be prised apart except at the peril of either side losing coherence.[121]

In 1868 Paul Janet wrote a response to Ravaisson's *Philosophie en France* where he explained how it was that while philosophy could not become religion, 'a religion can become a philosophy'.[122] For Janet, as for Ravaisson, spiritualism took the view that religion and philosophy were continuous yet distinct. Genealogically, religion preceded philosophy, along with every other basic aspect of human culture. Thus religion emerged spontaneously, as 'a human fact, a primitive act of reason and heart ... just like society, family, art, language'.[123] But philosophy, nonetheless, was seen to be implicated in religion. According to Janet, philosophy was the conscious reflection on the facts of human culture from which it emerged; philosophy was what happened when religion became aware of itself. Seen from this perspective, argued Janet, philosophy remained essential to religion, even as religion would remain irreducible to philosophy. The task of spiritualism was to enable the philosophical self-realization of religion in what Janet called a spirit of 'liberalism', by which he meant the position of Ravaisson and his followers:

> The spiritualists I will call liberals are far from being animated by bad feelings towards positive religions: they respect and they love conviction wherever they find it, and they are far from denying what is common to their personal beliefs and to Christian beliefs. Perhaps they would be even more willing than others to borrow something, albeit freely, from Christian metaphysics.[124]

The initial step to comprehending Ravaisson's philosophy of the spiritual life – which here elaborates the alternative philosophy of spiritual exercise introduced by Biran – then, lies in putting to one side the largely antagonistic way in which philosophers of recent times have tended to oppose mysticism to metaphysics, Christian religion to Greek philosophy – Augustinianism to Stoicism. Ravaisson takes a number of concepts drawn from the tradition of mystical and spiritual literature – the rule of love, of intuition and ineffability – and brings them into philosophical discourse. What results is a philosophy of this mystical knowledge. It is the active reflection on that in life which is mostly passive, spontaneous and involuntary in nature. As such it takes as its point of departure both Augustinian and Stoic imperatives. On the one hand it draws the philosopher to the edges of comprehension by means of prayer, questioning and supplication. Here, truth is received, not achieved; it is all involuntary assent, spontaneity, gift. On the other hand, it encourages the philosopher actively to work and reflect on what is given, to become the artificers of nature – for there is in this world of gifted life no nature without grace, no grace without nature. Beginning with Ravaisson, 'grace' becomes the term that encompasses this mode of knowledge, which becomes also a distinctive way of being and style of life.

Yet Ravaisson, as we saw, did not always find it easy to strike a balance between the two ideal polarities of Augustinianism and Stoicism. Despite his critique of manly virtue, the principal concept associated with spiritualism would become, overwhelmingly, that of spiritual effort, *l'effort*. Gabriel Madinier, in his study of French philosophy since Condillac, *Conscience et mouvement* (1938), shows the dominance of this motif, which continues through to Bergson and later thinkers.[125] As a result of this development we saw that passivity was viewed with suspicion, if not altogether denied. In a way it thus mattered very little that Cousin's spiritualism had been surpassed by Ravaisson, or that mysticism had been rescued from Cousinian rationalism, for what motivated Cousin's worry over mysticism – a dread of passivity – remained at the core also of Ravaisson's philosophy. Although Ravaisson took great care always to present grace as the effortless middle term between effort and passivity, any description of it in his work invariably is summarized by the active voice: the hero who gives, loves and willingly sacrifices themselves. This is a Herculean Christ, as courageous and determined in death as in life, awesome and inspiring, the greatest among the great. In Thomas Carlyle's lectures *On Heroes, Hero-Worship and the Heroic in History* (1841), delivered in England as Ravaisson was first coming to fame, the author popularized this idea, which is very close to the themes we have been discussing. In Christianity, writes Carlyle, one finds 'the highest instance of Hero-worship'.[126] To Carlyle, Hero-worship was the 'grand modifying element' of any ancient 'system of thought',[127] that without which religion was inconceivable: 'Religion I find stands upon it; not Paganism only, but far higher and truer religions,—all religion hitherto known'.[128] Those lines could have been written by Ravaisson. But such equivalences between hero-worship and Christianity are true only once the Easter passion, with its derelict victim crying out in weakness and fear, has been temporarily forgotten. As the theologians of the early church noted, while Christ was not unlike Hercules, Christ's suffering was not glorious, nor was it the result of courage; there was nothing to admire, in the accepted terms of classic heroism, about the cross.[129] Whatever it was that the nineteenth century in general, and Ravaisson's spiritualism in particular, conveyed about the art of life, it was thus not to be found in the suffering and self-doubt that characterized the Augustinian spirituality that had shaped Biran's original meditations. While Ravaisson's was still very clearly a religious mysticism, it was a religiosity oriented ineluctably towards principles that departed from those of the Christian gospels. Hence the ease with which the Augustinian ideal would be mostly forgotten in the decades to come among those most impressed by Ravaisson's work, and hence also the increased significance of Stoicism in the philosophy of spiritual exercise. It is this emergence of a modern, Stoic philosophy of the spiritual life that will occupy us in the next chapter.

4

Effort: Henri Bergson and Alain (Émile Chartier)

So far we have been tracing the characteristics of an Augustinian ideal in nineteenth-century French thought – the changing dialectical visions of effort and grace from Maine de Biran to Victor Cousin and Félix Ravaisson. Like subjects in a fugue, these visions compete and converge in the philosophy of spiritual exercise which they express. We now pass to another stage, one closer to the state of our thinking today. In this new development, the ideal of effort began to acquire for itself unprecedented recognition, and we shall ask why this was and how it shaped the thinking of the influential philosopher Henri Bergson (1859–1941). In Bergson's work mysticism also got another model for how the spiritual life works: Stoic philosophy, expressed most strikingly in a set of lectures on Stoicism which Bergson delivered at the *lycée* Henri–IV in 1894–5. The interest in Stoicism owed much to its example of effort: in the Stoics' ability to withstand misfortune and cultivate fortitude – in the ancients' reverence for Hercules. Finally, spiritualist admiration for Stoic philosophy was thrown into broader debates, notably in the positive portrayals of Stoicism by Bergson's younger contemporary, Alain (Émile Chartier) (1868–1951). Out of that reinvention of Stoicism came a fresh concept of the spiritual life based on effort. Stoicism, furthermore, had now become an elevated alternative to Christian spirituality: at once a revered source of ancient wisdom pre-dating Christianity and a contemporary voice with critical perspectives to promote.

I

Dominant in the work of Henri Bergson, effort was the key concept discussed and argued about by turn-of-the-century philosophers in France. In 1934, when trying to distinguish his method from other approaches, Bergson claimed that it could be summarized by the activity of effort. 'Thus I repudiate facility,' he explains in *The Creative Mind*, 'I recommend a certain manner of thinking which courts difficulty; I value effort above everything ... Tension, concentration, these are the words by which I characterise a method which required of the mind, for each new problem, a completely new effort.'[1] In its broadest sense effort, for Bergson, was to recognize the singular nature of reflection and the irreducible freedom of the will that created it. Or, as one commentator later put it, to regard 'the role of movement in thought and more precisely in the act of conscious grasping, in the constitution of an "interiority" '.[2]

Bergson derived his understanding of effort from the same idea found in the work of Biran, where effort signifies the 'cause' and 'substance' of selfhood. Before the advent of spiritualism, French philosophy had been dominated by the school of Condillac, which assumed that the self could be conceived of as an epiphenomenon of passive sensation. Biran had changed all this by introducing in the place of Condillac's passively constituted self the active, dynamic, self of spiritualism.[3] Likewise, in his work Bergson proposed that spirit resembled creative effort, analogous to what he called the 'vital impetus' (*élan vital*) of evolution. In one of his last books, *The Two Sources of Morality and Religion* (1932), Bergson also gives an explicitly mystical meaning to effort: 'In our eyes the ultimate end of mysticism is the establishment of a contact, consequently of a partial coincidence, with the creative effort of which life is the manifestation. This effort is of God, if not God himself.'[4] Though spiritualism as Ravaisson had devised it originally maintained also a strong critique of effort and a robust metaphysics of grace, it was Bergson's interpretation of the spiritual life in terms of effort that became popular currency, first in *Creative Evolution* (1907), his major work, and, after a temporary fall from fashion, again in Gilles Deleuze's 'Bergsonism'.[5] What additional and alternative content spiritualist philosophy was given in the process of this diffusion is the focus of discussion in this chapter.

Elevating one concept in a dialectic pair is much like suspending from thought the opposite or complementary part, and such shifts in perception do not happen in a vacuum. Certain conditions must be in place, conditions which reinforce the concept now emphasized and predispose it to be preferred over others. Bergson it was, then, who popularized the idea of effort for a philosophical audience, but he was expressing tendencies and fashions already present in the fabric of the French imagination. Vitalism had anticipated its significance and so too had evolutionary biology. Theodore Zeldin describes how, at the end of the nineteenth century, 'popularized science was drawn on to prove that struggle was the essence of life and that force was synonymous with virtue', with writers in all disciplines endorsing the idea that warfare was the basic state of human nature, a nature which Darwinism had proved to be 'red in tooth and claw'.[6] At the time most European intellectuals no doubt shared this view. In elevating effort, Bergson was participating in a wider trend already established at the beginning of the century with the success of medical vitalism. In shaping his philosophy of human nature around effort, Bergson brought to mind Xavier Bichat, the eighteenth-century physician who had argued that organic life was the result of those 'forces' or vital currents with which an organism resisted inertia. It was Bichat and his colleagues who planted the seeds of ideas that would later find their way into Bergson's philosophy.[7]

In France the philosophy of effort had its indispensable social conditions, too, which had been present long even before the scientific hypotheses of vitalism and evolution. Effort had always been prized in a military nation like France, where manly virtue, physical prowess and resilience in the face of misfortune were highly valued. Unlike many European countries at the time France supported a large standing army throughout the nineteenth century, and it was in the context of being a military nation that the ideal of effort found a natural audience. Zeldin again: 'France managed to be the apostle of fraternity but also chauvinism, egalitarian but also accepting a hierarchical military organisation, a parliamentary democracy but one proud of its military virtues.'[8] True, the total warfare in which France had helped to engulf Europe during the Napoleonic years was viewed by many as an horrific savagery antithetical to the aims of a civilized nation, but, even so, it was taken for granted that peace could be purchased only at the price of considerable military action. Virility and prowess thus continued to be generally admired and praised as the nineteenth century turned into the twentieth, with the mass media catering to a reverence for physical culture and the male nude which would decline only after the Second World War.[9] It is this generalized and widespread belief in effort which, rather than Bergson's philosophy or spiritualism as such, was mainly responsible for its appropriation in French philosophy. It is this context which would give the concept of effort a concrete pathos, a sign guiding the ideal of spiritual exercise towards human self-improvement and apotheosis. With the consolidation of this belief in effort a new stage in our subject begins.

II

The period in recent French history which saw the rise of Bergson's philosophy of effort and the high point of military morality was also the time when many philosophers were drawn, appropriately enough, to Stoicism. The prominence of Stoicism in fin-de-siècle French culture, its popularity among philosophers and its widespread interest for the general reader are rarely appreciated. But in the heyday of the Third Republic, Stoic ideas were a persuasive source of inspiration; Bergson and Alain, the subjects of this chapter, are only two prominent examples. Strictly speaking, however, their attempts to appropriate Stoicism begin with – and in Bergson's case confine themselves to – isolated occurrences. In embracing Stoicism, Bergson and Alain were moving beyond the traditional limits of spiritualist discourse. Throughout most of the nineteenth century, as in earlier periods (before spiritualism was reinvented by Victor Cousin and Félix Ravaisson to become a national philosophy), spiritualism had been a religious philosophy of introspection. Essentially its task had been to use the methods of spiritual exercise to transform philosophical practice and so recover humanity's connection with the divine. The spiritualist was bound to be interested in the tradition of Stoic meditation and self-examination, a topic to which Biran had attended with enthusiasm in his private journal. But this interest was principally critical; the purpose of engaging with Stoic approaches was to sharpen the contours of the religious position – hence Biran's eventual rejection of Stoicism, as discussed in Chapter 2. Ravaisson had begun to reverse this order of priorities when he published his *Essay on Stoicism* in 1857, and later in his *Philosophical Testament*, where he seemed to incorporate some Stoic ideas – such as the heroic ideal and the concept of divine force or *tonos* – into spiritualism. But Ravaisson too remained within spiritualism's Augustinian framework and thus hesitated, for instance, to endorse Stoic morality. The full reversal of priorities did not become evident, however, until the 1890s, when Bergson and a new generation of philosophers indebted to spiritualism but distinct from the original movement began to take an interest in Ravaisson's work on the Stoics. This younger generation preferred to talk about Stoicism in positive terms as a way of life, a guide to happiness and a path to inner ecstasy in its own right, rather than use it polemically to clarify their position.

In addition, all French nineteenth-century thinkers writing after the Revolution were to some extent the inheritors of Stoic ideas and so present another important connection, besides Bergson's work, between that ancient school and the philosophical interest in spiritual exercise that develops during this time. The connection has been studied extensively by Michel Spanneut, who shows how the French revolutionaries took from Stoicism a lesson in fortitude, heroism and the ability to withstand suffering. 'Reborn when the Roman world rises and … reborn when the West is torn apart in political and religious struggles', writes Spanneut, Stoicism had a long history of offering consolation to French writers at times of war and political uncertainty.[10] It had done so in the seventeenth and eighteenth centuries, when Stoic can be found in soldiers' manuals, and it did so again in the nineteenth, when it consoled the thousands employed in France's professional standing army. But the atmosphere that had once shaped revivals of Stoicism at the time of the Counter Reformation was now quite different. The increasingly secular context of republicanism meant that, instead of contending with Stoicism in the tradition of its entanglement with Christianity, philosophers in the nineteenth century were creating their own accounts of Stoic morality, accounts in which the ancients conveyed readers in a bold leap beyond the anxieties of God, grace and eternity, into an art of living focussed on self-assertion, on autonomy and on the efforts of the will. Here, Stoicism seemed to provide a morality in a neutral context free of dogma and separate from institutional religion. In the writings of Marcus Aurelius and Epictetus especially, readers could find instructions on how to live a good and Godlike life: how to discipline the mind, purify the will and achieve unity with the divine – without a church. Such teachings were particularly attractive to French republicanism, which, as Spanneut explains, was fuelled by a search for philosophical and spiritual approaches distinct from yet comparable to the outlook of Christianity: 'Since the eighteenth century, [Stoicism] embodied republican virtue, particularly with the revolutionaries. With the progress of positivism, France sought a new morality which no longer required Christianity ... This [Stoic] morality fascinated republicans and free thinkers well into the twentieth century.'[11] Hence the special affinity between the ideas of Stoic morality and the ideals of French culture, and the distinctive appeal that Stoicism exercised over French philosophers shaped by and also actively shaping those ideals, such as Bergson. During the nineteenth century there was thus 'a great effort ... to duplicate and replace Christian morality by an independent morality, inspired, whether indirectly or directly, by Stoicism'.[12]

From the nineteenth century onwards, three notions dominated the intellectual milieu of republican philosophers in post-Revolutionary France: the definition of religious outlooks based on principles and experience rather than denomination alone; an emphasis on effort, resilience and autonomy as the ideals informing the spiritual life; and the frequent identification of Stoicism as the crucial anticipation of this new ideal. The most changeable of these were the last two – which still in the nineteenth century had about them the whiff of heresy. Both Biran and Ravaisson, writing from an Augustinian tradition, were among those who had rejected both Stoicism and the ideal of effort on the grounds of grace. But they had also been fascinated by Stoicism and written extensively on the concept of effort from a psychological and theological perspective. Despite – if not, in part, because of – their work, Stoicism was a popular creed among many, reaching back to the Christian Neostoics of the eighteenth and even seventeenth centuries. Now those who were dissatisfied with Christianity but still desired guidance in spiritual matters could turn to Marcus Aurelius instead of St Paul. In fact, Stoicism was often seen simply as an older and therefore more authoritative spirituality than the Gospels.

In France, a popular and influential presentation of the philosophy in question – a philosophy drawing heavily on the ideal of Stoic exercises – came from Alfred de Vigny (1797–1863), a poet, playwright and royalist aristocrat who also served as a garrison officer in Napoleon's army. Vigny developed his ideas independently of Biran and the spiritualists. But his work illustrates strikingly the approach to Stoicism and to Stoic ideals that has since become characteristic in the philosophy of spiritual exercise.

In 1814 Vigny joined the restored bodyguard and served in the military for the next thirteen years, retiring in 1823. Vigny joined at the point when the French army and indeed Napoleon's empire was heading towards its most devastating defeat, and Vigny himself did not have the opportunity to take part in any larger campaign. Like many in his position, the experience at the Battle of Waterloo in 1815 caused Vigny to balk at the terror and bloodshed into which Napoleon had driven France, and to question the ideals which had facilitated Napoleon's popularity. On the other hand, Vigny was suspicious of the Bourbon monarchy and while denouncing Napoleon still dreamt of a time when chivalry had not yet been corrupted by empire. The result was an attitude of, as his English translator puts it, 'a sort of confused nostalgia for glory, behind a bewilderment and alienation'.[13] Fortunately, French philosophy had a remedy for disillusioned soldiers like Vigny: Stoicism. In the 1830s, when Vigny began publishing extracts from his diaries – later collected and published as *Servitude and Grandeur of Arms* – Stoic ideas, if not outright references to the ancient school, crowd the pages. In the pagan philosophers' admiration for heroism and human effort Vigny could find a classic description of the chivalric ethos, and read about how the good rested with a person's strength and power, their *virtù*. In their moral psychology he also found a subtler understanding of effort, one where heroes would be prized not only for what they were seen to do but what they did invisibly by suffering hardship with equanimity and self-possession. And in the process, through the practice of self-possession and self-governance, lay the potential for glory even in the lots of soldiers like Vigny.[14]

Like the republican intellectuals described by Spanneut, Vigny was drawn to pagan philosophy on account of effort. Vigny concluded that the ancients' famous ideal of 'resignation' did not really mean the state of inactivity with which it was commonly associated. In *Servitude and Grandeur* he writes how even resignation draws its efficacy from a 'strange, proud virtue ... animated by a mysterious vitality'. In this vitality, Vigny argues, people trust as if in God, 'a god around whom many greater gods have fallen' – and concludes his reminiscences by declaring the pagan virtue of Honour to be the soldier's true religion.[15] In *Servitude and Grandeur,* Christianity is a more or less successful iteration of the mysticism of force which the soldier discovers through his service; where Christianity celebrates heroism and endurance it may be seen as a development of an ancient insight common to all true spiritual traditions. Through their contact with vitality, every soldier has the opportunity to live closer to divine power. As Spanneut shows, Vigny's Stoicization of Christianity becomes especially evident in his notebooks, published posthumously in 1867 as the *Journal d'un poète* (A Poet's Diary). Here Vigny asserts: 'honour is Stoic Christianity' and 'the Stoics were the *trappists* of antiquity'.[16] It seems that at the end of his life Vigny was even planning to write a play on the life of Julian the Apostate. It was to be called: 'The Stoics, an historic and epic drama'. Even without this crowning piece on the Stoics, Vigny's admiration for them is obvious and made a profound impression on his readership, which was widespread. Parts of *Servitude and Grandeur,* for instance, first appeared in the popular magazine *Revue des deux mondes*, and no fewer than six editions of the collected volume followed in Vigny's lifetime alone.

During the nineteenth century, many French-speaking writers took impression from Vigny's descriptions of honour, virtue and effort as spiritual ways of life and paths to happiness. As a result, they learnt that for moderns the good – not to say God – was expressed and accessible through effort: that honour, for instance, was the result of self-willed fortitude; that inertia must be overcome; and that humans are not that different to God, because both share in a flow of vitality and power. While Stoicism was often seen as the progenitor of these ideas, the ideal of effort could also be interpreted as part of a more general, Hellenistic worldview that had fed into Christianity. Others argued that it belonged to a distinctly pagan outlook incompatible with Christianity's emphasis on grace and so posing a challenge to established religion – a challenge many now embraced as a sign that a new world and way of life were approaching. In poetry especially, Stoicism now became less intimation of Christianity and more antinomian spirituality, reflecting political realities of revolution and revolt that accompanied the latter half of the nineteenth century. Many of these ideas –

including the valorization of Stoicism and the elevation of heroic values – are found in the work of Friedrich Nietzsche, whose widespread popularity in the years leading up to the First World War reinforced, in France as elsewhere, 'the cult of action and energy, and of the heroic virtues generally'.[17]

By the end of the nineteenth century, then, there was a pronounced shift in the way philosophers in France thought about the relationship between philosophy and spiritual exercise: from a perspective shaped principally by Augustinian currents (stretching back to the older 'spiritualism' of Fénelon), to a perspective shaped by reinterpretations of Stoic ideas. If we put to one side its accuracy as an account of historical Stoicism, the importance for our discussion of these late Romantic ideas about the spiritual life is that they begin not with a consideration of grace and abandonment to God but with the discovery of active power and of self-willed apotheosis. That crucial step from one kind of spirituality to another has also become the major theme in the philosophy of spiritual exercise as it has since developed. It was made possible by Stoic ideas revived over many decades during the nineteenth century by writers like Vigny. But it was also a new development, a complete revaluation of the spiritual life in light of modern aspirations. What techniques of self-improvement do spiritual exercise and mysticism present, philosophers subsequently would ask. What ecstasies could be achieved by perfecting the divine power within?[18]

III

At around the same time that Vigny's posthumous praise of Stoic effort was published, there was born a new generation of philosophers who would bring the ideal of effort finally into the heart of the spiritualist thought-world we have been considering here; the face of a new philosophy of spiritual exercise was emerging. In this development the trail blazers were two of Ravaisson's younger contemporaries: Bergson and Alain (Émile Chartier) (1868–1951). What they wrote and taught between the 1890s and 1940s transformed the spiritualism of Ravaisson from a religious mysticism of grace to a spirituality of effort inspired by Stoic ideas. This development underscored the distancing of spiritual exercise from its religious and mystical origins, even as the continued influence of Biran and Ravaisson perpetuated Augustinian themes under new guises. Alain – to whom we will return shortly – was the younger contemporary of Bergson. A passionate humanist intensely attracted to Stoicism, Alain described the ancient school as an 'art of living' and a form of natural religion common to all peoples.

Bergson, for his part, progressed from secular agnostic to mystic with Christian and Stoic sympathies, and maintained spiritualism's link with the tradition of spiritual exercise while also modifying this tradition in significant ways. The mature statement of his position, *The Two Sources of Morality and Religion*, was published in 1932 and translated into English three years later. Presented as a critique of conventional religion and a plea for universal mysticism, the book ends with an historical survey of extraordinary religious figures and their religious experiences – their ecstasies, visions, trances and so on – in diverse traditions, focussing particularly on Greek philosophers and Christian mystics, and giving special mention among them to Plotinus, Teresa of Ávila, Catherine of Siena and Joan of Arc. Bergson identifies their form of religion with mysticism and gives it the name 'dynamic'. In two places, special mention is given also to Stoicism. 'Before Christianity,' writes Bergson, 'we find Stoicism and, among the Stoics, philosophers who proclaimed … that all men [sic] were brothers, having come from the same God.'[19]

To Bergson the difference between Stoicism and Christianity lay not in their respective messages – 'the words were almost the same' – but in the conviction with which the message was delivered: 'if [the Stoics] did not succeed in drawing humanity after them,' he explains, 'it is because … the impetus was not there which would have made them spring from the static to the dynamic.'[20] So Bergson accepts Stoicism as a philosophical precursor to dynamic religion, a form of Christianity in all but practice. What the Stoics lacked in religious 'impetus', the Christian mystics made up for by their actions, dreams and ecstasies. It is in the context of his description of dynamic religion that Bergson gives his famous definition of mysticism as 'the establishment of a contact … with the creative effort which … is of God', from which we quoted earlier.[21] 'The great mystic,' he goes on to say, 'is to be conceived as an individual being, capable of transcending the limitations imposed on the species by its material nature, thus continuing and extending divine action. Such is our definition.'[22]

In *Two Sources*, Bergson is building on the subject Biran had made his special theme: the borderland where a philosophy of human effort meets a mysticism of divine grace. But the critique of effort which the experience of grace elicited for Biran and which he had laboured to articulate is mostly absent from Bergson's account of mysticism; indeed, the whole theme of grace, so important to spiritualism in general, is not developed at any length in *Two Sources*. In Bergson's view, 'mystic experience is a continuation of the experience which led us to the doctrine of the vital impetus'.[23] Vital, creative effort, in the sense envisaged by Bergson, simply *is* mysticism. Each mystic is a person who, through their own effort, has made contact with divine force, each having realized that they are themselves expressions of that force and able to direct it at will. So connected and interwoven into one creative effort are humans with God that it requires 'just the extra effort' on the part of humans for joy and mystical intuition to diffuse 'throughout the world'. So great is the ability of human effort that 'men [sic] do not sufficiently realise', writes Bergson, 'that the future is in their own hands'.[24]

Such faith in human effort had been challenged, of course, by Biran in his descriptions of grace, and even before that by Fénelon and the Augustinian tradition of spiritual exercise. But Bergson had to his advantage the spiritualism of Ravaisson, which hinted at a more positive appraisal of effort and a more action-oriented understanding of grace. We saw that in Ravaisson's work the most important of these active manifestations of grace was heroism: a person giving their life for others and so imitating God's self-giving to humanity through the birth and death of Christ. In some cases, Ravaisson had argued, pre-Christian philosophy intuited this heroic sense of grace without having any knowledge of revealed religion, as when the Stoics imagined creation to be the result of God relaxing the intensity of divine power, thus 'giving' of God's self in order for life forms to grow and flourish – an idea outlined by Ravaisson in the *Essay on Stoicism* and again in his *Philosophical Testament*. Bergson, who said of Ravaisson's ideas that 'they have so thoroughly permeated our philosophy, a whole generation has been imbued with them to such a point', would have been familiar with the new, mystical relevance Ravaisson had given to Stoicism and to Stoic ideals like effort.[25] Bergson's own treatment of mysticism, his *Two Sources*, owe much to Ravaisson's work, but his interpretation of Christianity is unusual, at least from the point of view of the Augustinian tradition with which Ravaisson's spiritualism to that point had been associated. Throughout *Two Sources* Bergson suspends from the discussion any mention of grace, pictures the mystic's relationship to God wholly in terms of effort and compares Christianity favourably to Stoicism.[26] While Bergson's desire to align mysticism with philosophy thus shows him to be operating still with the same convictions that characterized the work of earlier spiritualists – the conviction that philosophy was a form of spiritual exercise and in essence a method for mystical ascent – his idea of what that exercise entailed and how the mystic's ascent ought to be understood has shifted: from repose and calm, to action and effort.

Very quickly, scholars concluded that for this reason Bergson's philosophy amounted to something like a modern iteration of Stoicism – as when Nathalie

Frieden-Markievitch, for instance, argued that Bergson's philosophy presented the reader with an 'unconscious Stoicism', or when Vladimir Jankélévitch described Bergson's philosophy as a 'heroism', 'an asceticism of the spirit', with the Sage of antiquity as its ideal.[27] Perhaps the relationship between Bergsonism and Stoicism was best summed up by Gilbert Murray, the Oxford classicist, in his 1909 Conway Memorial Lecture on Stoic philosophy. The Stoics, he declared, find their best analogue in the philosophy of Bergson; here the ideas of Bergson – of *élan* and spiritual action – are traced imaginatively to the Stoics. On Murray's account, Stoicism and Bergsonism are kindred through their idea of vitality and divine force.[28]

The links between Bergson's philosophy and Stoicism have been noted by several philosophers, and we shall soon consider some of these connections. First, however, I would like to explore more thoroughly the question of Bergson's own interest in the ancient school. What were his opinions of Stoicism and how did they relate to the tradition of interpretation established by Ravaisson? Curiously, and despite the historical link between Stoicism and spiritualism, this approach to the question of Bergson's Stoicism has not been common among commentators, who have focussed instead on comparing Bergson's philosophy to historical Stoicism rather than to the spiritualist Stoicism disseminated via Ravaisson's influential essays. In part, this is due to the fact that Bergson published very little on Stoicism and left us with only a handful remarks on Stoic philosophy in his published work.[29] At the same time, what he does say about Stoicism is suggestive. For instance, in addition to the passages from *Two Sources* mentioned above, there is a striking reference from an essay (composed in 1905) where Bergson writes (à propos Biran's philosophy): 'The phenomenon of effort brings [Biran] to a doctrine of internal tension and concentration, analogous to that of the Stoics.'[30] Given the significance of 'effort', 'tension' and 'concentration' in Bergson's own work, and the close historical connection between Bergson's philosophy and the spiritualism of Biran, we may assume the comparison to be a positive one. There is also a brief aside on Stoicism in *Creative Evolution* (1907). Here, in a chapter where Bergson critiques and rejects aspects of ancient Greek philosophy, and where one would expect to find a discussion of Stoicism, there is only a casual reference to the ancient school: 'the main lines of the doctrine that was developed from Plato to Plotinus', writes Bergson, alluding to the Greek concept of 'ideas', 'passing through Aristotle (and even, in a certain measure, through the Stoics)'.[31] The careful wording – '*even, in a certain measure*' – coupled with the fact that this passage is the full extent of Bergson's engagement with Stoicism in a book that spares no ire on Plato,

Plotinus and Aristotle, suggests Bergson's tacit approval. Put differently, while the purpose of *Creative Evolution* – to challenge the assumptions of classical metaphysics – necessitates Stoicism's inclusion in the list of philosophies under scrutiny, where the Stoics themselves are concerned it seems Bergson cannot find in their position substantial ground for serious disagreement.

Taken together, these scattered remarks on Stoicism in Bergson's published oeuvre indicate that Bergson favoured Stoicism in some way, but it is left to the reader to work out the finer details. A more rewarding approach, though as yet not explored among commentators, is to look at Bergson's unpublished work, especially his lectures. Where the published work betrays only hints of an admiration for Stoicism, the lectures confirm unequivocally Bergson's enthusiasm. We find Bergson's opinions of the Stoics described and recorded in great detail by Antoine Vacher, a student of Bergson's at the *lycée* Henri–IV who attended a survey course on the history of Greek philosophy that Bergson taught in the academic year 1894–5. The sheer volume of notes accorded Stoicism in this course indicates something of its importance to Bergson at the time: while the Stoics receive thirty-two manuscript pages, Plato is accorded sixteen, Aristotle eighteen and Neoplatonism only thirteen.[32] In this survey course Bergson speaks at length and with enthusiasm on Stoicism, paying attention in particular to the Stoic doctrine of effort, which he declares the 'first principle' of Stoic philosophy: 'the principle that governs Stoic morality is the same which governs physics and logic; the principle of tension, of effort.'[33] The doctrine of effort is illustrated by Bergson through Stoicism's stereotypical link with the Cynics and their hero-god, Hercules, styled in these lectures evocatively as the 'god of effort': 'In pleasure, man [*sic*] becomes the slave of his desire. Thus, the object of human life is emancipation, freedom. It is through effort that we liberate ourselves. Hercules is the god under whose invocation the Cynics place themselves, Hercules is the god of effort.'[34] Under the heading of Stoicism Bergson – like Ravaisson – also includes Heraclitus' cosmology, where effort, Bergson thinks, is so fundamental it may describe the essence of a Godself who holds together the universe through the alternating tension and relaxation of a vital effort or *tonos*. The similarities between the Stoics' idea of effort and the concept of effort as it appeared in Ravaisson's spiritualism were obvious to Bergson. 'From the idea of effort, the idea of force', Bergson concludes his presentation of the Stoics, these ancient philosophers regenerate thought by 'spiritualising it, giving it a soul'.[35] So crucial is the idea of effort to Bergson in these lectures that it appears any philosophy which discovers it may be considered spiritualism *avant la lettre*.

The importance of a connection between Bergson's *Two Sources* and his lectures on Stoicism is this: read alongside one another, the two texts dramatize the advent of those features of a modern philosophy of spiritual exercise that sets contemporary approaches apart from the Augustinian mystical tradition that has been occupying us in previous chapters: the ideal of grace and the paradox of active passivity. For Bergson's is not merely a rehearsal of Ravaissonian themes. True, it seems that Bergson's enthusiastic treatment of Stoicism in his 1894–5 survey course was prompted by his study of Ravaisson's *On Stoicism*, for this is the first time in Bergson's work that *On Stoicism* is cited and discussed.[36] But while Bergson draws heavily on Ravaisson's essay, especially on its descriptions of the Stoic doctrine of effort which Ravaisson lays out in such vivid detail, Bergson's approach to Stoicism itself is quite different. In contrast to *On Stoicism*, where Ravaisson interrogates Stoicism at length, Bergson does no such thing. The way Bergson describes it, little remains of the hesitations over the philosophy of effort that had characterized Ravaisson's account. To the contrary, Bergson anticipates what would become the familiar, twentieth-century response: he finds the idea of effort fascinating, and its presence in Stoicism is enough to justify his favourable opinion of the ancient school. Of course, the influence of Stoicism was superseded historically by the rise of Neoplatonism, and Bergson's survey course reflects this, passing from Stoicism to Plotinus and showing how Stoic ideas were absorbed into Neoplatonism and sometimes improved in the process. Pantheism, for instance, is one aspect of Stoic philosophy that Bergson thinks Neoplatonism challenged constructively. But he does not, like Ravaisson, find it necessary to refute Stoic doctrines. Instead, he devotes to them long and vivid explanations that draw in the audience. As the editors of Bergson's lectures on Stoicism explain: 'That is probably the main lesson of [Bergson's] lecture course, which some will find dull as dishwater – until the moment the Cynics and Stoics enter the stage. At this moment the philosopher awakens, as if he were suddenly in his element, and we are witnessing an extensive, deep and lively reflection, in which the author of *Matter and Memory* (then still in progress) converses with those from whom he came to draw inspiration.'[37] With the venerable 'Monsieur Ravaisson' as unwitting herald, Bergson's Stoics are well on their way to becoming a new sort of philosophical ideal for the spiritual life.

Unique though this account of Stoicism is in Bergson's oeuvre – he did not again pay attention to Stoicism in such detail – the parallels between what Bergson says here about the Stoic god of effort and what he says much later in the *Two Sources* about mysticism's God who *is* effort serve as a useful guide to understanding the new direction in which Bergson takes the philosophy of spiritual exercise: a confidence in the spiritual efficacy of human effort which goes against the grain of an older Augustinianism and corresponds to a more general enthusiasm for force and for Stoic values in French thought and European letters at the time. If looked at from the point of view of Ravaisson's spiritualism, Bergson's 'dynamic religion' in *Two Sources* becomes only a very loose Christian spirituality in which 'the future is in the hands of men [sic]' – hardly the receptive attitude required, traditionally, by the mystic for the receiving of divine grace. But when this mysticism is broadened to include Bergson's enthusiastic appraisal of Stoicism and the wider French ideal of effort, its coherence begins to become apparent.

The chief theme in Bergson's 1894–5 lectures on Stoicism is the idea of spiritual effort: the belief, in Stoicism, that the Sage could, by their own willpower, free themselves from slavery to the passions and become one with God, described by Bergson as 'this ever-vigilant activity, this concentrated ardour'.[38] This equivalence between God and spiritual effort, as has already been hinted at, would also become one of Bergson's own ideas, and it is sketched out in these lectures in the context of a description of Stoic philosophy. Virtue, Bergson contends here, was for the Stoics not the gradual result of becoming more and more Godlike (as it was, Bergson explains, for Aristotle or Plato), but the immediate result of having attuned oneself to God's vital tension through an 'intense effort' on the spiritual plane of the inner life.[39] For the Stoics, God's tension, penetrating everywhere like a 'vital fluid' and so holding together the most diverse things, could change abruptly and thus compel matter to take on wholly new qualities, Bergson observes. The inner tension of each particular thing in the universe was seen to be distinct and yet it could become something different as its tension was increased or relaxed (as when separate elements formed new chemical compounds). Humans too, by focussing their minds and exerting an effort, could alter their spiritual composition and become new spiritual beings. In all this, Bergson saw the Stoics narrating a universe constantly pushed from within to become more like God. Spirit tries to assert itself, attempting to overcome the sluggishness of its relaxed, material state in order to ascend to God's state of superlative tension. Thus the Stoics produce, Bergson argues, 'a positive formula for liberty, for the emancipation of the soul'.[40]

A theology based entirely on effort was the foundation for Bergson of a new, more intense mysticism in Greek thought. The Stoics understood that ecstasy could be the work of the individual, not a mere desire to be asked for in prayer and hoped-for in supplication. The Stoic philosopher must exert themselves spiritually to the utmost degree, until no part of their former way of looking at things remained. They must become, like God, the expression of effort. By becoming pure effort, the philosopher could see the world as God saw it: as so many diverse and constantly changing degrees of tension, a spectacle of vitality and power. 'God is, above all, active force, tension, *tonos*,' explains Bergson.[41] It is this force, he goes on to say, which the Stoic loves and which is the measure of all their actions. 'It follows from this,' according to Bergson,

> that virtue consists less in the acts themselves than in the interior disposition; it resides in the inflexible rectitude, in the perfect tension, in that which the Stoics called *orthos logos*, 'right reason'. Now the *logos*, this ever-vigilant activity, this concentrated ardour, is fire, ether, is the primordial element, active in the original purity. To live according to right reason, then, is to replace oneself at the heart of the active principle, at the principle of universal life – it is to return to God.[42]

For the Stoic, explains Bergson, a continuous act of concentration, the concerted effort at attention, could remind them that they too were, in essence and at the core of their being, a vital expression of God's creative power. But if concentration was broken, the whole thing was lost. The mere fact of God's identification with perfect tension rendered all relaxed states imperfect by comparison. 'Either virtue remains what it is, or destroys itself,' he summarizes, paraphrasing Seneca: 'Virtue is a straight line, which cannot be deformed without absolutely ceasing to be what it is.'[43] To attempt to maintain such states for long periods through an interior effort, to fight consciously against the distractions that threaten to put an end to attention and to strive for spiritual transformation was to pursue a superlative awareness of the divine energy within.

For Bergson, the Stoic concept of effort proves itself most strikingly not only when studied on its own but when compared to the status of effort in other philosophical and spiritual traditions. Towards the end of his presentation of Stoicism, Bergson reflects: 'What constitutes rectitude, then virtue, is the interior effort. One understands how, on this point as on so many others, it is possible to draw connections between Stoicism and Christianity in general, between the Stoics and Kant in particular.'[44] That a religious life should require much internal exertion and effort, real and experienced, is axiomatic to Bergson's idea of religion in these lectures. He would not have Christianity confused with a mysticism of repose – teaching persons to shrink from effort, distrust human abilities and so (in Bergson's view) relinquish any chance of becoming like God. Effort, inner strength, virtue, ardour, fire – these are what matter in Bergson's comparison between Christianity and Stoicism. Hence he aligns Christianity with Kant's philosophy, in this way emphasizing to his students the importance of willpower and autonomy in the spiritual life. A little while later, Bergson returns to the idea of religious effort as he stops to explain briefly the Stoic concept of *apatheia*, or 'equanimity'. It has been misunderstood, he says, to mean a state of mental and spiritual relaxation. But this is to confuse Stoicism with the philosophy of Epicurus: 'If Epicurean *ataraxia* is to let go,' he says, 'if it consists in being carried away by things, Stoic apathy is – to the contrary – the state of a soul that gathers itself together, that concentrates on itself and lives by pure reason,' and continues: '[the Stoic Sage] will seek the opportunity to exercise his reason and effort, the opportunity to do well. He will therefore prefer social life to isolation, for only social life makes justice and friendship possible, that is, charity.'[45] In order to practice charity – here the essence of Christian as well as Stoic morality – the philosopher must resist letting go and focus instead on the will, 'concentrating on itself'. Once again, what to Bergson defines the good is effort, physical as well as spiritual. Hence he rejects the whole tradition of voluntary 'isolation', as he puts it, of spiritual retreat and temporary withdrawal from the world. Everywhere, passivity is held in suspicion: the impediment to charity is inactivity, while the facilitator of the religious life is effort. With this equivalence between charity and effort Bergson brings to a close his lectures on Stoicism. Few philosophers have been more intent on defending Stoic morality from a religious point of view – on equating effort with the spiritual life, and spiritual exercise with the efforts of spirit.

In 1894–5 Bergson describes philosophy as a life of intense, spiritual effort and grace ('charity') as an expression of that effort. Earlier, in his very first book, *Time and Free Will: An Essay on the Immediate Data of Consciousness* (1889), he had observed a hidden effort in the phenomenon of grace. 'We could hardly make out why [grace] affords us such pleasure,' he declares, 'if it were nothing but a saving of effort.'[46] Philosophers would look at the graceful movements of a professional dancer, or the curved lines issuing from an artist's pen, and conclude that the smoothness of their gestures was a result of a relative absence of effort. Grace is attractive because it is effortless, on analogy with divine grace, which gives itself without effort. 'But the truth,' he writes, 'is that in anything which we call very graceful we imagine ourselves able to detect, besides the lightness which is a sign of mobility, some suggestion of a possible movement towards ourselves.' If the dancer's movements cease, if the artist's hand pauses, Bergson is saying, we find ourselves compelled irresistibly to complete the movement, responding with the physical sympathy established by grace. 'It is this mobile sympathy, always ready to offer itself,' argues Bergson, 'which is just the essence of higher grace.'[47] Ravaisson had observed something similar in his analysis of grace, when he compared grace to the superlative effort of self-sacrifice compelled by love and compelling others to love. And Bergson drives home the point: to give of oneself, to be always ready to offer oneself, is nothing but activity – mobility, effort! A more striking assertion of this claim is made by Bergson in his essay on 'The Life and Work of Ravaisson', originally delivered as a formal eulogy to his predecessor at the Académie de Sciences Morales et Politiques in 1904. The essay describes Ravaisson's concept of grace according to the Augustinian formulation: 'in everything that is graceful we see, we feel, we divine a kind of abandon, as it were, a condescension.'[48] To which Bergson adds another definition, this time based on movement and effort: 'And it is not by mistake that we call by the same name the charm we see in movement, and the act of liberality characteristic of the divine goodness: the two meanings of the word *grace* were identical for Ravaisson.'[49] Ravaisson's spiritualism, Bergson muses, paves the way for a mysticism of effort, a religion of concrete experience and action, anchored to the achievements of humanity.

According to Bergson, the spiritual life has in every respect a base in effort: it descends from God by an act of superlative effort, and it is realized in human beings through a reciprocal activity of creative effort. The true purpose of mysticism, of spiritual exercise and *askesis*, in other words, is nothing less than the apotheosis of human effort, or the achievement of the most divine, God-like humanity possible. Philosophers like Heraclitus, the Cynics and the Stoics were describing with their concepts of vital force, *tonos* and reverence for Hercules the primitive intuitions of what nineteenth-century thought had confirmed through its identification of human with divine effort. And it was this idea of God emerging through humanity's own efforts that Bergson made the central claim of his philosophy. It became the principal legacy of Bergsonism to twentieth-century French thought.

IV

Himself a kind of culmination of spiritualist philosophy in the nineteenth century, Bergson is also the figure with whom French thought enters its more recent, contemporary form. Within a few decades of Bergson's arrival on the philosophic scene in the 1890s, philosophers were drawing connections between the spiritual life and Stoicism in the very ways Bergson had suggested to his students, including the idea that the key to mysticism was to be found in a pre-Christian doctrine of effort. Given that Bergson's opinions on Stoicism were not published until long after his death and so would have had only a limited influence on philosophers at the time, this is remarkable, and shows the extent to which both Stoicism and the philosophy of spiritual exercise evidently were already 'in the air'. It is also not inconceivable, of course, that Bergson's lectures did contribute directly to this new moment. One imagines the report of his lectures – with their evocative portrayal of Stoicism – spreading by word of mouth in Paris' Latin Quarter. Whatever the case, from the twentieth century onwards several philosophers now pursued enthusiastic readings of Stoicism as a mystical way of life, readings clearly inspired by Bergson's ideas or by spiritualism more broadly. Émile Bréhier, an important scholar of Hellenistic philosophy and also an interpreter of Bergson, declared that the Stoics had '[produced] in their school the abandonment of discursive logic to the benefit of the impulses (*élans*) of moral and religious activity'.[50] That claim appeared in the final sentence of Bréhier's 1908 doctoral dissertation on Stoic epistemology, *La théorie des incorporels dans l'ancien Stoïcisme* (The theory of incorporeals in ancient Stoicism). A few decades later the same idea made its way into Bréhier's immensely influential multi-volume *History of Philosophy*, published between 1926 and 1948. In the first part, we learn how Stoicism offered the closest analogue to the spirituality of Judaism and early Christianity. 'If the God of Aristotle and the Platonists is the transcendent God of a scholarly theology,' writes Bréhier, 'the God of the Stoics is the object of a more human piety ... [ordaining] direct, special relations between God and men, whereas in Aristotelean or Platonic theology ... the general relation of God [is] to the order of the world, not with a relation peculiar to man.'[51] The 'God of the Stoics', of course, was none other than Hercules, the hero of Bergson's lectures and now the principal figure also in Bréhier's account: 'neither the assimilation to God that Plato envisioned nor the simple civic and political virtue depicted by Aristotle [but manifesting his divinity in] his acceptance of the divine work and collaboration in this work through his knowledge of it.'[52] Bréhier was not the only one to focus on the idea of effort when considering the merits of Stoicism. Thus Léontine Zanta, a scholar of Neostoicism, chose to open her 1914 study of Stoicism in the Renaissance with a description of *tonos*. In the Renaissance, she writes, 'power becomes the prerogative of force':

> and this is certainly a favourable condition for the development of energies, the glorification of effort; such is the best practical translation of Stoic *tonos*. Humanists thus find themselves enveloped in an atmosphere of Stoicism: everywhere struggle, effort, and effort followed by success; everywhere this flourishing of individualism, which allows each person to give fully of themselves.[53]

Such a description of *tonos*, with its portrayal of effort as 'energy', 'success' and even 'self-giving', would have been unthinkable without the influence of Bergson's philosophy on the intellectual climate, as would Bréhier's reflections on Hercules as a god of 'more human piety'. Within a few decades, Victor Goldschmidt would make use of Bergson's ideas to interpret Stoic philosophy, and Pierre Hadot would later cite Bergson when developing his account of ancient Stoicism as spiritual exercise – Hadot would also refer to Bréhier as an important teacher and would draw on Ravaisson's description of *tonos* in his analysis of Stoic philosophy.[54] By the mid-twentieth century, Stoicism was associated, in many philosophers' minds, not only with spiritual exercise in the sense of meditation and introspection, but in the sense of mystical ecstasy and spiritual effort – and it was this connection that would become decisive. Thus Gilles Deleuze was able to look back with excitement at a near-half century of a new Stoic ideal in philosophy, announcing, in his *Logic of Sense* (1969), that the Stoic Hercules had effected a 'reorientation of all thinking'.[55] And *Logic of Sense*, like Hadot's *Philosophy as a Way of Life*, is concerned with philosophy as a 'style', a spiritual endeavour and 'art', and, like Hadot's work, cites both Bréhier and Bergson. For this generation of French philosophers, Stoicism and Bergsonism together seemed to reclaim an art of living more in tune with the real demands of truth and life than the old mysticism.[56]

Needless to say the adoption of Stoic ideals into the philosophy of spiritual exercise was more nuanced than this brief sketch allows. For a number of philosophers, the idea of *spiritual* effort seemed to offer a welcome alternative to the increasing profusion of positivism and rationalism at the universities. They imagined Stoicism could provide a new way to save intuition, will and experience from the ravages of abstract reason. As Thomas Bénatouïl has pointed out: '[such] French uses of Stoicism are firmly anchored in ... a philosophy of experience, of sense, and of subject.'[57] To philosophers seeking a reaffirmation of the spiritual life outside of theological doctrine, Stoicism came to represent for many a welcome bulwark against encroaching secularism. For Gustave Loisel, zoologist and author of *La mise en œuvre du Marc-Aurélisme ou la nouvelle stoa* (1930) (The Uses of Marc-Aurelianism, or the New Stoa), the interest of Stoicism was even more outspokenly spiritual or mystic: Stoicism was 'a Religion, the Religion of the universal Good', a spiritual path rather than a system of doctrines.[58] For still others, such as the Catholic philosopher and theologian Teilhard de Chardin, the convergence between Stoic ideas and Bergsonism provided an opportunity to reinforce the universal quality of the mysticism which, he hoped, would put humanity back in touch with the living, energetic pulse of divine reality.[59]

In many ways, then, what was happening among philosophers indebted to Bergson was still continuous with the direction in which Biran had first taken French thought: to a discovery and rediscovery of the 'spiritual' in the exercise of philosophy. In particular, there had arisen among Bergson's generation an entire 'reflexive philosophy' chiefly concerned, as Biran had been, to establish truth through introspection and rigorous self-examination. It was a half-secularized *askesis* in which Biran's early works were important and 'action' a key word, but in which older, Augustinian ideas continued to resurface. Most, if not all, of these young philosophers were fascinated by the idea of spiritual effort, and many had taken impression from either Biran or Ravaisson or both. Some moved Biranian ideas into the clinic and applied them to the study of mental illness, developing a psychology based on the notion of an interior or psychic 'tension'. Others, such as Maurice Blondel, would continue to work on the religious philosophy of spiritual action, those heroic efforts – such as voluntary suffering and self-sacrifice – said to shape the moral life through extraordinary displays of willpower.[60] These approaches, while they did not as a rule invoke Stoicism, inevitably took impression from the same military morality that suffused Gallic philosophy more broadly and influenced Bergson's philosophy of the spiritual life in particular. A good example of such Stoic ideals surfacing amidst Augustinian currents in the 'reflexive' or Biranian philosophy at this time may be seen in the work of Jules Lagneau, a contemporary of Bergson who taught for some years at the *lycée* Michelet before his untimely death in 1894. In 'Simples notes pour un programme d'union et d'action' (Brief Notes Concerning a Programme for Union and Action), published in 1892, Lagneau imagines Ravaisson's spiritualism in the terms that for many centuries had been associated with the Stoics – as the expression of resilience in the face of misfortune – while at the same time invoking the old mystical ideals of suffering and renunciation. 'There is no other way to restore social harmony: a high spiritualism preached by example first, by action' and: 'We want to make known within ourselves the benefit of rule, discipline, resignation, renunciation; to teach the necessary perpetuity of suffering, to explain its creative role'.[61] The concept of spiritual *action*, however, takes precedence over the course of this essay, and Lagneau eventually follows Ravaisson in redressing charity itself as heroic effort, and ends by invoking manly virtue and military morality: 'Our charity,' he explains,

> is the true gift, the only gift, and the perfect instrument of salvation. To be loved by loving the manly love which is absolute will, that is to say sacrifice, and thus learn to love, everything lies there … We create in the light of day, without

ulterior motive and without any mystery, an active union, a militant secular order of private and social duty, the living nucleus of the future society.[62]

While Lagneau never seems to have paid Stoicism much attention, he did lecture on Spinoza, and Spinoza's philosophy was well known for its association to humanist Neostoicism. Spinoza showed Lagneau that spirit and effort were inextricable, and that suffering was useful only if put to creative use.[63]

Concurrent with these nascent philosophies of spiritual exercise centred around effort – and one that would also give to Stoicism a privileged place – a parallel conception was emerging in the work of one of Lagneau's former students, Émile Chartier, better known by his pen-name Alain. In the 1890s Alain was studying at the École Normale Supérieur and preparing his master's dissertation on the epistemology of the Stoics. He was then in his early twenties and had never before studied Stoicism, though its ideas seemed to resonate immediately with his earlier training: here was the doctrine of effort and action he had learnt from Lagneau, here too was the commitment to endurance and spiritual discipline that his teacher had imparted. The resulting dissertation, eventually published posthumously in 1961, is a work that concerns not only Stoicism but the nature of philosophy, which Alain thought about in terms of 'effort' and 'concreteness': 'the Stoics have left us a philosophy of concreteness,' he writes, 'of effort, and progress.'[64] Upon graduating, Alain persisted in his enthusiasm for Stoicism, writing on Stoic themes and becoming one of Stoicism's most striking advocates. He died in 1951, the author of several popular books on philosophy, art and literature, and the inventor of his very own philosophical style, the *propos* or short essay, where most of his mature reflections on Stoicism are to be found. Over the course of his career Stoicism appears as a philosophy concerned with the art of living, with returning philosophy to the practical and experiential, but also with the spiritual – though Alain always stops short of engaging closely with spiritual exercise in the Augustinian sense popular in previous centuries. In the opinion of André Comte-Sponville, Alain's spiritualism was secular:

> And that is why the Stoics win, for Alain. For man [sic] is in the world, certainly, but the world itself is only a world by the spirit, which judges it. It is therefore the man who matters, not the world, nor God. Alain's secular spiritualism is also a humanism.[65]

From Alain's forays into Stoicism and his development of Lagneau's work there emerges a distinctly modern philosophy of spiritual exercise, where 'spiritual' itself no longer forms part of a discussion nonetheless devoted to reclaiming philosophy as a practice for beatitude in the tradition of Augustine and

Ignatius. On the whole, Alain's is a philosophy of spiritual exercise untied from Augustinianism, though in important respects it remains deeply influenced by aspects of Ravaisson's thought, as we shall come to now.

One theme dominates Alain's philosophy: the idea of spiritual action or effort. In a *propos* on Stoicism, published when he was fifty-four years old, Alain writes: 'there is nothing favourable to man [*sic*] except what he has made through his own efforts.'[66] From his student days onwards, that had been Alain's principal philosophical thesis. Nature is a harsh and unforgiving place, full of meaningless suffering and devoid of inherent purpose or goodness; the human being must therefore become literally like a god, creating purpose through their willpower alone, refusing to be sad at the chance misfortunes the world puts in their way and remaining determined instead to turn suffering into a test of strength and perseverance. A more apposite embodiment of this creed than Stoicism never commanded Alain's attention, unless it was Jansenism, with which he also seems to have sympathized.[67] Where Stoicism is concerned he is drawn to the doctrine of effort, perhaps a reflection of Lagneau's sense of effort as the criterion of goodness and sanctity. This is the overarching theme of the dissertation he submitted in 1891: *La théorie de la connaissance des stoïciens* (The Stoic theory of consciousness).

Effort, vital tension, *tonos* – these are the inevitable principles of Alain's Stoicism. They seem a direct response to Ravaisson's vivid description of *tonos* in the essay *On Stoicism*.[68] Yet Alain – just like Bergson – also departs from Ravaisson's interpretation of effort and insists on its positive relevance for a philosophy of the spiritual life. When the Stoics articulated the doctrine of effort, Alain argues, they hit upon the truth of nature and of humanity's relation to God. At any given moment our thoughts, our body, our whole constitution, are the result of many different physical and mental efforts (some conscious, others unconscious) to hold together the organism. From the very beginning of his dissertation, then, Alain must contend with the one widely accepted argument regarding the Stoic doctrine of *tonos* that would controvert his theory, namely, that the closest modern parallel to *tonos* was to be found in the philosophy of Spinoza: 'one is tempted, for example, to compare the *tonos* of the Stoics with the *conatus in suo esse perseverandi* [the tendency to persevere in one's being], which is also the essence of each being.'[69] Perhaps the analogy had been suggested to him by Lagneau, the scholar of Spinoza and Alain's former teacher. But, striking though it is, for Alain the analogy between *tonos* and *conatus* can be disregarded, and this by virtue of one concept: effort, which, he argues, belongs uniquely to the Stoic account, where it defines the essence of a being in terms of motion rather than substance. So compelling does this hypothesis appear that Alain is confident it will render any comparison with Spinozism merely superficial:

> *tonos* implies an idea of effort, of tendency, of wanting; the strength of the *conatus* is the very force of the definition of a being which subsists as it is by a kind of rational inertia. For the Stoics life is change, perpetual progress; for Spinoza, life is immobility in the rational, it is the eternity of a definition that has no intrinsic reason to become other than what it is … Spinoza fashioned a philosophy of the abstract, the motionless, the eternal; the Stoics have left us a philosophy of concreteness, of effort, and of progress.[70]

The remainder of Alain's dissertation continues in this vein. As he reflects on the role played by movement in Stoic philosophy, his admiration becomes unreserved:

> [The Stoics] understood that the synthesis of the one and the many could be realised only by movement, but they renounced what might be called the metaphysics of motion; they reduced the inevitable conception of the universal mechanism to its subjective condition … For the Stoics, therefore, it is neither a question of a metaphysics of the object, exceeding the representation, nor of the metaphysics of the subject, rejecting the representation, but of a physics of the soul, in the ancient sense, that is to say: a study of the soul in its concrete life, an analysis of psychical facts leading to one's finding in each of them the fundamental unity of a simple movement.[71]

The result of this heaping of praise upon the Stoic philosophy of effort is to dispel any doubts a reader might have had about the possible negative aspects of the doctrine. When movement is made the focus of philosophy, Alain is claiming, its whole nature is transformed. No longer a subject reserved for mechanics, movement is replaced at the heart of philosophy as that through which a person lives and has their being. Then those aspects of a doctrine of effort which had made the Stoics the subject of opprobrium, such as their belief in the power of the mind to conquer the body, will become, instead, sources of insight. Understanding that movement is indispensable to human experience, Stoicism rejects the idea that truth could ever be definitively mastered – rather, it is in constant progress and evolution towards higher and better states of 'superlative clarity'. Philosophy, according to the Stoics, he writes,

> is not the results, but the method; it is not the state of our mind, but the progress of our minds … To find a solution, to arrive at an absolute, definitive truth, would be the death of thought; for life, for thought, is research, it is progress towards superlative clarity.[72]

Such is his belief in the significance of effort that Alain does not hesitate to hold it up as an ideal for the contemporary philosopher. For Alain, what contemporary philosophy needed is what Stoicism achieved several millennia ago: a return to earth, to movement and 'concreteness'. This is the 'physics of the soul' by means of which Stoicism will prove its relevance to the present day.

Alain would later refer to his dissertation on the Stoics as a turning point in his intellectual formation and as the 'only work of erudition' he had ever undertaken (Alain chose not to pursue doctoral research).[73] To be sure, he would go on to write more about other philosophers – about Descartes and Hegel, for instance – than he ever did about the Stoics, and would find much to praise in the philosophy of Plato. These thinkers all showed Alain new ways of interpreting the progress of the human mind. Moreover, he went on to take an enthusiastic interest in Epicureanism and in the question of pleasure, thereby expanding his idea of human happiness. But for all these excursions into the history of ideas, the Stoics' simple, stark, correlation between truth and effort remained the key to Alain's way of thinking. Throughout his life he was convinced that in any experience of the good only one thing mattered: the effort of the will that made it so.

Undoubtedly the explanation for Alain's interpretation of Stoicism and his emphasis on the doctrine of effort arises from his earlier philosophical training and in Lagneau's passionate, almost religious, conviction that action was the key to humanity's spiritual self-realization. Further, Alain would later assert that Lagneau had met with him frequently during his student years at the École Normale, and that, to Alain, study of the Stoics in particular helped give him a better understanding of his teacher's work.[74] At that time, Alain writes in his memoires, *Historie de mes pensées* (History of my ideas) (1936), he had become uneasy about Lagneau's high opinion of Spinoza, whom – as Alain's dissertation shows – he considered to be an abstract thinker lacking the firm, concrete sense of effort that Lagneau, despite his Spinozism, had so inspired in Alain. The Stoics were a way for Alain to reconcile himself to Lagneau's philosophy without embracing Lagneau's high regard for Spinoza. His memoirs make it quite clear that what Alain found in Stoicism was the same doctrine he had learnt to admire in Lagneau:

> The Stoics, it seems to me, have pressed closer, seeking what would be the very knowledge of the world without the will to know. And their formulae are very striking, though very obscure. For in seeking the criterion of truth (the object of polemics at that time), they said that truth resides in the tension itself, or

the tone, of the will that seeks it ... This is violent ... It's the same as saying that energetic research is the sign of truth.⁷⁵

The effort of the will decides which 'truth' among competing conceptions should survive in the progress of the human spirit. After the decision has been made the mechanics of a kind of natural selection takes over. Just as nature selects the strongest specimen, so truth selects the most intense example of willpower and interior 'tension'. Only when philosophers forget about the effort and focus on some idea of truth at the end of the search does the whole pursuit dwindle into abstractions. 'I now insist on this doctrine, certainly taken from Lagneau,' writes Alain, 'of the will in judgement.'⁷⁶ We do not need to look very far in Lagneau's work to find the same unequivocal equivalence between effort, willpower and truth as the one stated by Alain in his reflections on Stoicism. In 'Simple notes', the essay I cited earlier, Lagneau writes: 'To those who ... think that the truth is the good of the man [sic], that he should ... seize it with a firm embrace and attach to it, to those who seek the peace of certainty and know that it must not be conquered once, but always reconquered ... we say: "You are in the right".'⁷⁷

The significance of Stoicism for the philosophy of the spiritual life as it develops around the turn of the nineteenth century has already been studied in relation to Bergson. For the moment we will point out the distinct way in which Alain's work on the Stoics reinforces the connection and how he develops it further: as secular exercise. Michel Spanneut has pointed out that Alain was the one philosopher in early twentieth-century French thought who 'went even further [than others] in the understanding and exploitation of Stoicism ... [penetrating] to the heart of the Stoic doctrine of the inalienable person'.⁷⁸ 'The reader is impressed to find formulated in these lines,' writes the editor of Alain's dissertation, 'and five years before the publication of *Matter and Memory*, the outline of a psychology which would come to replace that of Bergson.'⁷⁹ Alain was drawn not only to what the Stoic doctrine of effort had to say about the nature of God and of spiritual experience; he was drawn to the Stoic doctrine of effort for what it had to say about the human quality of these lofty topics. Where Bergson may be said to begin the reinvention of philosophy's spiritual exercise according to Stoic ideals, Alain completes and perfects the process; where Bergson establishes the spiritual nature of effort, Alain defines the spiritual life itself as effort. In Alain's work a new kind of humanist spirituality becomes increasingly evident. And where Bergson still spoke principally to a largely classical conception of religious mysticism (the *Two Sources* is interested in Teresa of Ávila and Joan of Arc), Alain appealed to the more anticlerical tastes of a younger generation. Between 1909 and 1944 Alain taught philosophy at the *lycée* Henri–IV, and during this thirty-four-year tenure conversed with and influenced many of the students who passed through his class room, including among them Simone Weil. He was also politically outspoken and published prolifically in the popular press, making him France's first public intellectual and a philosopher whose reputation at one point ranked higher even than Bergson's.[80] This peculiar nature of Alain's impact justifies a brief look at his mature writings on Stoicism, with the aim of uncovering a distinctly Stoic ideal emerging in modernity's philosophy of spiritual exercise.

As late as 1931 Alain incorporated Stoic doctrines into what would become one of his best-loved philosophical works, the *Éntretiens au bord de la mer: recherché de l'entendement* (Seaside conversations: in search of understanding). In it two friends strolling along the waterfront encounter a nameless 'old man' – the mysterious *le vieillard* – who engages them in conversation and imparts a Stoic perspective on the meaning of life, thought and piety. In the ninth 'conversation', as the topic turns to God, the old man maintains that God is not hidden (*secret*) but composed of power (*puissance*) accessible to humans through acts of courage, and thus the old man rejects every attempt by theologians of the past to identify God with weakness. What people fear, he says, is not power as such but ugly power, for what people fear can never be beautiful – and courage, he insists, is beautiful. All the proofs for God's existence, the old man explains, comes down to the 'contemplation of bare power'. Soul, preference, decree, for instance, all these are derived from the power with which spirit expresses and asserts itself. And the Stoics might be seen as the guardians of this truth, which allows a person to face difficulties with courage rather than flee hardship. 'It is courage,' says the old man, 'it is courage which is God.'[81] In the *Éntretiens,* Alain goes on to extend this theology of effort to include Stoicism and those ideas of spirit as effort or force which he had discovered as a young student: the cosmic principal of effort which, for Alain's Stoics, is also the criterion of truth.

No doubt some readers would have found Alain's perspective on God curious. But Alain was, by all accounts, an exceptionally charismatic person and his ideas were taken up enthusiastically by many, not least his pupils. One former student – the novelist André Maurois – remembers vividly how, when the professor entered the classroom for the first time, 'that day, for me, everything in the world was changed'.[82] After all, Alain's philosophical position – his emphasis on action, his belief in the effort of the human spirit – responded to a widely diffused military morality, according to which humanity communes with God through daring acts of heroism and tests of strength, a transformation of suffering and dejection to opportunities for courage and glory. Alain himself had instanced these ideas in his personal life. In 1914, despite being exempt from conscription on account of his profession, Alain joined the army. Though a committed pacifist and against war in principle, nonetheless Alain thought it a poor show of solidarity not to fight alongside one's fellow person – in addition, he supposed warfare to be a human art and a means for any person to confront their death bravely and make something of their life. 'He who goes to meet [death] and calls it, so to speak, into the arena, such a man feels stronger than death,' he writes in 1911, adding: 'there is, therefore, a kind of poetry in war.'[83] Towards this more enlightened understanding of action and courage all philosophy should work.

During this time – the years leading up to and immediately following the First World War – Alain's thoughts never strayed far from Stoicism. Of particular interest is the collection of *propos* entitled *On Happiness* (1928), where, with the aid of the ever-present Stoics and Cynics, Alain argues that,

> man's [*sic*] only resource is his own will ... [I]nner strength is proved through its accomplishments ... [I]f I had my way, children would be told about Hercules' labours so that they would learn to overcome external forces: for that is what living is all about, and the other choice – the cowardly choice – is nothing but a slow death.[84]

To Alain, the guiding principle of life is effort. As a general rule, a person prefers to act rather than to be acted upon; in light of this, only work willingly chosen qualifies as 'a form of happiness'.[85] 'Fundamentally,' writes Alain, 'the only thing we like is power.'[86] From the myth of Hercules and from Cynic and Stoic philosophy Alain draws many more examples of effort, including the idea that nature in its 'natural' state is devoid of purpose and indifferent to moral ideas such as good and evil. From this doctrine Alain concludes that it is through effort that meaning is created, and that without the efforts of human beings 'the face of the earth would be brushwood and pestilence; not hostile, but not friendly'.[87] The indifference of a world without effort, he notes, haunts the human spirit and is the reason why she will not desist from imposing on it her will and willingly accept hardships, finding 'peace ... in strength' – or something very like what Hercules experienced when, according to one tradition, he decided to immolate himself and pass quickly out of the world rather than suffer a slow and painful death.[88]

There was in Stoicism's doctrine of effort a good deal more play with relaxation than Alain ever wanted to reveal. But otherwise the myth of Hercules can be seen as bringing effort into special focus for the ancient Cynics and Stoics. And this idea of effort was connected to another one which we find also in Alain's work: the necessity of effort in human nature, which was contrasted to the passive and sensitive life of plants and animals. For Alain effort was, as we suggested earlier, the indication of consciousness. Without effort, he had argued in 1891, there could be no progress of the human spirit. In the essays *On Happiness* Alain states that while a 'torpid state is good for man ... and is always restful', repose is all the same an 'animal state ... the essence of Epicurean virtue'.[89] Happiness can be had by giving in to one's passions and living like an animal, but it can also be had by '[awakening] completely and, as it were, [leaping] all the way up to Stoic virtue'.[90] It is not difficult to see which of the two virtues – the Epicurean or the Stoic – Alain prefers. Pleasure is the only good, this much Alain admits, but true pleasure is to accept hardships willingly and with an alert mind; it is to speak like an Epicurean but live like a Stoic. Such, Alain argues, is the 'virile wisdom' preserved for posterity in the writings of the Stoics.[91] And like his younger self, the Alain of *On Happiness* is wary of passivity and critical of its association with the spiritual life. It is the contradictory belief of Alain's philosophy that a life of intense effort will result in a more peaceful existence. While forced labour and suffering is always an evil, without the opportunity for voluntary hardship there is no real pleasure, no true courage and no authentic 'art of living'.[92]

Alain's Stoicism found instruction also in the tradition of spiritual exercise. In a *propos* from *On Happiness* entitled 'Prayers', composed in 1913, Alain argues that religion may be very useful, insofar as it contains 'prodigious practical wisdom'.[93] In essence Alain argues that the spiritual exercises of religion supplies psychological techniques for coping with suffering – provided, of course, that metaphysical ideas about God and so forth are put to one side. If a man who has survived a terrible ordeal 'wears himself out and redoubles his misfortune by useless agitation', prayer offers an effective treatment. For in the case of the miserable man reasoning will not help; then it is better 'to force him to kneel down with his head in his hands ... for, by this bit of gymnastics ... you thwart the violent state of his imagination, and for a moment you halt the effects of despair and anger'.[94] With this description of prayer as a form of 'gymnastics', Alain manages at once to recognize the usefulness of spiritual exercise and reject its metaphysical commitments, resisting the idea that such practices represent any real intuition of a more-than-human presence. Alain goes on to explain how religion arises through the false belief that things are 'given' from beyond. As he did in the case of the Stoics, Alain reflects now that where religion is concerned there is no divine agency in nature. 'Superstition,' he writes, '... always consists in explaining real effects by supernatural cause'.[95] But, says Alain, this should not detract from the fact that praying may be very effective psychologically. Whatever aids the person in her pursuit of happiness is good; insofar as religion can be a means to this end, it is useful and true.

Alain's Stoic philosophy of the spiritual life, and his secularized spiritual exercises, are anticlerical and pay homage to humanist ideas of religion. The collection of essays which present this position on religion the best, and that provide the context for Alain's work on Stoicism, are the *Propos sur la religion* (Remarks on Religion) (1936). Religion, Alain thinks, should be political: concerned with changing the world for the better and supplying persons with the courage necessary to effect change. But all around him Alain saw French religious thought dominated by a form of Augustinian mysticism which Alain though incompatible with the political aspirations he detected in Christianity: 'Quietism'. Quietism was, he thought, an impediment to action and a threat to the freedom of spirit. It was an approach to life that went against every faith in effort, indeed encouraged an attitude the very opposite to effort: repose. 'So theology can teach the purity of the heart,' says Alain, 'but it does not grant the courage to change the course of things according to justice. And the forces of faith are spent in the void, as is shown by this mystical doctrine called Quietism, in other words, the doctrine of repose.'[96]

In Quietism, then, was a philosophy of spiritual exercise fundamentally at odds with the one proposed by Alain: a religion that could instruct in 'purity of heart', yes, but which proved unable to educate heroes; an outlook more interested in God than in human life, elevating God's grace above every human achievement. Through its long history in France it had established many elaborate arguments for referring human activity to divine grace and more prosaically through its catechisms. But according to Alain, what theology had tried to explain away – effort – could still be found at the heart of Christian doctrine. In a *propos* entitled 'La Fête-Dieu' (The Feast of Corpus Christi), composed in 1922, Alain imagines a traveller from a non-Christian land who, while passing through a French village on the feast day of Corpus Christi, happens upon the sacramental procession and converses with the local vicar regarding the significance of the monstrance. The traveller, writes Alain, can well understand why people would bow down and revere a piece of bread, for who could live for two days without this hard-won substance? But the traveller is perplexed at the priest's insistence that such is not the meaning of the procession and that furthermore what the bread represents is not a nourishment provided by human hands, but a spiritual gift no merit could secure. '[The Vicar] seemed to me,' speaks the traveller in Alain's fable, 'to possess a secret doctrine regarding [the bread], and to pity those who were ignorant of it':

> 'So I pretended to understand [the priest]; but it appears to me that I understand him much better than he understands himself. It is well known that ... bread is the [support] of all wisdom and all spirit in this world. I would like to say in this regard that the good deeds of God reside less in maxims of wisdom and principles of knowledge than in the more humble conditions that make knowledge and wisdom possible.
>
> And if some proud man claimed to be the master of thinking and willing without these outside helpers, I would like to see him go for two days without ... bread. I am willing to call "grace" these aids which enable us to know a little and to want for the better. That this grace comes to us by ... bread is apparent to everyone, and it is therefore in the [form of] bread that it is proper to celebrate the benefactor. But it seems to me that, following this, it is our business to will and think properly, and it would seem impious to thank the benefactor for what we ourselves have done well in this world – because that is our business, once we are provided with wheat. It is remarkable that universal religion is always wedded to some superstitious belief, counsellor of laziness and weakness'. Thus philosophized [the traveller], because he had witnessed a Corpus Christi procession.[97]

In this short fable the traveller with his religious outlook untouched by Christianity, inwardly shaking his head at the secret doctrines of the Catholic priest – is a foil for Alain's own non-Christian spirituality. Alain understands well the need to honour the material gifts provided by nature. Without grain, how could one make the food necessary to 'think and will properly'? Food fuels the mind. So giving thanks for this 'grace' seems fitting. But to Alain it is not right to conflate the gift of wheat with what a person achieves by means of food. Thought and will – these are the result of human effort, thus 'it would seem impious to thank the benefactor for what we ourselves have done well in this world'. So Alain renounces the religion that would obscure the glories of human endeavour and lift the responsibility for human deeds from human shoulders. This was the faith so admired by Alain's students, such as Maurois, Weil and Simone Pétrement. A 'human and not inhuman' religion, derived from life rather than doctrine.[98]

When Alain used Stoic ideas to extract from spiritual exercise an 'art of living' distinct from metaphysical commitments – in effect, distinct from 'spirit' – he was anticipating an approach that was soon to become widespread and significant. After the Second World War, Stoicism would become a principal image of what philosophers would look to when they wanted to think about philosophy as something more than abstract ratiocination – as a subjective method leading to experiences beyond the ken of discursive reasoning; as *mystical*, in some deep-seated and indefinable sense. Mysticism, however, had undergone profound changes in the process. When did grace cease to be recognized alongside effort in the spiritual life? Was it when vitalism came to discredit the very idea of passivity? Or was it when nineteenth-century culture claimed the man of action as its paragon? Alain did not engage with these questions but focussed instead on explicating the principle of effort in fables and myth. But regardless of whether the philosophy of effort was discussed in the context of 'natural religion' (Alain's traveller from a non-Christian land) or pre-Christian Hellenism (the figure of Hercules), it was evident to Alain, as it was also to Bergson and Bréhier, that here was an art of life which articulated, from the depths of pre-Christian history, a compelling and current truth.

From the 1950s onwards, several influential French philosophers – not only Hadot and Deleuze, but also Michel Foucault – would take inspiration from Stoicism and use it to rethink the nature of philosophy. Hadot's contribution will be discussed in more detail in the following chapter. For now, it will suffice to point out that when these thinkers alight on the idea of philosophy as a spiritual exercise or art of life, they do so, on the whole, without engaging with the Augustinian tradition of mystical prayer from which the philosophy of spiritual exercise first emerged in France. The most striking consequence of this shift in perspective is that grace – both conceptually and thematically – diminishes in importance while effort increases in significance. Insofar as philosophy is, once again, identified as a spiritual exercise and art of living, it is an art centred on the individual and their efforts. As Thomas Bénatouïl has shown, there is an obvious connection here not only to Bergson's philosophy – with its emphasis on the efforts of the self and the view of autonomous spirit – but also with existentialism, the most popular philosophical current during the mid-twentieth century (and indeed, Jean-Paul Sartre showed a keen interest in Stoicism).[99] For Sartre, as for the new interpretations of Stoicism that emerges in French twentieth-century philosophy, human beings find themselves thrown into a world without meaning in which they are compelled to create truth through their own efforts, and Stoicism (mediated, as it already was, through the effort-oriented philosophies of Bergson and Alain) seemed to reinforce this insight in significant ways. And philosophy itself agreed with such outlooks, at least so far as the younger generation of thinkers was concerned. But the work of Biran and Ravaisson was another matter: a religious position that insisted on the idea of grace and so looked towards spiritual exercise as a way of challenging rather than affirming human effort. Such an outlook, however, was not really part of modern thinking, and it transpired to be much simpler to keep it separate from the new currents that appeared in the wake of Alain, Bergson and existentialism. To many, no doubt, it must have seemed a certain kind of spiritualism was to blame for French philosophy's languishing over-long in the shadow of Catholic theology, a fact which would only have increased the respectability of Stoicism as an anti-clerical alternative to Christian spirituality.

Neither Bergson nor Alain ever seemed to show much interest in the conceptual difficulties that arose from this bracketing of grace from the philosophy of the spiritual life. Most likely the long-standing reality and threat of war had indicated the principal outlines of the focus on effort. Aside from responding to a generally diffused military morality Alain was thinking more specifically about the battle field as he wrote his mature essays on Stoicism, spiritual exercise and religion. For instance, in *Mars: Or, the Truth about War* (1921), Alain addresses Stoicism explicitly from the perspective of war: 'Under the protection ... of the good Hercules, the only god who is venerable,' writes Alain, 'I drew here the ambiguous face of Mars, god of war.'[100] To Alain, the ambiguity of war was clarified through the concept of effort which Hercules embodied. On the one hand, war seem to pay homage to Hercules, since in war virtue was at last inseparable from power. 'I do not turn away from this thought,' Alain affirms: 'all human force ... pleases me and reassures me inasmuch as it approaches his divine example.'[101] On the other hand, in war there were no real heroes because everyone was frightened into action and no one really approved of what they were doing or acted freely. 'In this human storm,' writes Alain, 'I can only see ... weakness unchained, passions triumphant, and virtue decapitated.' 'Hercules,' he concludes, 'is humiliated.'[102] This view of the human condition, of its purpose in effort and its affinity with Stoic ideals, had been expressed as early as the 1830s by Alfred de Vigny, and had initially emerged out of a general disillusionment with the terrors of the Napoleonic war mingled with nostalgia for the glory days of chivalry and honour. In the twentieth century it was possible to see the same ideas resurfacing in the aftermath of another terrible combat that had left France shaken. The immensity of the death toll and the reports of soldiers' conditions in the trenches had made the old descriptions of war as the site of glory and heroism questionable. Yet for Alain this fact did not controvert the principle of effort. To the contrary, if modern warfare had left Hercules 'humiliated' it was not because soldiers no longer exerted themselves, it was because soldiers were not active enough. In the trenches what looked like action was in truth unthinking passivity, merely 'weakness unchained' as he puts it in *Mars*.[103] So heroism was thwarted. According to Alain, war was an experience that had torn the veil of superstition from religious ideals, leaving them naked and bare. Hereafter, philosophers were free simply to survive in the world, and to make of survival a spiritual discipline and training. Now the radicals in the French intellectual milieu would gravitate, unconsciously or not, towards Stoicism and a philosophy of effort that would echoed the soldier's dream of being one's own master, able to defend justice justly.[104]

The irony in this elision of Stoicism with a philosophy of spiritual exercise was that while Stoicism offered an ideal that agreed with an influential philosophical movement, it also undermined that movement's coherence. According to the spiritual philosophy of Biran and Ravaisson, effort was a factor that must emerge in human experience but which did not exhaust it; for Bergson and Alain, effort becomes the defining factor of the human condition – creativity, religiosity, consciousness – as such. The two positions were at odds with each other and would inevitably come into conflict. The first and most significant such encounter would appear in the work of Alain's most famous student, Simone Weil: in her writing the two ideals of the spiritual life – of grace on the one hand and effort on the other – are drawn into confrontation as she writes her account of philosophy's spiritual exercises. For most of her adult life Weil adhered to the humanist Stoicism of her former teacher. Then, a few years before her early death in 1942, a religious experience caused her to rediscover the tradition of Augustinian mysticism. In her reading of the mystics Weil is led to question the elevation of effort in philosophical method, even challenging the authority of Bergson, and mounts a formidable enquiry into the concept of activity and the ideal of effort. By the end of her life Weil had wrested an uneasy truce between the Stoicism of Alain and the Augustinianism of an older Catholic tradition. Rather than claim the triumph of either side, Weil equivocates between grace and effort, between passivity and activity, much as Biran had done at the beginning of the previous century. And much like Biran, what Weil produces in her work is an account of philosophical method which anticipates the modern love of connecting method with spiritual exercise and philosophy with art, while at the same time taking with utmost seriousness the 'spiritual' in spiritual exercise.

To Weil's account of the spiritual life, questioning of effort yet not dismissive of its significance for human experience, Gianni Vattimo and other critics have turned in recent decades.[105] They have tried, and we shall see how Weil gives them ample reason, to find in the idea of passivity and weakness alternatives to the language of force in both philosophy and religion. Such ideas are of the utmost importance to the understanding of philosophical practice today. Most theologians have understood by now that it is no longer possible to leave weakness and vulnerability out of a description of God or indeed of the good. But philosophy remains strangely attracted to the ideal of effort, especially where the legacy of the modern Stoicism we have been studying in this chapter is concerned. As a consequence, some negotiation between the graced and exercised aspects of life needs to be articulated, some co-extensiveness recognized between intuitions of finitude and acknowledgements of power.[106] Thus in the twentieth century, Weil's philosophy becomes part of a much larger debate between revivals of Bergson on the one hand and phenomenologies of suffering on the other. But in whatever way it is construed, Weil's work is a turning point in conveying spiritualist insights out of the history books and into philosophical awareness.

5

The paradox of attention: Simone Weil

The rapture which seized Maine de Biran on 27 May 1794, and which is recounted in the fragments of an early journal, characterizes the experience of spiritual exercise. Remember how Biran describes the event. At sundown on a beautiful spring evening, as he is out for a walk, the young philosopher is overcome suddenly by a 'sweet calm', 'an occasion too sweet, too remarkable in its rarity that I should ever forget it'.[1] Attempting vainly to recall this repose, and sensing the return of his ordinary state – where he suffers not only an agitated mind but a body in pain and discomfort – Biran detects at the core of his rapture a tension and contradiction. Calm is precisely what an agitated person can never attain, at least not by their own effort. So Biran must be passive in relation to the good, and yet he is, now more than ever, compelled to want and work for it. It is as if Biran had set out to discover, through an examination of his own inner life, the foundational paradox of spiritual exercise: the paradox of effort and grace. The basic form of this paradox recognizes in human experience the reciprocity of action and passivity, the co-extensiveness of doing and receiving. A person who exerts all their effort meditating will reach a point where activity seems to lead them nowhere – they become frigid and 'dry'. In most accounts of mystical prayer, active meditation is then said to give way to passive contemplation: here, effortless attention – not arduous concentration – is what counts for spiritual exercise and facilitates the sweet repose and tranquillity sought by the practitioner. Such tranquillity allows them to act without exercising their will, achieving a synthesis of effort and spontaneity. Actions performed by a person in this state will be felt to have had their source elsewhere, as if gifted by some divine desire which now moves the will, abandoning it to God. Repose thus becomes linked theologically to the perceiving – and receiving – of grace.

It has been argued that an important but neglected theme in the modern theorizing of philosophy as spiritual exercise has its origins in this ideal of tranquillity, which François Fénelon described as the result of an 'abandonment to God', and which once figured so prominently in French philosophy.[2] In previous chapters I examined, first, the emergence of this ideal in Biran's philosophy of the spiritual life ('spiritualism') and, later, traced its demise in the late nineteenth century, a story that helped us to understand how it was that *effort* rose to such prominence in modern philosophies of spiritual exercise and how passivity came to play such a vanishing role in the popular work of thinkers like Pierre Hadot. The purpose of the present chapter is different. Here I return to the ideal of tranquillity, but this time as it appears in the work of Simone Weil (1909–43), a philosopher who, like Hadot, comes out of a tradition of late nineteenth-century French philosophy descended from Biran, and like Hadot is committed to thinking about philosophy as a way of life and spiritual exercise. But Weil was also a late outpost of the Augustinian mysticism that had influenced Biran but which had begun to recede from the philosophies that most influenced Hadot: Henri Bergson and existentialism. Consequently, for Weil the experience of passivity is at the core of philosophical method as the experience of grace is at the heart of the spiritual life, and her account of philosophy as a spiritual exercise is thus quite different from that of Hadot. In this story Weil represents a counterfactual to Hadot's influential school of interpretation – a picture of what might have been but also of what could be in the future, providing not only an alternative viewpoint but an experiment in constructive thinking, for where Weil discovers passivity structuring the spiritual life it causes her to enquire more deeply into the nature and limitations of human effort in the practice of philosophy as such.

The critique of effort recovered here does not narrate a loss of faith in human ability, however. Biran's account of his state of rapture was shaped by the Augustinian ideal of tranquillity, but he stopped short of the pessimism often associated with French Augustinianism.[3] As pleasurable as it was to feel passive when the rapture seized him – to do nothing, and yet receive so much – it was frustrating, after the event, to feel passive and powerless in relation to the good. There must, Biran thinks, be something a person can do, some habit they can acquire and cultivate, some effort that will not contradict the good. If there were not, all the teachings of the ancients – of Socrates, Plato and the Stoics – would be for naught. Thus his concluding remarks on the evening's event are a prayer to ward off that melancholy which threatens to descend on him now once the rapture has fled, to 'dispel the veil [that] had covered my heart, as the sweet purple of the dawn hunts the sad darkness'.[4] Here Biran brings together two wholly different approaches to life: a compulsion to trust in the self-sufficiency of human ability on the one hand, and an equally keen intuition of dependency on the other. Since the Renaissance, the two approaches have been symbolized, typically, in the opposition between Stoicism and Christianity, and this is how we find them referred to in Biran's philosophy. In many places, no doubt, the opposition is merely rhetorical, used as a placeholder for serious argumentation. But just as often it is the outward sign of a contradiction deeply felt, a paradox which animates the whole introspective style of philosophy as such – its conclusions and its method. This particularly is the case among the French philosophers who claim a special line of descent from Biran, such as Félix Ravaisson, whose work we studied earlier. In this chapter, I will consider three sets of more or less striking variations on the effort and grace paradox in the work of Weil, a philosopher, poet and syndicalist who would go on to become a celebrated mystic. For the sake of simplicity, I have labelled the three sets of passages philosophical, practical and mystical respectively. They represent distinct but related moments in Weil's writing career: essays and lectures written during her student and teaching years (1929–34); notebooks kept during her 'factory year' (1934–5); and miscellaneous writing from the brief years of intense speculation that took place between her major religious experience in 1938 and her death in 1943.

I

The young Simone Weil was taught philosophy by Alain (Émile Chartier), from whom she learnt a love of philosophy and an appreciation for the concept of effort which was the principal content of Alain's approach. Effort was significant in turn-of-the-century French philosophy and Alain was not alone in focussing his work around this idea: the same tendency is evident in Bergson's philosophy, as we saw in the previous chapter. One would expect effort, then, to occupy a prominent place in Weil's work, and while we will note points of affinity between Weil and Alain (the *practice* of philosophy being one), the differences are striking, and nowhere more evident than in the work Weil submitted for her university examination (two years after graduating from Alain's class): 'Science and Perception in Descartes' (1929–30). In it Weil writes as a disciple of Alain but also as an inheritor of Maine de Biran's revision of philosophical method. Drawing together Alain's striking sense of philosophy as effort with a Biranian meditation on the limits of effort and experience of passivity, Weil produces an account of philosophical meditation that is questioning of effort and comes very close to the spiritual exercise tradition that had originally influenced Biran. Few French thinkers since have succeeded in making relevant an Augustinian method of introspection or captured with more clarity its significance for a critique of philosophical method.[5]

At the point in the essay where Weil begins her examination of passivity she has already introduced the reader to a sweeping history of humanity's quest for knowledge – what Weil, here, calls 'science' – as well as an evaluation of René Descartes' own contributions to the same. In those opening sections, Weil recognizes the unsatisfactory nature of Descartes' conclusions about the world – a world where reason is wholly divided from matter and from ordinary perception – but argues that these conclusions do not follow necessarily from Descartes' method, which in itself is nothing but attention carefully and rigorously directed at every aspect of experience, including the senses.[6] At the end of her initial evaluation of Descartes, she suggests that for this reason Cartesian science will always be misunderstood unless approached via the method itself, that is, unless preceded by a meditation that takes nothing for granted and attends to everything equally:

> Cartesian thought is not something that one can comment on from the outside; every commentator must become, at least for a time, a Cartesian … Let us therefore have no hesitation about imitating the Cartesian stratagem in commenting on Descartes [but] imagine another Descartes, a Descartes brought back to life. This new Descartes would have at first neither genius, nor knowledge of mathematics and physics, nor force of style; he would have in common with him only the fact of being a human being and of having resolved to believe only in himself. According to Cartesian doctrine, that is enough … So let us listen to this fictitious thinker.[7]

Still, while Weil professes fidelity to Descartes' method, her own execution of Cartesian 'attention' is distinct. Or rather, if (as we saw in an earlier chapter) there are in Descartes' *Meditations* (1641) two approaches to spiritual exercise – the autonomous meditator with their ideal of effort on the one hand, and the dependent meditator with their ideal of grace on the other – Weil is very keen not to forgo, as Descartes did, the discoveries that come with an analysis of the latter approach. So in the remainder of the essay Weil casts herself as a 'new' Descartes, examining her experience of the world just as Descartes had done in the *Meditations* yet all the while questioning Descartes' procedures as well as his conclusions.[8] What she discovers is the inadequacy of Descartes' equivalence between the meditator's self and pure activity, or mind. Though she recognizes a distinction between the activity of her mental faculties – principally, her will – when compared to the mostly passive nature of her body's sensations, she hesitates to separate definitively action and passivity, or to elevate action above passivity. A mark of how significant the latter concept becomes for Weil is the prominent role passivity plays in the final part of the dissertation. Here, halfway through her Cartesian meditation, Weil asserts not only the indivisibility of action and passivity, but the need to reunite them in philosophical method:

> I am always a dual being, on the one hand a passive being who is subject to the world, and on the other an active being who has a grasp on it ... Can I attain perfect wisdom, wisdom in action, that would reunite the two parts of myself? I certainly cannot unite them directly, since the presence of the world in my thoughts is precisely what this powerlessness consists of. But I can unite them indirectly, since this and nothing else is what action consists of. Not the appearance of action through the uncontrolled imagination that makes me blindly turn the world upside down by means of my anarchic desires, but real action, indirect action ... or, to give it its true name, work.
>
> It is through work that reason grasps the world itself and masters the uncontrolled imagination ... Only through the intermediary of the world, through the intermediary of work, do I reunite them; for if through work I do not unite the two parts of myself, the one that undergoes and the one that acts, I at least can cause the changes I undergo to be produced by me, so that what I am subject to is my own action ... I must use cunning, I must impede myself by using obstacles that steer me where I want to go.[9]

It is curious, especially if one is familiar with Weil's later work on the virtues of passivity, to see her here commending action, effort – and 'work'. But Weil, who would come to love the idea of the soul 'waiting' for grace and desisting from muscular effort, was by all accounts obsessed with the phenomenon of work, and was forever devising schemes that would bring her into closer proximity to manual labour and the life of the working classes. Weil's reasoning on this point is simple, and it is all contained in the passage from her Cartesian meditations quoted above. Action, Weil explains here, is usually pictured as the opposite of passivity, yet a close examination of experience does not support this conclusion. Whatever I do to the world – however cleverly I seem to grasp or lay my hands on it – I remain subject to it because the world, like my body, is never wholly within my control. Of course, in my imagination I may be able to 'turn the world upside down', as she writes, while meeting no resistance, but this idea is a fantasy. In life, there will always be impediments and so my action will always be in some manner 'indirect' and passive: 'I am always a dual being, on the one hand a passive being who is subject to the world, and on the other an active being who has a grasp on it.'[10] Action and passivity are thus two sides of a coin, and are naturally reunited when a person's activities make them conscious of the fact, such that they can say – with the farmer who rubs their aching limbs after a hard day's work – that 'the changes I undergo [are] produced by me, so that what I am subject to is my own action'. We can see that Weil regards such conscious reuniting of the two sides of human nature as the ideal form of life – the life of the skilled labourer. It is an expression of the reaction to factory work and the nostalgia for an older, pre-industrial idea of craftsmanship, a nostalgia that had been on the rise for well over half a century. But we can also see that Weil regards this ideal life of skilled labour as the life of the philosopher, for whom 'meditation' (the Cartesian method, to which Weil is committed, however critically) should consist in the same reuniting of passivity to effort – rather than in a valorization of effort and a suspicion of everything associated with the opposite of effort. A distinct political tone can be heard in this passage, but also a distinctly religious one, for what Weil (much like Catholic critics of industrial capitalism at the time, such as David Jones or Josef Pieper) is trying to get at by describing the ideal mental labour as an effort that, paradoxically, will involve and be shaped by passivity, is something like theology's understanding of contemplation or intuition as a passive mode of knowing whereby the mind learns by being 'open' and 'receptive' rather than by grasping actively at ideas. So Weil happily accepts that meditation must involve a voluntary passivity to the thing contemplated and reconciles what – then as now –are often seen as wholly opposite approaches to effort: joy and undergoing, or happiness and inactivity.[11]

What interests us here is Weil's ability to equivocate between action and passivity as she meditates. In *Science and Perception* philosophical practice is an exercise, but an exercise that maintains a double recognition of effort and repose. The typical starting point for such an equivocation is the desire to avoid falling on the side of either pure activity – voluntarism – or pure passivity – determinism; it is the desire for the middle. 'There is no longer any contradiction between freedom and necessity,' she writes in the final pages of her essay, nor between 'idealism and realism'.[12] It is important that Weil's philosophical career begins, in *Science and Perception*, with equivocation reached through what is, in essence, a spiritual exercise of meditation, because attention and contemplation (what, later on, will become 'prayer' in Weil's philosophy) are for Weil the principal means of perceiving her middle and keeping it in view. In a way the remainder of Weil's writing is the result of viewing the middle repeatedly from fresh vantages with the aim of articulating better the duality of activity and passivity which it reveals and which structures the practice of attention which it performs. There are very few philosophers who have been more explicit about the importance of duality, of contradiction and paradox, to philosophical method. In *Science and Perception* Weil explains that the recognition of contradiction can lead to a heightened awareness of reality. When I acknowledge that the limits to my power are also what give them their actuality, then I am not powerless but at home in the world. Was this not how Descartes discovered the existence of God, by recognizing that he was *not* God? 'It is enough,' she writes, 'for me to know that my power is not absolute to know that my existence is not the only existence.'[13] Hence the world too, as Weil says, appears to me as a paradox, it is both obstacle and means, both that which constrains and restricts me but at the same time that through which I know myself and know myself to be the recipient – rather than author – of my existence.[14]

In her conclusions Weil combines well-known aspects of Augustinian anthropology with a psychological approach inherited from post-Biranian philosophy: it is a study of philosophy as spiritual exercise, an examination of philosophy's spiritual exercise. As she discovers herself to be a 'dual being' yet, *pace* Descartes, a single person, she invokes the familiar theme, adapted by Biran from St Paul and Augustine, of the *homo duplex in humanitate, simplex in vitalitate*, the 'human who, while twofold in humanity, is simple in vitality'.[15] The *homo duplex* is the divided self of Paul's Letter to the Romans, the self who feels themselves torn between spirit and flesh, mind and body; it is the philosopher who struggles to reconcile active with passive being, and rails at their material embodiment. The *homo simplex* is the self for whom mind and body are attuned and in harmony; it is the philosopher who has reunited active and passive being in such a way that there is no perceptible distinction between them and so no sense of internal struggle. In this way the *homo simplex* may resist the tendency towards melancholy and sadness which the *homo duplex* seems to provoke. For if self were in truth pure mind then its material embodiment would be a tragedy and a cause for grief; but if self is not fundamentally distinct from matter then such sorrow is unwarranted. From the discovery of her 'dual being', writes Weil, she thus derives not sadness but a kind of bliss, explaining that 'not only do I have a grasp on the world, but my thought is, as it were, a component part of the world, just as the world, in another way, is part of my thought. From now on I have a share in the universe; I am in the world'.[16] The *homo duplex in humanitate, simplex in vitalitate* provides a means for thinking about duality in human experience without accepting a tragic dualism of substances, for it asserts that while the distinction between activity and passivity is real, nonetheless it is what Biran elsewhere calls 'logical' rather than real.[17] A person is of necessity neither disembodied mind nor mindless matter but an embodied life; she is active and passive at the same time but not in the same way, and meditation – practised attentively – can initiate the philosopher into a realization of this state.

Nevertheless, and in spite of what Weil knows about religious philosophy, Weil's understanding of meditation in *Science and Perception* is shaped as much by humanism as it is by the Augustinian current of French philosophy to which it is conceptually so closely tied. Later Weil would write of how, at this time in her life, she had identified as an 'agnostic' and 'Stoic' (Weil had been brought up in a secular Jewish household).[18] For four years, moreover, she had been under the tutelage of Alain, whose sympathies with Stoicism were well known; Weil had attended Alain's gatherings even after graduating from the *lycée* Henri-IV, and there can be little doubt that she admired Alain's striking portrayal of Stoic ideas. When Weil writes about the transformative potential of work, it is Alain the advocate of Stoicism whom we hear. Yet even the mark of Alain's Stoicism does not prepare a reader for the noticeably religious tenor that Weil's thinking acquires in *Science and Perception*, a piece which shows the influence also of an older spiritualism – though what precisely Weil read at this point is not easy to ascertain.[19] One senses, at any rate, that for Weil there is in meditation no contradiction between the ideal of effort and the ideal of passivity, or between Stoicism and Christianity. It is a position which she will elaborate on in more detail in her first piece of major philosophical thinking after the essay on Descartes, her *Lectures on Philosophy* (1933–4).

The *Lectures on Philosophy* – originally delivered at the girls' *lycée* in Roanne where Weil was now employed – begin with the same question that occupied Weil in the dissertation on Descartes: the paradoxical nature of philosophical method, of introspection or attention. Taking 'attention', or the 'study of oneself', as her starting point, Weil declares that there is an incompatibility between introspection and attention, because in those moments when one is most attentive and 'actively involved in something' one is also least conscious of what one is doing. So, intense attention resembles passivity.[20] Weil attributes this paradoxical state of affairs to habit – the effects on the body of repeating continually the same action over a long period of time. Habit, for Weil, is what makes activity feel like passivity. Learning a new skill – especially one that involves physical labour – is difficult at first but eventually becomes easy, so that 'we never feel pure activity'.[21] As a result, we tend not to notice how much work is still required of us even when the activity we are performing has become, itself, easy and effortless. 'In most cases,' explains Weil, 'the feeling of effort is inversely proportional to its being voluntary: effortlessness is always a sign of a real exercise of the will.'²² This is an important point for Weil, and she repeats it to her students. 'The feeling of effort is a sign that the will is no longer at work', she says; 'effortlessness is ... the sign of heroism', and 'sensation is always something one undergoes, something passive, even when one feels the will powerfully at work'.²³ Implicit in this statement is a critique of the popular admiration of effort in French philosophy and culture. Resembling a Quietist or Quaker rather than the Hercules of Alain's *propos*, Weil's 'hero' will prove themselves through a kind of inactivity – their ability to undergo and be passive – rather than through their ability to shape the world through their efforts. There are to be no transports of achievement, no apotheosis of human effort, nothing at all like what one finds in the vitalism and effort-oriented philosophy of Henri Bergson's *The Two Sources of Morality and Religion* or, indeed, in the philosophy of Alain.

Particular differences between Weil and the popular current represented by Bergson and Alain become evident as she refutes, in the next sentence, the connection between mysticism and effort. Since complete attention is not available to consciousness, the idea that there could be a 'feeling of effort' which would equate to contact with God is, she says, 'an illusion': real holiness, in her opinion, consists in 'trying not to think that one is being virtuous'.²⁴ This 'trying not to think' about what one is doing as one does it is difficult to articulate and, to Weil, is what worries any simple alignment between effort and mysticism, or between effort and attention. A phenomenon like attention – the mystic's principal tool, but also the method of the philosopher – seems to contradict all notions of passivity, since in order to manifest attention one must be alert and vigilant, and yet it is only when a person is 'tired and [thinks] ... almost dreamily, unconsciously', that what they are seeking for finally becomes apparent. 'Men [*sic*] of genius, one thinks,' says Weil, 'are those who have unconsciousness of genius.' Such persons no longer pay attention, they *are* attentive; to them attention has become habit and second nature. Is this not also how true mysticism works; how grace is received, unsolicited and unlooked-for, when the mystic is least expecting it? Weil would therefore define attention in terms of the unconscious and habit, and she declares that there may even be 'some unconscious knowledge in habit' though admits that it is 'a difficult question'.²⁵

Here Weil is stating again the paradox of meditation in terms similar to those she had used in her dissertation on Descartes. In *Science and Perception* she had spoken of the necessary passivity in mental or physical effort, of the undergoing involved in any volition and of the simultaneity of action and passivity in human experience. That concept had conveyed to Weil a middle between determinism and voluntarism in the idea of 'indirect action'. And now Weil, finding the same middle in the idea of habituated attention, draws from it the same duality of experience. As she was when writing her Cartesian meditation, in her *Lectures on Philosophy* Weil is certain that action and passivity, doing and undergoing, are not contradictory but intimately linked, morally as well as psychologically. As she says at one point: 'Complete attention is like unconsciousness.'[26]

Though Weil at this point does not yet consider herself a 'Christian' (the religious experience she has in 1938 is still four years away), her certainty regarding the significance of passivity for philosophical method stems from her understanding of mysticism and of the spiritual life. In the final part of her lecture course – entitled 'Ethics and aesthetics' – Weil repeats that 'those who believe that they can come into contact with God through experience (mystical) are guilty of blasphemy'.[27] The emphasis is on 'believe'. She has already shown the limits of volition and of the feeling of effort when what is sought is the genuinely unknown – God or illumination. Like Weil's 'men of genius' who discover truth when they are no longer conscious of making an effort to reach it and no longer directing their attention at will, the real mystic is someone who is not conscious of their effort to reach God. As Weil had shown in her dissertation on Descartes, the meditator's evidence for God – if evidence it can be called – is not arrived at through effort but through the arresting of effort: I discover that God exists because it is impossible to grasp God; this is how I know that the infinite being whom 'God' describes must exist.[28] All the same, Weil is certain that many philosophers have the right idea about God (later we will also see her revise – or at least revisit – her opinions on the necessary impossibility of the mystic having 'contact' with God). This position she arrives at through a survey of Greek and Hellenistic philosophies, principally Stoicism.

Weil regards Stoicism as an example of true philosophy: and true philosophy, it transpires, is philosophy practised in such a way that it becomes indistinguishable from reverence and holy joy. The Stoics, she explains, were pantheists who loved the world because it was divine; for them philosophy was continuous, loving contemplation directed towards everything that was – spiritual exercise (though Weil does not use the term). At the same time, the Stoics did not think that God was the world; rather, according to Weil, what they contemplated as 'the world' was that which allowed human beings and gods to communicate: '[The world] is divine in so far as it allows divine beings (men [sic] and gods) to live in it. The religion of the Stoics is this relationship between the world and man; one is reasonable in so far as one loves the world.'[29] Put differently, and in the terms Weil had used in her essay on Descartes (and now repeats here), what the Stoics contemplated was the connection between invisible spirits and visible matter, between action (spirit) and passivity (matter): 'So [Stoic] pantheism follows naturally from a way of thinking of the relationships of the soul and the body, of the relationships between theory and practice.' In *Science and Perception,* when Weil had written about how meditation on the self revealed a 'dual being' at once active and passive, and how meditation might be able to reunite the two, she had not mentioned religious feeling. But to the Stoics in Weil's *Lectures,* who now become the vehicles of her own thought, the religious nature of philosophical method is obvious: real attention, the kind that is so intense it becomes almost unconscious, is here Weil's definition of the spiritual life.

Nor does Weil confine her approval of spiritual exercise as a philosophical method to the historical Stoics. Interpreting Stoicism as a general attitude towards the world rather than as a school of thought, she detects its principles in Christianity too, especially among its mystics and poets. According to Weil, the best examples of Stoicism are to be found in the poetry of Francis of Assisi and of Johann Wolfgang von Goethe – in Weil's letters and notebooks we find references to Francis' 'Canticle to the Sun' and to Goethe's *Faust*.[30] Weil does not separate Stoic writers like Marcus Aurelius from the Christian poets she admires. Her mention of Francis and Goethe is prefaced by a long list of quotations from Marcus Aurelius' *Meditations.* These writers, like their work, are for Weil part of a general religious inspiration. 'Ancient Stoicism was a universal love for everything,' she says, 'not the so called "stoic [*sic*] resignation" as is commonly said today.'[31] How could it be otherwise in a philosophy which taught that the world itself was divine? So it would be impossible, for a real Stoic, to 'resign' themselves to the world, if that world were understood to be the gateway to gods. Rather, like Francis or Goethe, a real Stoic would love the world in so far as it manifested – albeit indirectly – divine presence. As she concludes her summary of the Stoics, Weil's approval of their 'love for everything' becomes evident:

> Let us think of pantheism in connection with the Stoics. The question arises in connection with the opposition there is between a transcendent God (who is beyond our grasp) and an immanent God. Plato thought of God as transcendent. The question is one which is related to the ideas one has of the relationship between the mind and the body. One thinks that there is a relationship of harmony between the mind and the body just as one thinks that there is one between God and the world.
>
> Now, we have to think of matter as an obstacle and as a means ... So, we have to struggle against the world as a swimmer does against the water, as the dove struggles against the air, but we have to love it as the swimmer loves the water that bears him [*sic*] up, etc. The Stoics brought these two feelings together and it is the second which seems more important – that of the love of the world.[32]

Overall, there is a noticeable similarity between the pantheism of Weil's Stoics and the religious anthropology that emerged from her Cartesian meditations. Although Weil now attaches more importance to the question of how creatures relate to God, she frames the creator-creature relationship immediately in terms of the question that had preoccupied her in *Science and Perception*: the relationship between mind and body, or between action and passivity. On the one hand I am thwarted by the matter which puts up so many obstacles for me, on the other hand I am 'held up' by it; on the one hand the world is what separates me from God, on the other hand it is that which allows me to know God. Hence I will make an effort but I will also be passive – and it is passivity on which Weil now lingers and which she thinks the Stoics emphasized in their idea of 'loving the world'. The Stoics are here engaged in reuniting humanity's dual nature. Struggle is not the principal objective in life, nor is it the purpose of philosophy; repose is equally significant, if not more so (the swimmer cannot swim efficiently without also relaxing a little). Effort and repose are not mutually excluding phenomena but two terms of a contradiction which relate to one another in the form of a paradox, and attention to this paradox is what makes for that attention to the world which is also the matter of philosophical method.

Later, in 'Forms of the Implicit Love of God' (1941–2), Weil would again locate the key to both philosophy and spiritual exercise in a 'Stoic' recognition of repose. At one point in this essay Weil describes the effort which brings a person to salvation. She has just named that effort 'attention', and explained that it is neither wholly active nor entirely passive, but a 'kind of passive activity' that is different from volition while being, at the same time, an arduous task ('there is an easiness in salvation which is more difficult for us than all our efforts').[33] No wonder, she says, that salvation should be so difficult to talk about or even imagine. And yet something very similar to what happens between the human soul and God takes place everywhere in the natural world:

> The weeds are pulled up by the muscular effort of the peasant, but only sun and water can make the corn grow … It is because the will has no power to bring about salvation that the idea of secular morality is an absurdity. What is called morality only depends on the will in what is, so to speak, its most muscular aspect. Religion on the contrary corresponds to desire, and it is desire which saves.[34]

Salvation is not compatible with effort in so far as effort is understood purely in muscular terms, as a result of deliberate action. When God reaches a person and 'grace' descends – that word appears in the following section – it is not because of anything they did consciously, but because of the unconscious desire that turned them in the right direction, just as plants receive the light of the sun by means of nothing but an instinctual tendency to open their petals towards the sun. Like the plant's instinct to seek out the sun, the human soul's desire to seek out God is not subject to control by the will. It is at this point in her essay that Weil compares religious morality to Stoicism. 'The Roman caricature of Stoicism also appeals to the muscular will', she says, alluding to that idea of 'resignation' she so despised, '[but] true Stoicism, the Stoicism of the Greeks, from which Saint John, or perhaps Christ, borrowed the terms of "Logos" and "pneuma", is purely desire, piety and love. It is full of humility'.[35] The key to Weil's interpretation of philosophical method, what will transpire in her later writings as a dialectic of effort and grace, is that in attention mystical passivity is the same as Stoic effort.

But to return to Weil's *Lectures*. Even in those passages where Weil writes from a Stoic perspective, praising the Stoics' idea of philosophy as a way of life, she does not imagine Stoicism to be something separate from Christianity or mysticism. Besides naming Francis of Assisi a Stoic, Weil repeatedly describes Stoic philosophy in terms of religious feeling and spiritual exercise. The essence of Stoicism, as Weil saw it, was the discovery of dependency (finitude, passivity) in the midst of power. Over a century after Biran had first wrestled with the difference between Christianity and Stoicism – 'the spiritual life is higher: it does not come from man [sic] ... [whereas] everything that is most sublime in Stoic morality is nothing but human virtue, the force of the human *moi*, having support only in itself' – Weil proposed a way for Stoicism to be reconciled with Christianity.[36] In the 'Miscellaneous topics and essay plans' which Weil provided for her students as part of her lecture course, she encourages them always to look at philosophical questions in light of that paradox which constitutes the fundamental experience of human life and so must provide philosophy with its method: the paradox of passive activity, of weak power. In an essay plan addressing a quotation of Francis Bacon's, 'Man [sic] can only gain control over nature by obeying it', Weil thus suggests to her students that true mastery is not power but humility. Her thoughts on Bacon's slogan provide a good summary of her teaching in his lecture course, and of her 'stoical' position more broadly.

Our general character, Weil begins, is to feel both miserable and great, to be sometimes 'at the centre of the world, and sometimes ... nothing in contrast with it'.[37] This is the twofold nature of human beings, to be both active and passive at the same time but not in the same way, and an essay on the topic, Weil suggests, could open by stating this paradox: 'man [sic] seems sometimes to possess a great power over nature, sometimes to be its plaything.'[38] Then, she says to her students, consider writing separate sections on power and powerlessness respectively. Examples of the first could be modern technology, which allows us to master nature; examples of the second could be death and illness, which remind us that we are always mastered by nature. This leads to a preliminary conclusion: 'man's [sic] power does not belong to him; it is given to him and taken away without his knowing why.'[39] But to grasp the paradox, and see the relationship between effort (mastering) and passivity (being mastered), we must understand correctly the nature of human power; we must, says Weil, analyse 'the idea of systematic work'.[40] This analysis of work would correspond to the third and final section of the student's essay, and recapitulates themes from Weil's dissertation on Descartes. To illustrate the idea of work, Weil refers to the art of navigation. What one sees in the case of navigation, she says, is human ingenuity mastering nature, and yet power is not being executed directly on matter. Rather, what the skilled navigator does is alter the conditions just a little so as to bring about a 'a great change in the effect'. When the sailor tacks against the wind they are not manipulating the wind; they are placing themselves in such a position as to make use of the wind's power, which does not change but remains unaltered, and entirely beyond human control. It is the same with human action in general, which is never the result of changing the world at will and through effort, but of figuring out how to obey it. 'What is always at stake, as far as man [sic] is concerned,' she says, 'is never a matter of concentrating his energy, but of having a method. It is the way the effort is directed, and not the effort as such, which makes human power what it is.'[41] In other words, no human effort is pure action; it is always a question also of undergoing, of being passive. But the example of navigation shows that while nature is never wholly within our control, it would be absurd to say that we are powerless in what we will and act, for manifestly we do make choices that change the world. Yet those changes were not wrought directly by us. Rather we should say that our power is exercised 'indirectly … according to the conditions of a phenomenon, and not on the phenomenon itself'.[42] In moral terms, it is to say that we are never masters of anything before recognizing that we are in the first place and principally servants. This, for Weil, is what philosophical 'method' really means; it is what the Stoics discovered in their religious attentiveness to the world. Bacon's paradox, as a result, becomes in Weil's work the founding paradox of the spiritual life in small.

Weil's reasoning here follows the assumptions of spiritualist philosophy as laid out by Biran. What we effect through our will as agents of power depends, finally, on the relinquishing of the claims to author that power. Where the will is concerned, perfect activity is perfect passivity; true effort is complete repose – it is being at home and at ease in the world; it is mastery as 'obedience'. Weil's position here is like the one Biran describes in his last work, where the philosopher-mystic is able to experience God at the point where the effort to meditate no longer is meaningful, where 'there is no more struggle, no more effort or resistance'.[43] But in Weil's *Lectures* it is expressed rather differently, for Weil chooses to describe her faith not as Christian mysticism but as 'Stoicism'. And though her Stoicism may be closer to Biran's Augustinian mysticism than to Alain's humanism, the fact that she is thinking in terms of Stoicism changes things. It means that effort, for Weil, matters – even, or especially, where repose is concerned. For if, as the example of Stoic theology suggested to Weil, repose is prepared for by passivity, which emerges from a state of active concentration, then how can effort and grace be thought to signify an opposition? Skilled labourers, who know the feeling of unconsciousness that descends on complete attention better than other persons, reveal the unity of action and passivity and so provide us with an exemplar of their indivisibility in human nature. The skilled labourer not only senses but also actually reunites effort with passivity. When they perform their art willingly yet without making a conscious effort, they become a model to the person 'trying not to' try for God's grace. What they attain through manual labour the philosopher can attain through spiritual exercise.

II

No part of Weil's oeuvre confirms the relevance of her Stoicism – with its religious feeling and intimations of mysticism – more strikingly than the project she embarked on immediately after delivering the *Lectures on Philosophy*. In 1934 Weil applied for a year's leave of absence from teaching in order to gain first-hand experience of the manual work that so interested her, and made arrangements to find employment in a factory where she could be hired as an unskilled labourer. In the end she worked in not one but three different factories for a period of roughly ten months, and the journal from her factory year may be read as an exercise in the Stoic acceptance she had described to her students: 'At Renault [one of the factories where Weil was employed], I had arrived at a more stoical attitude,' reads the final entry, 'Substitute acceptance for submission.'[44] Although Weil was at this time not yet religious, most of the singular characteristics of Weil's 'Factory Journal' (1934–5) are the direct result of what one commentator has called, aptly, her 'asceticism of work'.[45] It may not be easy to say exactly what Weil was aiming for, but knowing the spiritual resonances 'stoical acceptance' had to Weil at the time we are not left in much doubt that she felt the factory year had yielded some insight. Observing the way in which Weil persists in returning to the factory when there was no outward compulsion for her to do so we can only surmise – or so the biography would suggest – that Weil's willingness to undergo the suffering involved (exacerbated by Weil's ill health, which made her remarkably unsuited to hard physical labour) depended on a conviction as to the moral and spiritual benefits of such passivity. The critique of effort that she had presented to her students less than a year previous would then have been motivated by an admiration, if not indeed a yearning, for violent forms of undergoing. The kind of passivity associated with self-denial had given Weil access to the spiritual life.[46]

But the significance of the 'Factory Journal' is more complex than this biographical observation would suggest.[47] Because Weil takes seriously what, to her students, she had called the 'effortlessness' of the stoical attitude – the way the swimmer who 'struggles' against the waves also 'loves' the water that bears them up, and that it is this latter, relaxed, feeling which is the most important – her entries on accepting suffering and on suffering in general have about them a polemic character. Taking it for granted that effortlessness is impossible under conditions of fear and duress, Weil does not think that the way in which factory workers are made to accept their sufferings and, as it were, 'grin and bear it', carries any resemblance to the 'acceptance' she has in mind. From the very beginning, Weil is clear that she disapproves of the way factory workers are forced – by the demands of speed and productivity – to submit to their work rather than consent to it willingly and with pleasure. Enjoyable factory work, of course, would be possible only were factories completely reorganized, and much of Weil's 'Factory Journal' is devoted to sketching an outline of improved working conditions that would allow employees to work freely and without fear. (Later she would use these notes to write *The Need for Roots* (1943)). Repeatedly she enables her personal fascination with suffering to play against her equally real desire to end needless suffering, so that her evident admiration for factory workers' endurance appear alongside acute reactions to their pain. Although Weil's personal desire to suffer vicariously is evident everywhere in her journal, its purpose is critical, and this shapes every description of factory work that we find in its pages. In this way Weil's 'Factory Journal' belongs to the same thought-world as her earlier writing, and has very much in common with the founding paradox that she introduced there and which will feature so prominently in her religious writing: the paradox of effort and passivity.

That feature of Weil's 'Factory Journal' which makes apparent the connection to her previous writing is, above all, her analysis of the work itself. On closer scrutiny, manual labour presents with craftsmanship and moral agency the same double aspect that Weil discovered in the phenomenon of attention – the duality of action and passivity. Like the virtue that manifests itself in a person when they are no longer 'trying' to do good, successful manual labour stands at the intersection between deliberate effort and unconscious passivity. Weil discovers that too much effort makes the work exhausting; it is impossible to meet the 'rate' and she makes mistakes and blunders. It is only when she is able to keep her mind focussed without paying too much attention to what she is doing that Weil finds she is able to relax and even enjoy the work a little. As in Weil's earlier analyses of what makes for virtue (or philosophy itself for that matter) Weil discovers that the key to successful manual labour lies in the admixture, into work, of a degree of passivity, or in the knowledge that can be derived from habit. 'Speed that comes automatically, without artificial obsession, effortlessly, and merely by maintaining the "uninterrupted tempo", Weil notes, adding: 'Feeling of relaxation.'[48] For Weil, 'work – the hard, routine, manual work of the proletariat – is oppressive, but can become a means of going beyond the limits imposed by it: work consciously done can become a form of asceticism.'[49] At the same time, Weil does not romanticize factory work. True, she records many moments of joy, even pleasure. What interests her fundamentally, however, is obviating the need for others to undergo the same experience, or at least, to undergo it on the same terms. Consequently, in the 'Factory Journal' Weil returns frequently to how different, in the end, the 'feeling of relaxation' is when experienced in the factory, compared to the same feeling accompanying other types of work. While it is possible to feel relaxed in the factory, relaxation is fleeting and always hedged about with anxiety. Weil finds that fear – fear of being reprimanded, 'bawled out' and injured – makes it almost impossible to relax and creates a formidable impediment to mastering the knack of the 'uninterrupted tempo'. 'Worked another year and a half in a state of constant nervousness (fear of doing badly),' Weil reports of a female colleague, 'although she was working quickly and well. Only at the end of 2 years did she become sure enough of herself "not to worry".'[50] If Weil found in the factory evidence to prove her theory about the importance of effortlessness in the sphere of free action, she also discovered how very different such effortlessness was from the kind of facility attained by one for whom passivity was the result of fear rather than joy. In the factory, facility involved a great degree of anxiety and very little of that genuine relaxation without which acceptance, Weil found, became grudging submission and passivity was evacuated of all generative potential.

The effect of fear on facility – the problem posed by the 'uninterrupted tempo' – becomes the principal theme with which Weil wrestles in the 'Factory Journal'. The three factories in which Weil worked specialized in the production of electrical equipment for metro carriages and streetcars, and the work was heavy and often dangerous. Immediately she is overwhelmed by the speed at which she is expected to work: 'the speed is dizzying,' she writes, 'especially when in order to throw yourself into it you have to overcome fatigue, headaches, and the feeling of being fed up' (Weil's ill-health and the difficulties it adds to her 'experiment' are a frequent topic). In the factory, to work well and become good at what one does it is essential to suppress all feeling; otherwise, one botches a piece or, worse, loses one's job. One becomes, says Weil, a 'slave' without real choice in what one is doing. Those remarks appear in the third week. Weil over-exerts herself: 'a certain joy in the muscular effort ... but in the evening, exhaustion.' The other workers pity her.[51] By the fourth week, when the Christmas holidays come around, she is 'worn out with fatigue'.[52] But there are moments of respite. In the second month of her experiment Weil is moved to the furnace, where work is more dangerous but also more complicated, so workers have to team up. There is also no foreman, and Weil discovers a 'relaxed and brotherly atmosphere'.[53] But a week later she is back on the factory floor, struggling again to achieve the 'uninterrupted tempo': 'continued – fast tempo, in spite of feeling ill. An effort, but after a while a mechanical, rather degrading sort of happiness.'[54] One has become good at what one does, but at the price of becoming like the machine which one operates; again, the feeling of being a slave, of losing self-respect and dignity. And thinking about it all only makes the suffering worse. It is easier not to think – 'to work in an irritated state of mind would be to work badly, and therefore to starve'. One must keep to the rhythm of the machine! 'We are like horses who hurt themselves as soon as they pull on their bits – and we bow our heads. We even lose consciousness of the situation; we just submit. Any reawakening of thought is then painful.'[55] On the factory floor loss of consciousness is an aid to survival; one becomes oneself only on Saturdays and Sundays, which makes the return to the factory all the more painful.

The rest of the 'Factory Journal' continues in the same vein. Feelings of happiness and relaxation are precious but give rise to bitterness since relaxation is the result of relinquishing thought, of becoming like the machine. 'I profoundly feel the humiliation of this void imposed on my thought. I finally manage to go a little faster ... but with bitterness in my heart.'[56] Not to think is a relief. It makes the hours fly past and the work relatively easy. But even the force of habit cannot dull the tedium of the routine. 'I feel no pleasure at all at having mastered a trick of the trade', Weil writes in the sixteenth week, and then: 'profound disgust, which slows me down'.[57] The battle to keep up the uninterrupted tempo intensifies. Weil finds she can do it when she is not afraid of botching a job or else when she is not thinking over-much, but then afterwards she feels disgust at being forced *not* to think. Eventually, she is laid off. She finds another factory job but within a month is laid off a second time; finally, she is hired by the Renault plant. It is to be her last job. Feelings of bitterness increase; the sense of being like a machine returns. Walking to work every day is painful, both physically and morally. And yet it seems she is able to achieve the 'uninterrupted tempo' more easily and feel relaxed at times. However, this relaxation is never free of anxiety, or indeed of a kind of nervous effort. 'As always when I don't single-mindedly strain every fibre to reach the rapid cadence,' she writes, 'I slow up.'[58] Thus her sense of ease and happiness is the ease and happiness of an automaton that has no choice but to work at top speed. Real joy comes to her in those moments only when she is going slowly, at her own pace. But those moments are few and far between. Mostly it is 'prostration, bitterness at stupefying work, disgust' – and 'fear ... of the cutter coming loose'.[59] Then it is August, and Weil leaves the factory. The experiment is over. What has she learnt? That 'an obviously inexorable and invincible form of oppression does not engender revolt as an immediate reaction, but submission'.[60] In the factory, any plan that would encourage revolt – any plan, that is, which would involve thinking – is discouraged by the criterion of speed which makes elaborate thinking impossible. Thus in the factory the one impediment to co-ordinated action – the loss of consciousness – is the only means of securing day-to-day survival and staying in the job. As passivity enables relaxation, it may also facilitate oppression and bitterness. And there seems to be no way to cast off that stupefying passivity, not least because it seems so closely tied to those moments of pleasure which make factory life bearable.

I have linked together in these two preceding paragraphs lines where Weil reflects on the nature of passivity and its relation to effort. These reflections reveal a dialectic of passivity that develops, I would argue, her earlier analysis of the phenomenon. At Roanne, Weil had pointed out to her students the knowledge to be gained from habit and the connection between habit and attention, or philosophical method. Is not our thinking at its most generative, most complete, when our attention has become habitual and to a certain degree passive? It is when the mind wanders – when the 'man of genius' is *not* focussing on the problem in front of them, or when the holy person (for attention is, to Weil, a religious as well as philosophical method) is *not* trying to be virtuous – that what they seek is given to them. But in the factory such generative passivity is not possible. One must be constantly on the alert. True, Weil does produce her best work when she is no longer paying much attention to what she is doing, but this loss of consciousness is not like the 'unconscious attention' (note the similarity of expression) she had discussed with her students at Roanne. There it was a question of trying not to think in order to relax; here, in the factory, it is a question of trying not to think in order to stay focussed. Always, at the back of Weil's mind, is the thought of the rate and the fear of the foreman. As a result, she finds herself achieving 'uninterrupted tempo' only through a sustained voluntary effort to remain at a certain speed, and it is this underlying effort that directly opposes the possible benefits of habit and makes true relaxation – not to mention real happiness – impossible.

The difference between the two forms of passivity – the generative passivity which follows from labour willingly undertaken and the humiliating passivity that results from the work to which one has acquiesced only grudgingly – is illustrated by a passage Weil writes several years later in *The Need for Roots* (1943), for which the 'Factory Journal' provided Weil with valuable field research. *Need for Roots* offers a programme for social reform and towards the beginning of it Weil makes a distinction which is of special interest to us. Here Weil is arguing that the problem with factory work is less the work itself (though this too needs to be reorganized in places) as it is the manner in which work is undertaken. To illustrate what she means, Weil compares the attention of 'a happy young woman, expecting her first child … busy sewing a layette' to the attention of a 'female convict' sewing in a prison workshop.[61] While both women, she says, 'are having their attention absorbed by the same technical difficulties', their mode of attention is different, for the pregnant woman's attention is motivated by love for her baby while the convict's attention is motivated by fear of the foreman. As a result, while the first woman is happy to accept the work, the second submits to it with bitterness. To Weil the purpose of social reform is to ensure that the first mode of attention – the mode of joy – is aspired to, while the second mode of attention – the mode of fear – is everywhere resisted.

The difference between the attention of the two women in this example is the same as the difference between the kind of passivity Weil described to her students at Roanne – the kind of passivity that is undertaken freely, and so becomes generative – and the kind of passivity that Weil experienced in the factory – a passivity that is undertaken against one's will, and so becomes a form of blind submission. Hence Weil can both praise passivity and rail against it. And it is significant that what she claims to have learnt from the experiment is not, in the end, 'submission' but 'stoical acceptance', keyword of Weil's inner striving to arrive, through attention, at an attitude in which the action desired by the will would be in perfect conformity with the limitations imposed on the will by circumstance and so allow a person to reunite within themselves the two aspects of their being, the active with the passive, thus resolving the contradiction between freedom and necessity, God and world.

III

A few years after Weil had written about passivity from a stoical perspective, a formative encounter with Christian mysticism made her return to the idea with renewed interest. In the late 1930s Weil underwent a major religious experience and in August 1941, while staying in Marseille (she had been forced to leave Paris because of the anti-Jewish legislation), she was given a copy of the complete works of John of the Cross in Spanish.[62] Weil is reported to have enjoyed John's writing – describing it as 'extremely beautiful'[63] – and evidently his work made an impression, for the essays, letters and notebook entries she composed in the years between this event and her death in 1943 may be read as an exercise in digesting and conveying the central idea of John's thought: 'passive loving attention'. John's 'passive attention' is modelled on the idea of Augustinian repose: it is the state in which the soul does very little but accomplishes a great deal because it is now God who acts through it.[64] In John's method of spiritual direction, natural, human effort is equated with activity while supernatural agency is aligned to passivity; so passive attention is compared to a state of 'tranquillity' and 'repose' – all standard Augustinian metaphors for divine agency – but also to 'waiting', 'detachment' and 'receiving'.[65] When Weil describes attention as a 'passive activity' and even uses the word 'waiting', she is echoing John. The most obvious evidence of John's influence, however, is Weil's habit of connecting attention to John's famous idea of the 'dark night of the soul'. In several places Weil explains that loving attention is possible only after the soul has passed through a 'dark night'. This is modelled on John's idea that passive attention appears spontaneously in a person once they have experienced disappointment with ordinary meditation and felt themselves to be abandoned by God. The predominance of both themes – the 'dark night' and 'waiting' – in Weil's late writing may be traced to this encounter with John's mysticism. It is his approach to the spiritual life that gives to Weil's late work its peculiar and striking character.[66]

Yet John was not Weil's first encounter with an Augustinian approach to human experience and psychology. French spiritualism, particularly Biran's philosophy, is structured along Augustinian lines and we have seen that through her education in this style of philosophizing Weil already possessed – by 1933 at the very latest – a fully developed idea of attention in which passivity is a central feature. Sensing, perhaps, an affinity between John's idea of 'passive loving attention' and her own concept of unconscious attention, Weil has no difficulty understanding the logic of mystical prayer and adopts seamlessly the tone of a spiritual director. The impression of Augustinianism in Weil's late work is a realization of the Augustinian tendencies already present in her own philosophy and in the philosophy of French spiritualism more broadly. In this way Weil's oeuvre may be counted among those spiritualist texts which, when taken together, have the effect of throwing suspicion on philosophy's confident belief in human effort, in much the same way as do the writings of Biran and Ravaisson. In both content and style, Weil's late work has much in common with that original mode of spiritualist writing.

Even though the evidence is not difficult to find however, a reader is not always guaranteed to notice Weil's commonality with the Augustinian elements of the spiritualist tradition, that is, with those philosophers who claimed a special affinity between philosophical method and spiritual exercise understood as a dialectic of effort and grace. Weil liked to describe waiting or attention by comparing it to the New Testament phrase *en hypomone,* which is often translated as 'with patience' but which Weil prefers to render as 'faithful immobility'. And she identifies it with grace: 'The notion of grace as opposed to virtue depending on the will and that of inspiration as opposed to intellectual or artistic work,' she writes, 'these two notions, if they are well understood, show the efficacy of desire and waiting.'[67] These are all ideas that repeat those fundamental connections between grace, repose and passivity that we find in John's mysticism and that go back to the same Augustinian spirituality that influenced Biran and Ravaisson. Ironically, however, the re-emergence in Weil's philosophy of this mystical gloss on philosophical method is obscured by aspects of the very same spiritualist tradition in which she writes, the most obvious example being the Stoic commitments which Weil brings to the spiritual life and which she never refutes nor relinquishes. From its earliest days Biran's philosophy had courted Stoicism and borrowed from it, suggesting that Christianity was a fulfilment of pagan philosophy. But it was nonetheless usually assumed by him that Stoicism was a this-worldly morality not to be confused with the way Christianity was in fact practised. In the main, when Biran reflects on Stoic techniques of meditation it is mostly to contrast them with corresponding Christian methods of prayer; in Biran's religious philosophy, Stoicism is thus juxtaposed, as a 'life of effort', with the Christian life of 'repose' and 'grace'. The effect of later spiritualism however – and especially of Alain's philosophy – was to bring Stoicism into a more favourable light.[68] Weil is perfectly aware of this: versed in Alain's admiration for Stoicism, she not only praises Stoicism, she identifies with it. 'At any rate if I really have the right to be called a Christian, I know from experience that the virtue of the Stoics and that of the Christians are one and the same virtue,' she writes in one letter.[69] And in another place, when describing the moment at which Christ entered her life: 'Until then my only faith had been the Stoic *amor fati* as Marcus Aurelius understood it, and I had always faithfully practised it.'[70] Because she identifies so emphatically with Stoicism, it is difficult at first to recognize that her approach to the spiritual life had been shaped, all along, by a basically Augustinian ideal. For Weil declines baptism into the Catholic church and at no point distances herself from her Stoic past. If anything, she defends it passionately. Convinced that Stoicism teaches universal virtue – the 'virtue of love' – she interprets Christianity's antipathy towards it as a sign that the church's true calling has been corrupted. 'Christianity will not be incarnated so long as there is not joined to it the Stoic's idea of filial piety for the city of the world,' she declares, and explains: 'When, as the result of some misapprehension, very difficult to understand today, Christianity cut itself off from Stoicism, it condemned itself to an abstract and separate existence.'[71] If we do not at once see the convergence between Weil's thought and the mode of Augustinian mysticism, it is in part because we are dealing with a peculiar, 'Stoic', version of the spiritual life and of grace.[72]

There is no part of Weil's late work in which this observation is more true than in her many descriptions of mystical attention or 'waiting' (*l'attente*). By 1942 Weil could confess to having met only two persons able to pay others what she called true attention. One of these persons was Weil's friend Joë Bousquet, a poet and literary critic who was permanently paralyzed as the result of a wound received in the First World War; the other was her spiritual director Joseph-Marie Perrin, a Dominican priest whose eyesight was failing and who was, by the time Weil met him, almost blind. What attracted Weil to these men was the courageous way they had dealt with their physical sufferings and with the social humiliation that came with their respective disabilities. Weil called this combination of physical and moral misery 'affliction' (*malheur*), and she thought it was an important contributing factor in facilitating the ability to pay attention, since, she reasoned, a person who had themselves suffered would be better predisposed to notice the sufferings of others and so to develop the kind of compassionate and loving attitude which Weil associated with mystical attention. But Weil also thought that affliction could give rise to the very opposite attitude, encouraging a person to bitterness rather than compassion; indeed, she thought that in most cases affliction operated in this way and so was a hindrance to attention rather than an aid. Hence her insistence that real attention was such a rare thing. In her first letter to Bousquet, she thus explains how she regards 'attention [as] the most rare and pure form of generosity' and how,

> [to] very few minds is granted the discovery that things and beings exist. Since childhood I have desired nothing but to have had received, before dying, the full revelation of this. It seems to me that you are engaged in this discovery. This is why I believe I have never met anyone since I came to this place whose fate was not a good deal inferior to yours; with one exception.[73]

A tall order! But we are used to such things. It is the logic of the hero – the logic of an Herculean Stoicism such as one finds it in the work of Alain – which has left its mark on Weil's philosophy and now comes into conflict with her increasingly Augustinian approach to the spiritual life. As if nothing beautiful and good could come without a high price in heroic deeds, we see attention presented in Weil's writing as a rare and exceedingly arduous thing. 'They must pass through years of a dark night where they wander about in affliction, far from everything they love and with the feeling of being cursed', Weil explains to Bousquet, using 'they' to refer to those few able to pay attention: '[This ability] is extremely rare. There is no other authentic greatness ... Most of those who think they possess it, do not.'[74] In Weil's mind, John's 'dark night' has become conflated with the quest ethos of the knight errant. As in most quest narratives the quester is a chosen individual whose abilities are elevated above those of the ordinary person. It is the same, Weil thinks, with the person able to pay attention. Their abilities are not like those of everyone else; they are chosen and, in some sense, unique. To Bousquet she writes that attention thus 'sums up the subject of the Grail legend' since 'only a predestined being has the ability to ask of another, "What is it that torments thee?" '[75] And in her notebooks, she links the Grail Knight to Christ, another comparison that emphasizes the uniqueness and rarity of attention.[76]

Still, Weil is not interested only in the arduousness with which she associates attention. In the quest romance that Weil is commenting on when writing to Bousquet, Wolfram von Eschenbach's *Parzifal* (*c.* 1225), the Knight must show compassion in order to win the Grail, but the compassion must be genuine:

spontaneous and free of premeditation. As a result, what really engages Weil is the easiness, even the unconscious, nature of attention. So when she describes attention as an ability that, paradoxically, does not belong to those who think themselves capable of it, the emphasis is on 'thinking' – in so far as thinking is a sign of premeditation and as such would interfere with the spontaneity required for genuine compassion.[77] This is quite different from Alain's idea of effort and altogether of a part with John's understanding of 'passive loving attention' as something distinct from deliberate mental activity (Ravaisson had held a similar view). Loving attention, John writes, 'happens when the soul's discursive acts and meditations cease'.[78] We might say that for John love is the mode in which attention is expressed and experienced as spontaneous desire rather than as deliberate act. In that same letter to Bousquet, Weil concludes something very similar when she writes that attention takes place in the domain of 'simple desire' and so is not to be confused with 'the will' (*la volonté*). She describes the nature of desire, the way it moves a person without their doing anything in particular to solicit desire; how all that is required to respond to desire is for a person to remain turned in the direction of the desired thing, and so on:

> [Attention] is a domain where the simple desire – if it is genuine – and not the will, operates; where the simple orientation makes one move forward, on the condition that one is always turned in the same direction. Whoever has been set once in the right direction is thrice-blessed. The others move about in a dream-state. Whoever is in the right direction will come to no harm. Though they are much more sensitive to affliction than others, though affliction puts in them especially a feeling of guilt and of being cursed, nonetheless, for them affliction is not an evil. Unless they betray themselves and turn away, they are always protected.[79]

Like the 'unconscious attention' that Weil described in her *Lectures on Philosophy*, mystical attention for Weil is suspended in that middle which stretches between pure muscular effort and willpower on the one hand and inactivity and changeless inertia on the other. It is the effort of the swimmer who struggles against the waves while loving the water that holds them up – with emphasis on the latter feeling, the feeling of acceptance and repose. At Roanne, Weil had called that middle 'Stoic', here it is recognized as 'mystical'; but it is the same middle. If there is a key to Weil's religious philosophy, then, it is not effort, nor is it absolute passivity as such (an impossibility in any case). Rather, it is spontaneity – the ability to act without deliberation and as it were straight from the heart: it is love, or desire.

But once this secret to the spiritual life has been discovered, how to manifest it? For desire cannot be willed and what genuine love requires is a forgetting of the motive to love. If there is a residue of the Herculean in Weil's late work it is in her peculiar obsession with how difficult is attention for one who *knows* what is required for attention to be genuine and spontaneous – easy and effortless.[80] Evidently it was a question that caused Weil much anxiety, for Bousquet comments on it in one of his letters. 'You do not have enough confidence in yourself,' he writes, adding: 'To be created by God ... must make us tremble, must make us feel our unworthiness – but it should not make us doubt the capacity for revelation that is in each of us.'[81] At the same time, Weil was certain that genuine attention was not impossible, even for her. 'I am speaking about this not at all as a blind man might speak about light,' she explains to Bousquet, but as one might who is partially blind.'[82] That 'partial' knowledge of attention Weil always attributed to her religious experience. In another letter (this time to Perrin) she writes about the event, which had taken place in the Benedictine monastery of Solesmes at Easter in 1938. Describing what had happened, she remarks how 'neither my sense nor my imagination had any part'.[83] Yet Weil is clear that some effort *was* involved – she had, she says, been 'praying' prior to her experience. But then the prayer had not been conscious, or not precisely. Weil recounts how she had been reciting a religious poem (George Herbert's 'Love (III)'), not trying to petition God or communicate with God. It was only after the event that she realized she had been praying: 'I used to think I was merely reciting it as a beautiful poem, but without my knowing it the recitation had the virtue of a prayer. It was during one of these recitations that, as I told you, Christ himself came down and took possession of me.'[84] Here, the effortlessness of grace – and the passivity of Weil herself – comports with the ardour of attention and yet seems wholly separate from it. As Weil receives grace she is not conscious of wanting grace and yet the arrival of grace was the answer to some deep desire obscurely articulated through her recitation of a religious poem about divine love. When Weil steps back to reflect on the event, she is thus presented with a structure very similar to the one that struck Biran after his state of rapture. Goodness had arrived unsolicited by effort and yet effort somehow came into it! To Biran the question had been how to define that effort and understand it, and the same question now occupies Weil. Without lessening the irrelevance of volitional effort for grace – and thus without diminishing in any way grace's formidable nature – Weil's experience of prayer means that she is convinced, nonetheless, that involuntary or spontaneous effort comes into it. What else would be the purpose of prayer? This is the question that we find at the centre of one of Weil's most celebrated essays from her late work, 'Reflections on the Right Use of School Studies with a View to the Love of God' (1942).

Starting from the assumption that most people are unfamiliar with the idea of an involuntary effort, Weil sets out her view on the matter and uses her mystical understanding of attention or prayer to do so. What is interesting about prayer, Weil thinks, is that when we pray our attention is not trying, actively, to achieve a goal, since God is not really something that can be possessed by the mind. And yet we are paying attention; we are making an effort. The difference is that our effort takes on a passive quality, as if we were 'waiting' for God rather than searching actively for God. 'Above all our thought should be empty,' says Weil, 'waiting, not seeking anything, but ready to receive in its naked truth the object which is to penetrate it.'[85] Though Weil does not mention John of the Cross in this essay, her description of attention as 'waiting' is very similar to John's account of 'loving attention' as a form of 'waiting', and Weil's description evidently is indebted to this mystical tradition. In *The Ascent to Mount Carmel* (1581–5) John describes how 'the soul delights to be alone, waiting lovingly on God ... in interior peace, quiet, and repose' and how there is 'nothing remaining except that knowledge and attention, general and loving.'[86] But then the idea of attention as 'waiting' is similar enough to Weil's earlier sense of the word to have been hit upon independently. Whatever the case, Weil discovers this mystical account of attention as 'waiting' to be applicable also to attention in the ordinary sense of the word, no doubt because in French 'waiting' (*l'attente*) is cognate with 'attention' (*l'attention*). The principal example in 'School Studies' is attention in the context of academic work, by which Weil has in mind everything from Latin to philosophy. School study demands copious amounts of concentration, and yet insights often come to a student when they are least expecting them, in the same way that grace arrives unsolicited to the one who prays.

Weil finds that in academic work there is thus a convergence with mystical prayer in such a way that school studies should be interpreted and taught as spiritual exercises, and vice versa: 'In every school exercise there is a special way of waiting upon truth, setting our hearts upon it, yet not allowing ourselves to go out in search of it.'[87] In the same way that a spiritual exercitant prays without any desire to solicit grace by their efforts, 'students must work without any wish to gain good marks, to pass examination, to win school successes'.[88] The lesson, in short, is that a recognition of passivity and conscious relinquishing of a certain kind of deliberate effort is necessary in the search after truth.

Weil's account here of attention as something involuntary, even passive, is symptomatic of her on-going reaction to the prominent role played by effort in modern philosophy as a whole. 'Most often attention is confused with a kind of muscular effort', she writes, as earlier – in her *Lectures on Philosophy* – she had rejected the idea that mysticism could have anything to do with effort. Then, as now, Weil does not mention the name of any philosopher when voicing this criticism, but scattered remarks in other essays written during her last years confirm that Weil had hesitations concerning Henri Bergson, especially the way Bergson's philosophy had been applied to religion. She feels uneasy about the language of the *élan vital* or 'vital impetus'; it comes dangerously close to what for Weil seems the wrong kind of mysticism – a mysticism of the muscular will. 'In Bergson, religious faith appears after the manner of a "Pink" pill of a superior kind,' she remarks in *Need for Roots*, 'which imparts an astonishing amount of vitality.'[89] And elsewhere: 'At the centre of the philosophy [of Bergson] ... there is a conception which is totally alien to any consideration of value, namely, the conception of Life.'[90] Yet it would be wrong to say that Weil is single-mindedly promoting passivity as such (or indeed, in light of this final quotation, 'death'). Notice how Weil's critique of Bergson repeats her critique of 'Roman' Stoicism – and in the case of 'Roman' Stoicism, what Weil questioned then was not Stoicism as such but those interpretations of Stoicism that would reduce its philosophy to a coping device for hard times. In the same way, her critique of effort in 'School Studies' is not a blank refusal to countenance the moral or indeed physical significance of effort in academic work and prayer. Attention, we read in 'School Studies', is 'an effort, the greatest of all efforts perhaps, but it is a negative effort.'[91] What Weil is questioning is not effort but the alliance of effort to force, or the idea that to act is always to be in control and to be exerting one's power in some way. She is protesting against a culture permeated by this Herculean ethos. Doubtless it is good for keeping up the rates of productivity, but, as Weil experienced in the factories, it also leads to misery and oppression. In her essay on school studies, then, Weil thus invokes 'relaxation' in order to characterize her critique of attention and to explain what she means by attention as a 'negative effort':

> Will power, the kind that, if need be, makes us set our teeth and endure suffering ... has practically no place in study. The intelligence can only be led by desire. For there to be desire, there must be pleasure and joy in the work ... The joy of learning is as indispensable in study as breathing is in running ... It is the part played by joy in our studies that makes them a preparation for the spiritual life ... Of itself, [attention] does not involve tiredness. When we become tired, attention is scarcely possible any more, unless we have already had a good deal of practice. It is better to stop working altogether, to seek some

relaxation, and then a little late to return to the task; we have to press on and loosen up alternately, just as we breathe in and out.[92]

The theme that connects this description of attention to Weil's earlier remarks on the topic is her opening polemic, directed at 'will power [that] makes us set our teeth and endure suffering'. It is very similar to what Weil says elsewhere about Stoicism – the Stoicism she dislikes, that is – and reminds one of her description of 'modern' Stoicism in her *Lectures on Philosophy*. In the essay on school studies the same ideas are at work, but presented in a more generalized form. Now it is modern philosophy and modern attitudes – secular morality – that display a fascination with effort, rather than Stoicism in particular. But the essentials of the argument remain unchanged. And contrasted to 'will power' we have 'desire', favourite concept of Weil's own Stoicism of love and of course also of John's Augustinian mysticism. Here it is the governing metaphor in Weil's account of attention. 'Desire' is significant because it is a power that compels without coercing. Attention motivated by desire thus becomes as it were spontaneous and relaxed, and it is this relaxed quality of attention that makes it, in Weil's words, a good 'preparation for the spiritual life'. Notice how for Weil the spiritual life is equated not only with leisure but also with 'pleasure and joy'. If the ethos of effort is dangerous, it is because it makes joy so difficult. When, as a consequence, Weil describes passivity in the context of spiritual exercise (attention), it is as a form of spontaneous or relaxed movement, such as the body performs 'naturally' – nature here being interchangeable with spontaneity.

Weil's description of attention as a form of 'relaxed' or 'negative' effort echoes her comparison between mystical attention and the Grail Knight's compassion, a comparison which appears also in this essay. Most of 'School Studies' has been taken up with comparing attention to prayer and contemplation; she now shifts to ethics which, she says, 'is made of the same substance'.[93] We are to understand that what Weil has been arguing regarding attention applies not only to love of God but to love of neighbour as well. What occupies Weil now is the idea of attending to God through attention to others, or the idea of attention as morality. The world, she says, is full of unhappy persons who have need of nothing except 'people capable of giving them their attention'.[94] She then enumerates a version of the strictures we saw earlier, on the rare and miraculous nature of compassionate attention, and how most people who think they possess the capacity to attend in this way do not. 'The capacity to give one's attention to a sufferer is a very rare and difficult thing; it is almost a miracle; it *is* a miracle,' she writes, paralleling her words to Bousquet: 'Nearly all those who think they have this capacity do not possess it. Warmth of heart, impulsiveness, pity, are not enough.'[95] This is another way of talking about the paradoxical, unconscious nature of attention – to understand how something can be easy to do while at the same time difficult to achieve. Such was, to Weil, the central insight of *Parzifal*. Hence she now turns to the Grail legend and to the Grail Knight's compassion. In *Parzifal*, the Grail is guarded by a king cursed with an incurable wound that emits an evil smell. The rightful inheritor of the Grail is the person who arrives to the castle and, instead of flinching at the sight of the king, recognizes his suffering and asks the compassionate question: 'what is it that torments thee?' This story, argues Weil, is about an action being difficult to achieve but at the same time easy to perform. That paradox of effort and ease is what unconditionally matters for attention. For a moment Weil allows the spontaneity of the Grail Knight's compassion to define her entire idea of attention. 'This way of looking [at one who suffers]', she says 'is first of all attentive. The soul empties itself of all its own contents in order to receive into itself the being it is looking at, just as he [*sic*] is, in all his truth.'[96] Then, quite suddenly, she returns to the question of academic work, and of attention as an exercise. If, in their studies, students pay attention, the activity will prepare them for one day being able to give those who suffer the same compassion the Grail Knight gave the wounded king. But only, she says, if they devote to their studies 'the right kind of effort'.[97]

That is how 'School Studies' ends. How are we to understand this twofold image of attention? It is relaxed, then effortful; on the one hand it expresses itself through spontaneous desire; on the other hand it emerges through exercise and deliberation. What is the meaning of attention here? On closer reading Weil's description of it transpires as an analysis of habit and its relationship to knowledge and action. In 'School studies' every instance of spontaneous or passive attention is linked to a prior effort of attention. When the Grail Knight pays attention and shows compassion, the spontaneous action did not emerge from nowhere: lengthy exposure to trials and suffering (what Weil, following John, calls a 'dark night') has made Parzifal into the kind of person likely to act in a compassionate way. Or Weil's imagined school student: years of practising attention has prepared them to be the kind of person likely to pay attention to strangers. The point becomes explicit in a line that Weil drops like a clue early on in the essay: 'each [task] will help to form in [students] the habit of that attention which is the substance of prayer.'[98]

The image of attention as habit evokes the paradox at the heart of the spiritual life. The will's concerted effort to achieve what it desires is juxtaposed to the passivity necessary to receive a desired thing. In Weil's late work, attention is what prepares for but does not solicit grace. Effort waits; action is passive. The juxtaposition represents both the power and the limitations of human effort. The way Weil describes prayer, one cannot say whether the practice is effective or ineffective – it is both, at the same time, though not in the same way. Many years earlier, in her *Lectures on Philosophy,* Weil had made the same observation in regard to Stoic philosophy, and again she comes to the same conclusion: one must make an effort, but passively; like the swimmer, one must allow oneself to be borne up by the waves. Yet she has now undergone what she once rejected as impossible – she has had a mystical experience, a real 'contact' with God. In the *Lectures*, before Weil's mystical experience, she had declared such experiences to be entirely separate from effort, but when she approaches mysticism now her opinion is – if not different – certainly more nuanced. Weil thinks that prayer is necessary as an effort, and as such cannot be discounted. Evidently this was the case in her own experience, where effort played an important role, albeit indirectly. So Weil takes seriously the effort that constitutes prayer and the concentration that contemplation requires. She is certain that passivity alone does not exhaust attention.

If Christian mysticism reinforces to Weil the relevance of passivity and the critique of effort that is so striking about her own 'Stoicism', it also brings to the 'Stoic' theme of effort a new meaning and purpose. In prayer, passivity emerges from effort itself – the effort that is of a kind with habit. For Weil as for John of the Cross, prayer is the activity that is experienced as inactivity: the intensity of being receptive. 'The receiver should act according to the mode of what is received,' writes John, 'and not otherwise, in order to receive and keep it in the way it is given.'[99] The early modern Spanish and French mystics sometimes compared this receptivity to the attitude of a plant. In the same way that a plant does very little and yet receives a great deal simply by keeping itself turned towards the sun, so the soul of the one who prays exerts very little active effort and yet receives all the grace it needs.[100] A similar image is used by Weil in an unfinished essay from her final years. In 'Some Thoughts on the Love of God' (1940–2) she compares prayer to the kind of effort a farmer makes when tending to their crops. Just as prayer can prepare a soul for grace but cannot solicit grace directly, a farmer can prepare their crops to receive 'solar energy' but cannot influence the sun in any way. 'It is not the farmer's job to go in search of solar energy or even to make use of it,' she writes,

> but to arrange everything in such a way that the plants capable of using it and transmitting it to us will receive it in the best possible conditions. And the efforts he [sic] puts into this work does not come from himself but from the energy supplied to him by good, in other words, by this same solar energy contained in

plants and in the flesh of animals nourished by plants. In the same way, the only effort we can make towards the good is so to dispose our soul that it can receive grace, and it is grace which supplies the energy needed for this effort.[101]

By this time Weil's outlook, to be sure, was articulated wholly by means of her mystical experience, which had been Christian in nature. But she never felt this experience to have stood in contradiction to her Stoicism. A century or so previously, Maine de Biran had attempted to hold both Stoicism and Christianity together in a similar way, but had concluded that the two were separate and that what they represented were two overlapping but distinct spheres: the life of effort and the life of the spirit or grace. After her mystical experience, Weil became adamant that Stoicism was inseparable from Christianity. In her late work, as if to test this conviction, she writes again and again about the paradoxical togetherness not only of Stoicism and Christianity, but of effort and grace. Eventually the very act of thinking this paradox and picturing it to oneself becomes inseparable, in Weil's mind, from the attention which the paradox is supposed to describe. There are several notebook entries from these years where she explains the importance of paradox or 'contradiction' as a method of attention. 'When the attention fixed upon something has revealed the contradiction in it ..., a sort of unsticking process takes place', she writes, and '[truth is] the search for the relation between things', it 'manifests itself as a result of the contact made between two propositions, neither of which is true; it is their relation which is true'.[102] To Weil the paradox of action and passivity – and its manifestations – *was* the spiritual life; every attempt to hold together effort with grace being itself an effective manifestation of the attention that bodied forth prayer and prepared the soul for God. But subsequent interpretation has compelled us to take the passive and as it were 'Christian' aspects of her thinking more seriously (although for Weil passivity is no more Christian than effort is Stoic): for a while, it is true, she was praised as a mystic with an acute perception of suffering, but then a reaction to her philosophy set in, and in the end her attention to passivity transpired as a morbid glorification of affliction.[103] The life of effort disappears behind the life of grace, of passivity. Quickly there is very little left except grace and passivity. The best evidence of this, of course, is Weil herself at this time: her own life. Weil had always been inclined to acts of vicarious suffering (the factory year being but one example of many such 'experiments'), but in her final years these tendencies became extreme. When, in 1942, her family managed finally to convince her to join them in New York, (where Weil would be out of danger from anti-Jewish legislation), she arranged immediately to be sent back to Europe. Her final months were spent in London working for the Free French, writing incessantly and eating very little, supposedly out of sympathy with her occupied compatriots. She died in 1943 of tuberculosis, which her weakened constitution was not able to fight off. Her friends reported that she wore a resigned look, as if overcome by sadness. One letter from her final year explains that she wanted to do everything she could 'in the hope that it would enable me to take a bigger and more effective part in … the dangers and sufferings of this great struggle'.[104]

IV

Over the past two decades much has been written, notably by Emmanuel Gabellieri, Gavin Flood and Lissa McCullough, on the tensions thought to represent what is most characteristic about Simone Weil's philosophy. Though these commentators have been concerned mostly with Weil's work, their interpretations are informed by a more wide-ranging, or at least potentially more wide-ranging, theory of the spiritual life, and of the practice of philosophy as a spiritual exercise. Flood made the connection most explicit in his fine chapter on Weil in *The Ascetic Self: Subjectivity, Memory and Tradition* (2004). Here, after refuting the assumption that Christian asceticism could be figured wholly as passivity, Flood nonetheless asserts': 'we … carry with us from Weil the understanding of the body as the abode of ascetic practice and asceticism as the willed conformity of the body to externally imposed conditions.'[105] What Flood is suggesting here is a twofold or paradoxical understanding of spiritual exercise based on Weil's religious philosophy. In itself 'ascetic action is a kind of passivity', he says, remarking on how the striving of the soul towards God appears to stand in direct opposition to grace in such a way that there is 'certainly a paradox here', one that Weil's work foregrounds to an impressive degree.[106]

Flood's is a useful way of approaching philosophies of spiritual exercise during the twentieth century, a period when much of the theory on the subject has been oriented, on the whole, away from passivity and towards the role of the active will. As Flood writes, 'self-assertion as agency is clearly a key feature of modernity in ways incompatible with the ascetic self of scriptural tradition.'[107] What we find in Weil's thinking is thus the basis for an alternative approach to thinking about philosophy as spiritual exercise. Following the typology used throughout this book, if Flood's characterization of modernity represents the ideal of spiritual exercise I have identified variously as 'Ignatian', 'Pelagian', and 'Stoic', Weil's position corresponds to the second kind of spiritual exercise, described as 'Augustinian', 'Quietist' and 'mystical'. In French philosophy, this tradition derives from a long history of philosophical engagement with Augustinian ideas about divine rest, ideas worked out systematically by Biran and influential through the tradition of spiritualism which he inspired.

With dazzling effect, Lissa McCullough has developed a similar critique of modern philosophy borrowed from Weil's account of the spiritual life. In *The Religious Philosophy of Simone Weil* (2014) McCullough begins by arguing that 'to lack contradiction or paradox is to lack an adequate grasp of the nature of created existence as such'.[108] She realizes that this could be true of any religious philosophy at any point in time. But she argues that there is a difference in quality, and that because Weil's philosophy operates through oppositions (effort-grace, body-mind, action-passivity, and so on) it not only addresses paradox but operates by means of it.[109] Oppositions, of course, are also what create difficulties for any reader of Weil; in this French philosophy, a Cartesian atmosphere has infused every page. But as McCullough argues (and as I have shown), the way in which Weil wants us to interpret duality – as a relational rather than oppositional truth – means that 'a more antidualistic thinking can hardly be imagined'.[110] Fundamentally, McCullough thinks, it is a question of Augustinian anthropology and of the 'twofold man', rather than of any strict substance dualism. Hence the importance of learning to think about philosophy through Weil's *religious* philosophy, because we find here that what characterizes the spiritual is also what characterizes the philosophical method: Weil's tendency to 'maximise dialectically' the relation between opposites, maximizing their interconnectedness, and, above all, maximizing their proximity.[111] This approach to the spiritual life, rather than being concerned with favouring one of either opposed terms – either action *or* passivity, effort *or* grace – is a method for speaking in a middle voice that conveys thinking to a place where dualities are logical structures transcendentally unified in experience and attention is at once supreme ardour and perfect spontaneity. Still, recognition of passivity seems to come into it in a special way and provide a catalyst for realizing this paradox. What profoundly matters in Weil's understanding of philosophy as a spiritual exercise is her critique of effort.

It is difficult to find a better characterization of the ideal of spiritual exercise that I have been tracing here: the critique of effort, which is at the same time the summation of effort. But if we wish to understand why these qualities are so singular to Weil, McCullough offers only partial answers. Spiritualism, to be sure, does not really interest McCullough; indeed, it has interested very few readers of Weil.[112] Though McCullough admits that the peculiar traits of Weil's religious philosophy must be traceable to some form of Augustinian anthropology, she does not recognize the relevance of spiritualism to her theory of an Augustinian ideal structuring French thought in the long nineteenth century.[113] Above all, McCullough overlooks the overwhelmingly dialectical portrayal of effort and grace by spiritualist thinkers such as Biran and Ravaisson. It would be difficult to imagine an environment more conducive to Weil's philosophy than the nineteenth-century French philosophy in which she was educated. Its influence on Weil's work is visible in that striking way she has of persistently perceiving the world according to a kind of double vision, looking at things from the perspective of matter and then again from the perspective of spirit, once from the perspective of active power and then again from the perspective of passive undergoing, and all the while letting attention make apparent the relation that would reunite these two aspects of being – in much the same way that Biran had done a century earlier.

However, the mainstream of philosophical approaches to spiritual exercise has not tended to interpret effort in light of passivity. This was Flood's point, and we have noted several times how Weil perceived herself to be in opposition to what was then the mainstream: the philosophy of Henri Bergson. Like the modern approaches to subjectivity in which self-assertion plays a fundamental role, Bergson's philosophy was also a philosophy of effort, and his account of mysticism connected spiritual exercise to an exercise of the will. His is an example of Flood's 'modern' asceticism, and while Weil shares so much in common with Bergson – not only the legacy of Biran but, via Alain, an admiration for Stoicism – her approach to thinking about philosophy as a way of life is quite different. Not only does she present spiritual exercise as a paradox of effort and grace, action and passivity, she articulates that paradox as a critique of effort and a defence of passivity. The impact of a position like Weil's on an intellectual thought-world dominated by the philosophy of Bergson should be obvious, and Weil, I suspect, was not being merely reactionary when she distanced herself from Bergson's approach to the spiritual life.[114] Perhaps this is the real reason why Weil has remained, at least where philosophy is concerned, a marginal figure and difficult to place, even within the tradition to which she so obviously belongs. It is also, I suspect, part of the reason why the whole approach to the spiritual life embodied in Weil's writing has been itself marginal in the history of recent philosophies of spiritual exercise, if not in the history of European philosophy as such. For as easy as it is to see Weil's critique of effort emerging out of French philosophy, it is just as easy to see that same atmosphere resisting Weil's critique. By the early twentieth century, ideas of how mysticism might relate to and constitute philosophical method had been shaped, in France, by ideals of effort rather than of grace, and so tended towards a picture of philosophy which aligned spiritual exercise with the power of the will, and that will to a Stoic will. Flood called this image of the spiritual life 'modern', meaning that it was characteristic of the period in history that came to an end with the Second World War. But even after the war, when philosophy as a whole took a turn away from explicit endorsements of the will to power, the idea of the self-sufficient individual who is master of their own destiny remained significant, not least for existentialists like Jean-Paul Sartre. These connections between modern French philosophy and the ideal of effort were indicated in an earlier chapter and I will not repeat them here, except to elaborate briefly on the work that has become particularly significant in the recent debate regarding spiritual exercise and which stands as both challenge and invitation to Weil's philosophy: Pierre Hadot's *Philosophy as a Way of Life* (1981–7).

Hadot's thought emerges from the same French intellectual milieu as that of Weil and in one chapter Hadot draws on Félix Ravaisson's work to provide a striking definition of Stoicism (Hadot was a scholar of Hellenistic philosophy and *Philosophy as a Way of Life* is a study of ancient philosophy in light of the Ignatian tradition). Ravaisson, we recall, had argued that Stoicism was essentially a philosophy of effort and interior tension. This view is cited by Hadot, who then aligns it to his understanding of spiritual exercise as such. '[A] philosophy like Stoicism, which requires vigilance, energy, and psychic tension,' writes Hadot, 'consists essentially in spiritual exercises.'[115] And again (citing Ravaisson): 'Attention ... is the fundamental Stoic spiritual attitude. It is a continuous vigilance and presence of mind, self-consciousness which never sleeps, and a constant tension of the spirit.'[116] Such descriptions paraphrase accurately what Ravaisson writes in the *Essai sur la Métaphysique d'Aristote* and the *Essay on Stoicism*, yet the critique of effort – and indeed of Stoicism – that Ravaisson voices in those works is entirely absent from Hadot's account. Instead, Hadot is fascinated by the idea of psychic effort being the key to spiritual exercises. Overall, his approach reminds one more of Bergson than of Ravaisson, and in particular it draws to mind Émile Bréhier, the scholar of Stoicism who was also an admirer of Bergson and who wrote so evocatively of the Stoic idea of effort. And in *Philosophy as a Way of Life* Hadot mentions how Bréhier was an important teacher and how Bergson had exercised a significant influence on his early thought.[117] Bergson is mentioned favourably at several points in *Philosophy as a Way of Life*. 'Not until Nietzsche, Bergson, and existentialism,' declares

Hadot, 'does philosophy consciously return to being a concrete attitude, a way of life and of seeing the world.'[118] In another passage, he compares Bergson's account of attention explicitly to spiritual exercise, drawing several comparisons that echo what Bergson says elsewhere about the idea of mental effort as a means of achieving mystical experience.[119]

There is little point in amassing examples: the omnipresence of Bergson's thought-world is significant mostly because it relates spiritual exercise to that ideal which Weil (and later Flood, drawing on Weil) had associated with modernity: the ideal of self-assertiveness and the willpower of the individual, for it is only through a prodigious effort of the will that the 'constant vigilance' prescribed by Hadot's Stoics can be maintained. But Hadot is not oblivious to the individualism which such a view of spiritual exercise seemed to entail, and a major theme of *Philosophy as a Way of Life* is to defend Stoicism – and, by extension, the whole tradition of spiritual exercise – from an individualistic and 'modern' interpretation. No single chapter makes this point more forcibly than 'Reflections on the idea of the "Cultivation of the Self" ', which Hadot wrote in response to Michel Foucault's use of his work in *The History of Sexuality*. Taking inspiration from Hadot, Foucault had investigated spiritual exercises as 'techniques' for cultivating the self.[120] The key phrase in Foucault's presentation of these techniques was Socrates' injunction, in the *Alcibiades I*, that a philosopher should 'care for the self'.[121] Though Hadot had initially drawn attention to the importance of construing philosophy as a form of self-care, he did not like the way Foucault chose to present ancient philosophy wholly as self-care. Self-care, he argued, weakened what Hadot saw as the ultimate purpose of spiritual exercise: to serve others and so make the exercitant a citizen of the world.[122] With the 'self' as the keyword to spiritual exercise, Hadot feared that Foucault was directing the practice of philosophy away from ethics and towards an individualistic project, becoming a 'Dandyism, twentieth-century style'.[123]

Whatever its shortcomings as an interpretation of Foucault, Hadot's keenness to understand spiritual exercise as something more than individual works of self-improvement is significant: it mirrors Weil's sense that the meaning of spiritual exercise for philosophy lay in its conception of passivity and relaxation, concepts which Weil argued could be used to question the prominence of the will in modern philosophy. Michael Chase has pointed out Hadot's critique of modernity, which evidently was of the utmost importance to the author of *Philosophy as a Way of Life*.[124] The Stoics recommended that philosophers work on themselves but the purpose of this effort, writes Hadot, was to efface the self and attain 'the view from above',[125] allowing the philosopher to 'regard both society and the individuals who comprise it from the point of view of universality'.[126] These practices were not designed solely for self-help, but for fostering sympathy and compassion. And again like Weil, Hadot intimates that passivity has something to do with the 'work' with which spiritual exercise is implicated. When discussing Epicurean exercises Hadot points out that while Epicureanism was very different from Stoicism it also had a critical function in relation to Stoicism: 'To cure the soul, it is not necessary, as the Stoics would have it, to train it to stretch itself tight, but rather to train it to relax.'[127] It was only when tempered by Epicureanism that Stoic effort became a guide for the philosopher.

The image of philosophy as a spiritual exercise leading to other-regarding compassion and care develops arguments similar to Weil's and does so by asserting a dialectic of effort and passivity. Yet the role of relaxation remains under-acknowledged in *Philosophy as a Way of Life*. While Hadot clearly appreciated what he saw as the Epicurean dimensions of spiritual exercise – the dimensions encompassed by passivity – his focus and overwhelming sympathy were directed, always, to the centrality of effort in attention. This is true also of Hadot's work on Plotinus and Plotinus' notion of 'contemplation'. Of Plotininan contemplation Hadot writes that 'it is the effort of attention through which the soul tries to maintain herself at the level to which God has raised her … the ever-renewed effort to remain in a state of contemplation of the Good'.[128]

There are several reasons for Hadot defining contemplation in this way, as a form of intense effort, but one significant factor – aside from the influence of Bergson – is undoubtedly Hadot's knowledge of the early modern tradition, which seems limited to Ignatius. When Hadot talks about 'spiritual exercises' and claims them to be 'nothing but a Christian version of a Graeco-Roman tradition', it is Ignatius' *Spiritual Exercises* (1522–4) he has in mind.[129] Elsewhere I noted the nuances in Ignatius' view of spiritual exercise, how there is space here for passivity and a recognition of effortlessness; but we also saw how Ignatius is fascinated by effort and emphasizes the importance of effort for the achievement of spiritual ascent. If Hadot's understanding of spiritual exercise relied mostly on a reading of Ignatius, this would help to explain why it is that spiritual exercise in *Philosophy as a Way of Life* corresponds mostly to a prodigious effort of the will. An approach like Ignatius' would have confirmed what Hadot had learnt about the nature of philosophy and mysticism from Bergson, and about the nature of Stoicism from Ravaisson and from Bréhier's Bergsonian study of Hellenistic philosophy in particular. Reinforced in this way from both the French intellectual milieu of his schooling and then later by the example of Ignatius, effort would have seemed the obvious way to think about the nature of spiritual exercise –

and the nature of philosophical practice – for Hadot. Hadot presents a critique of the individualistic, self-willed subject of modernity, but there are plenty of ways in which he also affirms this subject and elevates it. In other words, the same objections that Hadot raised against Foucault could be raised against Hadot himself.

But even when we raise such objections – and part of the purpose of this book has been to raise them – we are confronted with the tradition of interpretation that Hadot has inspired. And on the whole, while there are many who have seen convergences between Hadot's approach and Christian mystical prayer more broadly, the principal inheritors of *Philosophy as a Way of Life* have tended to emphasize effort, a point demonstrated by Alexander Nehamas, who argues that Hadot was not radical *enough* in his understanding of ancient philosophy when he attempted to understand it as a form of other-regarding ethics. To Nehamas, Hadot's interpretation of philosophy (with which he aligns the work of Foucault) has been far too concerned with the body politic and with spiritual matters to comprehend the radically immanent nature of ancient *askesis*. By contrast, Nehamas wishes to develop an unapologetic individualism free from those residues of religious ethics still evident, he thinks, in the work of Foucault. 'The care of the self ... precedes, or perhaps constitutes, the care of the other', he argues in *The Art of Living* (1998), explaining that Socrates' mission 'was personal: politics was irrelevant to it ... He addressed individuals individually and only as individuals'.[130] Insofar as philosophy is a way of life it is a personal project of self-elevation, an effort to rise above the demands of any group and perfect the genius within, with no help from the world or from God.

In Hadot's work, then, the philosopher's discovery of spiritual exercise initiates an understanding of philosophical practice that is quite different from what transpired in Weil's discovery of that same tradition. Their respective convictions – Hadot's sense that effort grounds mystical contemplation, Weil's sense that passivity is the key to attention – are reflected in the type of spiritual exercise to which they are drawn and to which they proceed to compare philosophy: Hadot to the Ignatian method with its emphasis on effort; Weil to John's spiritual direction with its recollection of Augustinian repose. But however removed Hadot is from the Augustinian thought-world of Weil, his work too is a striking product of many-faceted, French spiritualism. It embodies a view of life that may be traced to Biran's state of rapture in 1794. When Hadot intuits the significance of Epicurean relaxation for achieving the coherence of Stoic effort, he saw the beginning of a new stage in that paradox of effort and grace that is always found governing the spiritual exercise of philosophy.

In the late 1960s Iris Murdoch was impressed by how strange and shocking Weil's concept of passive attention still seemed, two decades after her death. Surveying the lay of contemporary ethics, the first thing that strikes Murdoch – as she explains in *The Sovereignty of Good* (1970) – is the modern ethicist's suspicion of passivity. Anyone who suggests that moral discernment might have something to do with a passive or contemplative attitude is laughed out of court. In modern ethics, she says, one thus finds instead an overwhelming elevation of activity and will power. ' "The man" of modern moral philosophy', she writes (amplifying the heroic ideal with a gendered pronoun), is one who identifies himself with his will and for whom the good is a function of the will.[131] For this 'man' the good is only possible when he is alert, vigilant and aware of his intentions; anything less is irresponsible and a sign of moral weakness. 'Since will is pure choice, pure movement, and not thought or vision, will really requires only action words.'[132] Aside from 'action words' like 'will' and 'choice' the characteristics of modernity's 'man' includes 'clarity of intention', and the idea that '[we] should aim at a total knowledge of our situation and a clear conceptualisation of all our possibilities'.[133] To be alert, aware and in control of one's thoughts – these are the ideals of the 'man' in modern philosophy but also, Murdoch argues, in politics and literature more broadly. This man 'is to be found more or less explicitly lurking behind much that is written nowadays on the subject of moral philosophy and indeed also politics ... This "man", one may add, is familiar to us for another reason: he is the hero of almost every contemporary novel'.[134]

That Murdoch finds 'the man' of modern moral philosophy dislikeable is clear, but she also argues that the ideal of agency which 'the man' represents is implausible and thus in a sense immoral. People, she writes, are simply not 'like that' and so '*ought* [not] to picture themselves in this way'.[135] When I choose the good, how much of it is up to me and my present action and how much is the result of desire, over which I have little or no control? It is as if philosophers had forgotten the fact that 'we are not free in the sense of being able suddenly to alter ourselves since we cannot suddenly alter what we can see and ergo what we desire and are compelled by'.[136] Does this mean that we are left entirely passive and powerless? Not quite. This is where Weil's 'attention' comes in. For Murdoch, attention invites us to understand moral agency as something distinct from choice but because Weil's sense of attention shies away from pure passivity, it does not deprive agents of their freedom. To explain what she means Murdoch uses an example from everyday life. A certain mother dislikes her daughter-in-law, but does so based on very little experience. As the mother spends more time in her daughter-in-law's company, her opinion begins to change. Those faults she at first found disagreeable now seem less so, and eventually the mother-in-law comes to love her son's wife. And yet the daughter-in-law has not changed. What has happened? Murdoch suggests that by paying attention to her daughter-in law repeatedly and over a period of time the mother has altered her opinion or vision of her son's wife. Because such alteration is largely unconscious (and slow) it is quite different from the kind of instantaneous change brought about by a judgement based on choice. Choice is driven by the will and is the result of conscious deliberation; attention, by contrast, is not really motivated by the will and is involuntary – it is the kind of knowledge which a person develops in spite of themselves and without trying.[137] In Murdoch's example, the mother-in-law who comes to love the person whom, on first encounter, she disliked, would not be able to say exactly when her opinion changed; she would know only that one day it was changed. Yet it would be absurd to conclude that because the mother-in-law had made no conscious choice in the matter her opinion had been forced. Say rather, argues Murdoch, that what the mother now chose to do coincided with what she found herself already doing – loving her daughter-in-law. 'If I attend properly,' writes Murdoch, 'I will have no choices and this is the ultimate condition to be aimed at.'[138] Yet precisely because it shapes action continually, attention is the kind of passive activity we can sometimes become aware of, and it is in this awareness that we may be said to come into our own as moral agents. 'The task of attention goes on all the time and at apparently empty and everyday moments we are "looking",' Murdoch reflects, 'making those little peering efforts of imagination which have such important cumulative results.'[139]

To Murdoch what finally is most striking about 'attention' – with its way of changing imperceptibly thoughts and feelings, so passive as to appear almost alien to the whole idea of agency as such – is its non-secular meaning. Attention is contemplation, meditation. Philosophy and spiritual exercise converge on the deepest level. While theological language as a whole for Murdoch is not particularly relevant (indeed, she openly eschews it), prayer most certainly is relevant. And she realizes that any argument in favour of contemplation will be seen as pseudo-theological. 'The idea of contemplation is hard to understand and maintain in a world increasingly without sacraments and ritual.'[140] By 'hard to understand' she means, among other things, that contemplation has become such a rarefied thing that it is impossible to think of it now without imagining some kind of monastic setting. 'Philosophy', she says, is partly to blame for this, because in throwing out religion it threw out contemplation also. But as

Weil's understanding of attention testified, the search for truth is no different, structurally, from prayer (the search for God). 'Unsentimental contemplation of nature exhibits the same quality of detachment,' Murdoch argues: 'selfish concerns vanish, nothing exists except the things which are seen.'[141]

What Murdoch sees in Weil's account of mystical attention, then, is not merely a method with interest for philosophy, but the method or way of life of philosophy as such. Philosophical attentiveness rehearses the basic tension in human experience that also happens to be the fundamental tension of the spiritual life: the paradox of action and passivity, effort and grace. The contrast between willing and desiring – between choosing consciously the good, and finding oneself drawn unwittingly towards it – dramatizes what is at stake for philosophical practice. Ignorance of it is, as Weil put it, the only obstacle to the realization of truth.

6

Epilogue: Reclaiming attention

It has been the aim of this book to provide an alternative way of thinking about the nature of spiritual exercise and its relationship to philosophy. At stake in this alternative account is the notion of passivity. Spiritual exercise and philosophy are both practices concerned with paying close attention to sensations, perceptions, thoughts. They are practices concerned with sustaining mental effort. But how much of what is desired by the persons performing these practices – whether it be the spiritual exercitant desiring contact with God or the philosopher desiring clarity and truth – is the direct result of efforts and how much is achieved spontaneously and as it were without effort? In other words, to what extent is passivity necessary for the exercise of attention? In the different variations of French Augustinian philosophy that we have been studying here (the meditations of Jean-Jacques Rousseau; the spiritualism of Maine de Biran and Félix Ravaisson; the religious philosophy of Simone Weil) this question was central, since it was thought that the aims of spiritual and philosophical meditation were analogous, if not identical; that the object of attention – God, truth – receded endlessly from comprehension and so necessitated something like repose or passivity on the part of the meditator: effort comporting with passivity, facilitating the mind's reception rather than possession of truth. But towards the end of the nineteenth century passivity dwindles dramatically as a factor in the philosophy of spiritual exercise and, while mysticism continued to be ever more closely and intimately linked to philosophical method, the meaning of mysticism shifts: from effort comporting with grace, mysticism becomes effort comporting with itself in feats of psychic tension. Hence Ravaisson's successor, Henri Bergson, could compare mysticism to philosophy and so rehearse the old connection between philosophy and spiritual exercise, while at the same time interpreting mysticism in ways that reflected new moods and persuasions: mysticism as an ever-vigilant effort by the individual to achieve apotheosis. Similar shifts are evident in Alain's work, where prayer is compared to gymnastics and piety to therapy. When we get to the work of Pierre Hadot it is thus *effort* which is the governing metaphor with which to theorize philosophy as a way of life and spiritual exercise, its conception connected to Bergson's thought in particular and to existentialist currents more broadly. Now that we have reached the century closest to our own, will the Augustinian approach prove an historical curiosity only? Simone Weil was a late, and in many ways unusual, representative of mysticism. She does not fit in with the dominant intellectual milieu, with Bergson and the philosophy of effort. Is the theory of attention that Weil proposes as the key to philosophy's spiritual exercise itself nothing more than a quaint throwback, its very oddness suggesting to us that the style of repose it recommends has been thoroughly superseded by the self-possessed subject of modernity?

It is significant and telling that the concept of passive attention should be studied not only, as one would expect, by a philosopher like Weil (who read and took inspiration from early modern mystics), but also by thinkers without any explicitly religious persuasion, such as Iris Murdoch. After the Second World War, the ideal of effort, self-possession and manly virtue which had so dominated philosophy began to be questioned in new ways that brought back into the discussion of philosophical method the concept and practice of passivity. It is instructive to see how, in the transition from modernity to post-modernity and beyond into our own era, passivity – and in particular, passivity as a spiritual style and mode of being – persists and is reclaimed.

In this concluding section, an epilogue to the book's historical chapters, I have space only to comment summarily on passive attention in its current role. But brief though it is, such an outline must be sketched because in the twenty-first century passivity has been joined to attention in the ethics relating to our most pressing concern: the environmental emergency. The present study, which began with a state of rapturous calm occasioned by one philosopher's close attention to the environment (the fair weather and beauties of spring), ought not to end before the advent of the Anthropocene.

During the latter half of the twentieth century the idea of 'attention' became significant to ecological thinking. We saw in an earlier chapter how there was a connection between sixteenth-century mystical theories of attention and a general sense of wonder and delight at the world. But this idea of attention had already been used – in all but name – by early Christian writers when describing what they called *phusike theoria*, or the 'contemplation of nature', an idea popular during the first centuries CE. To give one example, Evagrius of Pontus encouraged his monks to learn from nature by means of contemplation, and this idea was later taken up by Maximus the Confessor in his mystical theology. *Phusike theoria* certainly influenced how spiritual exercise developed, and there is even a sense in which the attentiveness proper to God was thought to be proper to and indeed derive from a prior attentiveness to the world: so, the monastic was supposed to relate to the creator of stones, birds and trees with the same attentiveness they showed those same stones, birds and trees in everyday life.[1] In the 1960s and the heyday of the Green movement the idea of *phusike theoria* resurfaced in discussions of spiritual exercise, as the following impressions from an essay by Thomas Merton, 'From Pilgrimage to Crusade' (1967), will illustrate.

When, in this essay, Merton wanted to define spiritual exercise for a modern audience he compared it to *phusike theoria*. The key to understanding *phusike theoria*, he argued, was attentiveness, which he described by likening it to the attitude of a pre-modern pilgrim. Such a pilgrim would have been in touch with the places and peoples they met, offering prayers at local shrines and eliciting the hospitality of strangers. Contrast this, he says, to the attitude of the crusader: happy to ravage fields, rape women and sack towns. In Merton's essay the crusader is an allegory for attention in modern, industrialized nations: so fixed on achieving a specific goal it loses the ability to be attentive to anything except that goal; while the pilgrim symbolizes the spiritual form of attention: attention that is open and able to notice its surroundings. The key to the pilgrim's mode of attentiveness, Merton suggests, is freedom from the pressures of time and planning – pilgrimages could take as long as one liked – and the absence of fear (there was no leader spurring on the troupes, as there was in a crusade). The pilgrim's was a relaxed attention, and indicated a mode of passivity or 'abandonment' – Merton's preferred term, and one that he learns from François Fénelon and the French Augustinian tradition.[2]

Among the different critiques of 'modernity' popular during the early decades of the Green movement, the idea of attentiveness was prominent and so too was the work of Merton. Spiritual exercise and its latter-day advocate combined attention with passivity for a context that was no longer confined to monastic life. To learn how to be attentive in this spiritual way was not a special skill useful only to a few ascetics; it was the skill of engaged and responsive living.[3]

Many ecological thinkers since Merton have run with the idea of attentiveness and made full use of it at key points in their arguments. Of course, most do not call attentiveness mystical nor refer to attention with the Augustinian language of abandonment. But there are in several recent works descriptions of a certain manner of looking at the world that evokes all the particulars of passive attention as it has transpired over the preceding pages: I mean receptivity, openness, humility and wonder – not the aura of dispossessed agency that 'passivity' so often recalls. There is in Jane Bennett's *Vibrant Matter: A Political Ecology of Things* (2010) a striking iteration of this theme. Bennett writes that most ecological thinkers agree that human beings need to become 'more attentive' and that sustainable living will rely on good management of perception as much as on good management of land and water use. The importance which Bennett attaches to attention is shown by the way she links attention to the work of Félix Guattari, one of the thinkers that inspires and informs her argument. Guattari, says Bennett, thought that good planetary living would entail the cultivation of what he called a ' "transversal" mode of perception', or the art of '[fixing] our mind's eye on the interlacing of the mechanosphere, the social sphere, and the inwardness of subjectivity'.[4] Perception can be improved, argues Bennett, and it should be cultivated, not with a view to 'inwardness' only, but for the sake of the outside and the other-than-human too. One is attentive to more than a single perspective, and so looks 'transversally' or diagonally at the world. The general tenor of *Vibrant Matter* towards improving ecological thinking is transferred to attention, which, Bennett says, is indispensable for a more 'dialectical, or dialogical, or phenomenological' way of relating to the world.[5] Attention as it is used today in science and philosophy is good for isolating the environment as an object 'over there' but it is not *attentive* and remains insensitive to the 'everyday experience of ... comingling' between selves and environment that attentiveness brings to light.[6] Bennett writes about attention as the art of being receptive to the ways in which a person is not, in fact, separate from nature but entangled with and dependent on it. 'Admit', she says,

> that humans have crawled or secreted themselves into every corner of the environment; admit that the environment is actually inside human bodies and minds, and then proceed politically, technologically, scientifically, in everyday life, with careful forbearance ... [and] remain present to the paradox of a self that is its own outside.[7]

Such a definition as this, of attentive attitudes towards the world, converges with the tradition of mystical contemplation and spiritual exercise, even where no such attribution is given. The 'paradox of a self that is its own outside' follows the logic of the mystic's union with God, especially when (as in the example from Merton) abandonment of the self to God is the same thing as abandonment of the self to the world through which God is revealed. And Bennett's recommendation that we 'admit' some degree of smallness and then act 'with careful forbearance' repeats the spiritual direction appropriate to the higher stages of mystical prayer, since here it is of the utmost importance not to upset attention by trying to grasp or possess the vision of God; that is, it is important to proceed with care. Which suggests that what ecological definitions of attention describe is the same practice that mystical accounts of attention prescribe.

Incidentally, this recurrence of mystical, passive attention in ecological thinking shows that the mysticism we have been studying here, though it rides on an internal opposition to 'muscular effort' (Weil's phrase), never entailed a renunciation of activity. Amongst the new uses to which attention has been put by thinkers like Bennett is environmental activism and ecological action. Cultivating attentiveness from an early age would help to prepare a child to become the kind of adult likely to be attentive to the entanglement and paradox which attentiveness brings to light. This would help the environmental cause, for neither entanglement nor paradox is the kind of truth easily correlated to precise, measurable targets in policy-making, and yet the success of any environmental policy – the question of policy being put into action and 'met' – will depend less on whether there is enough brute willpower to make the thing happen, and more on whether, at the time of crisis, there will be enough persons responsive to the demands necessary and able to act on them; that is, whether there will be enough persons already attentive and for whom ecological action seems not an imposition but a desirable future, even if the work to be done may not always be easy to achieve. As Bennett writes, while attentiveness will sometimes result in persons taking a step back in order to 'ramp down their activeness', at other times it will result in bursts of energetic work.[8] Here the 'passivity' of attentiveness is being used in relation to the 'action' for which it prepares, and the practice of attention, as a result, turning into something like spontaneity or desire.

When one sees in philosophy today the turn to an ideal of attention with close parallels in the spiritual tradition – Augustine, Fénelon and John of the Cross – articulated alongside environmental ethics and ecological criticism, and how the intellectual movement of the present epoch is reinventing these older approaches to attention, it becomes increasingly apparent that our environmental emergency should be studied in the context of the continuing influence of 'spirituality'.

And there are several theological writers, such as Sallie McFague and Catherine Keller, who have, over the past decades, written about 'attention epistemology' from a perspective that brings together spiritual exercise, philosophy and ecological thinking.⁹ But it is a philosopher of science, Isabelle Stengers, who gives us the most striking example of mystical attention reinvented for and through ecological thinking. I could point to any number of her recent volumes, most of them concerned in some way with attention; I choose one of her latest essays, *Another Science Is Possible: A Manifesto for Slow Science* (2013). At first glance, however, this essay by Stengers would seem an awkward ally for a book on mystical attention and its continued relevance to philosophy today, for here Stengers begins by seeking to distance philosophy and science from the ideal of spiritual exercise which, she argues, has exerted a negative influence in the past. She points out that it was only when science, in the early modern period, adopted from the tradition of spiritual exercise the ideal of undistracted attention that scientists began to lose their sense of attentiveness to the world and pay less and less attention to anything that was not part of the cognitive 'retreat' (matter, people, places). So on the one hand, Stengers is uneasy about philosophy's past borrowings from spiritual exercise, pointing out that, when undistracted attention is separated from its originally religious context (as it becomes in the modern laboratory), the emphasis on retreat precludes any serious engagement with places or persons. For Stengers, ecological carelessness seems built into undistracted attention, which encourages a researcher to detach themselves from the implications and applications of their work, not to mention from the actual places and cultures their work touches. She likens it to the mindset of a mobilized army of men at war: 'The only thing that matters is, "can we get through?", and the price that others will pay for their passing through (ravaged fields, devastated villages) will cause no hesitation.'[10]

Such, to Stengers, are the dangers of one kind of spiritual exercise. But Stengers also knows that there is more to spiritual exercise than the ideal of undistracted attention (always a trouble and temptation, in any tradition). In fact, the key to her own manifesto – the 'art of paying attention' – has been shaped through a series of reflections on religious practices of the same: in Stengers' case, reflections on attention as cultivated in modern initiatory Witchcraft, a religion sometimes known as the Craft. Starhawk (Miriam Simos), the American Witch who interests Stengers especially, began making a name for herself back in the 1980s by publicizing an earth-based form of Witchcraft and using rituals for environmental action, and her rituals appeal to Stengers on account of what she calls their 'pragmatic' and 'experimental' use of attention. The Witch's magic, writes Stengers elsewhere, 'forces one to pay attention ... that is to say in the first place and above all, not to think of oneself as sufficient unto oneself ... What we have proposed depends on this "paying attention".[11] 'Attention' was also the topic of a 2016 interview Stengers gave in London, where she elaborates on the connection between attention and spiritual practice. 'It is called an art,' she explains,

> because it needs a ritual in order to foster this possibility. And this is very interesting when we do it well and with joy. … It is just creating the occasion – a rather Quaker art, to 'bethink', to pay attention to what may lurk.[12]

Such spiritual attention is not, of course, for Stengers a matter of becoming a Witch or a Quaker (or, not necessarily), but rather of learning from and with Witches, Quakers and – we might infer, other similar, religious or non-religious groups – what is that modality of attention which makes for change. And to Stengers there is something that happens to attention in a ritual setting, something to do with the way the ritual steals from persons any ability to focus on the self alone, even to focus on the practice of paying attention. In a ritual one has the ability – if one participates – to disrupt ordinary perception-filters and let everything in. It is a kind of ecstasy of noticing, an opportunity to make (and feel) those robust connections and sense of dependency on everything and everyone that is the requisite for ecological thinking: 'Paying attention means "slowing down" and accepting that intrusive interstices open up even in the midst of an urgency.'[13]

That an attention like Stengers' – which invokes Quakerism, works negatively by 'slowing down', and invites passivity rather than effort by 'opening' attention to possibility's excess – descends from the same mystical spirituality of passive attention that we have been studying here, goes without saying. Stengers' 'slow' attention has as its function the same critique of effort that we saw in the Augustinian ideal of spiritual exercise identified in earlier chapters by David Marno and Gary Hatfield and elaborated by Biran and Weil. It also hardly needs repeating that the type of activity to which Stengers contrasts 'slow attention' – attention operating under the criteria of speed and efficiency – responds to the approach which forms with Augustinianism an ideal polarity: the ideal of effort, identified variously as 'Ignatian' or 'Stoic'. Stengers' narrative, which identifies both ideals of spiritual exercise as emerging differently from religious tradition, describes what is at stake for the argument we have been drawing out over the course of this book. Though the Augustinian approach as a way of recognizing the co-extensiveness of effort and repose in the practice of attention has become a model for thinking about the 'spiritual' and reinventing metaphysics for the philosophy of spiritual exercise, what it contends with is not 'secularity' but other ideals of spiritual exercise which in their origin and form are religious. Quakerism, the Christian mysticism to which Stengers refers, was once viewed with suspicion by church authorities, as was Quietism, the Augustinian mysticism of contemplation and repose (*quietas*) that thrived dangerously during the early modern period. In those days, anyone who sympathized with Quietist ideals, such as the Spanish mystic and poet John of the Cross, had to tread carefully, relying on the paradoxical nature of contemplation to defend the virtues of slowing down. In one of his books of spiritual direction, *The Living Flame of Love* (1585–6), John explains that the attention required for contemplation is not really possible without becoming (to a certain degree and for a little while) passive and 'receptive' but warns that most spiritual directors, accustomed to equate meditation with mental vigilance, will not understand what they see and will most likely think the practitioner is being lazy or idle, and laugh at their method: '"Come now", they will say, ' "lay aside these rest periods, which amount to idleness and a waste of time; take and meditate and make interior acts, for it is necessary that you do your part; this other method is the way of illusions and typical of fools".[14] That last phrase, which John puts in the mouth of the bad spiritual director, and which speaks from the perspective of speed and efficiency, rings true for us on two levels. Now as then, taking things seriously and being attentive demands not only doing something a little bit curious and different, it demands becoming the butt of jokes. There is no guarantee that people will 'understand'. It is, perhaps, this part of the art of attention that requires the most of its practitioners, whether they are philosophers or theologians. Who does not want to be taken seriously and recognized for what they do? At the same time, I see no reason to fear this mockery, which may, itself, be a formidable means of resistance, particularly with a view to climate change and environmental crisis. In a crisis, severity can become a dead weight and a measure of self-conscious foolishness would help attention remain receptive and alert to the dangers of its own sanctimony. As Stengers writes, 'it is also a struggle in which humour, laughter and mockery are crucial in face of the power of abstract ideals.'[15] Without such humour, without such methods 'typical of fools', to use John's expression, how will we – who may disagree with modernity's ideals of speed and efficiency yet have a hunch that jumping ship would be just as bad as unthinking obedience to the status quo – keep alive enough hope to keep practising attention, and practise it together?

Notes

Preface

1. Simone Weil, *Waiting on God*, ed. Joseph-Marie Perrin and trans. Emma Craufurd (London: Routledge and Kegan Paul, 1951), 55.
2. Weil, *Waiting on God*, 127.
3. Weil, *Waiting on God*, 54, 127.
4. Cf. Epictetus, *The Encheiridion (or Manual)*, 1.1.
5. Weil, *Waiting on God*, 126.
6. See for instance Pierre Hadot, *Philosophy as a Way of Life: Spiritual Exercises from Socrates to Foucault*, ed. A. I. Davison and trans. M. Chase (Oxford: Blackwell, 1995), 84–5, 130–2.
7. Maine de Biran, *The Influence of Habit on the Faculty of Thinking*, trans. M. Donaldson Boehm (London: Baillière, Tindall & Cox, 1920).
8. Weil, *Waiting on God*, 126, 128.
9. Weil, *Waiting on God*, 55.
10. Josef Pieper, *Leisure: The Basis of Culture*, trans. Alexander Dru (London: Faber, 1952) 36.
11. Peter Sloterdijk, *You Must Change Your Life: On Anthropotechnics*, trans. Wieland Hoban (Cambridge: Polity, 2013), 3.

Chapter 1

1. Plato, *Theaetetus*, trans. Harold N. Fowler. Cambridge, MA: Harvard University Press; London, William Heinemann Ltd. 1921.
2. Ignatius of Loyola, *The Spiritual Exercises of St. Ignatius: A Literal Translation and Contemporary Reading*, trans. David L. Fleming (St. Louis: The Institute of Jesuit Studies, 1978), 16 (20).
3. Philip Goodchild, 'Thinking and Life: On Philosophy as Spiritual Exercise', in *Intensities: Philosophy, Religion, and the Affirmation of Life*, eds. K. S. Moody and S. Shakespeare (Farnham: Ashgate, 2012), 165–76; *On Philosophy as a Spiritual Exercise: A Symposium*, ed. Philip Goodchild (Basingstoke: Palgrave Macmillan, 2013). For my understanding of spiritual exercise I am also indebted to Louis Martz, *Poetry of Meditation: A Study in English Religious Literature*, 2nd edn (New

Haven: Yale, 1962); Thomas Merton, *Mystics and Zen Masters* (New York: Delta, 1967); Amélie Oksenberg Rorty, 'The Structure of Descartes' *Meditations*', in *Essays on Descartes' Meditations*, ed. Amélie Oksenberg Rorty (Berkeley: University of California Press, 1986), 1–20; Jean-Luc Marion, 'Is the Argument Ontological?' in *Cartesian Questions: Method and Metaphysics* (Chicago: Chicago University Press, 1999), 134–55; Jacob Sherman, *Partakers of the Divine: Contemplation and the Practice of Philosophy* (Minneapolis: Fortress Press, 2014), 75–130; David Marno, *Death Be Not Proud: The Art of Holy Attention* (Chicago: Chicago University Press, 2016), 1–38, 218–28.

4   In what follows I take 'spiritual' in 'spiritual exercise' to indicate an invisible principle of life and hence to operate as a symbol of transcendence. For a different interpretation of spiritual exercise as concerned principally with the mind, see John Sellars, *The Art of Living: The Stoics on the Nature and Function of Philosophy* (London: Bloomsbury, 2003), 115.

5   Hadot, *Philosophy as Way of Life,* 84.

6   Hadot, *Philosophy as Way of Life*, 273.

7   Hadot, *Philosophy as Way of Life*, 265.

8   Hadot, *Philosophy as a Way of Life*, 284. Cf. *Philosophy as a Way of Life: Ancients and Moderns – Essays in Honour of Pierre Hadot*, eds. Michael Chase, Stephen R. L. Clark and Michael McGhee (London: Wiley, 2013); Ian Hunter. 'Spirituality and Philosophy in Post-Structuralist Theory', *History of European Ideas* 35, no. 2 (2008): 265–75; Jean-Louis Schlegel, 'La philosophie, un exercise spirituel', *Esprit* 404, no. 5 (2014): 29–42.

9   Hadot, *Philosophy as a Way of Life,* 283.

10 See for instance Plato, *Phaedrus*, 242b-c, 275b-c. Brian Inglis, *The Unknown Guest: The Mystery of Intuition* (London: Chatto and Windus, 1987), focuses on Socrates' *daimon* as that which compels action from without and independently of human reason, drawing connections between the *daimon* and intuition. I am greatly indebted to Inglis' study, which proposes – unconventionally – that intuition be interpreted in light of the Socratic *daimon*, and to the recent work of Peter Struck, *Divination and Human Nature: A Cognitive History of Intuition in Classical Antiquity* (Princeton: Princeton University Press, 2018).

11 Marno, *Death Be Not Proud*; 'Easy Attention: Ignatius of Loyola and Robert Boyle', *Journal of Medieval and Early Modern Studies* 44, no. 1 (2014): 135–61. Cf. Ignatius, *The Spiritual Exercises of St. Ignatius*, 4 (¶2).

12 Marno, 'Easy Attention', 154.

13 Marno, *Death Be Not Proud,* 38.

14 Weil, *Waiting on God,* 49–60.

15 Weil, *Waiting on God,* 55.

16 Marno, *Death Be Not Proud,* 1–38. On the concept of passive attention and its significance for critical theory, see Janet Martin Soskice, *The Kindness of God:*

Metaphor, Gender, and Religious Language (Oxford: Oxford University Press, 2007), 7–34; C. Falke, *The Phenomenology of Love and Reading* (London: Bloomsbury, 2016); Jonardan Ganeri, *Attention, Not Self* (Oxford: Oxford University Press, 2017), 169–92; Rolf Kühn, *Leere und Aufmerksamkeit* (Dresden: Text & Dialog 2014). One should also mention here the new interest in distraction and other 'passive' mental states by recent writers; see for instance Paul North, *The Problem of Distraction* (Stanford: Stanford University Press, 2012); and Anne Stillman, 'Distraction fits', *Thinking Verse* 2: 27–67. My thanks to Christian Coppa for drawing my notice to this discussion.

17 Iris Murdoch, *The Sovereignty of Good* (London: Routledge, 1970).

18 T. C. Wall, *Radical Passivity: Levinas, Blanchot, and Agamben* (Albany, NY: Southern University of New York Press, 1999). On Gianni Vattimo and 'weak thought', see *Weakening Philosophy: Essays in Honour of Gianni Vattimo*, ed. Santiago Zambala (Montreal & Kingston: McGill-Queen's University Press, 2007); *Weak Thought*, eds. Gianni Vattimo, Pier Aldo Rovatti and Peter Carravetta (Albany, NY: Southern University of New York Press, 2012), especially Alessandro Dal Lago's essay on Weil, 'On the Ethics of Weakness: Simone Weil and Nihilism' (111–37). See also John D. Caputo, *The Weakness of God: A Theology of the Event* (Bloomington: Indiana University Press, 2006); Marika Rose, *A Theology of Failure: Žižek Against Christian Innocence* (New York: Fordham University Press, 2019).

19 See for instance Herbert Marcuse, *Eros and Civilisation: A Philosophical Inquiry into Freud* (Boston: Beacon Press, 1955), where Marcuse critiques the valorization of effort in modernity by thinking with Narcissus as an alternative icon to Prometheus (my thanks to the series editors for reminding me of this seminal image). For a more recent treatment of these ideas, see Michel Onfray, *A Hedonist Manifesto: The Power to Exist*, trans. Joseph McClellan (New York: Columbia University Press, 2015).

20 On Nietzsche's critical recovery of asceticism, see the fascinating accounts by Michael Ure, 'Nietzsche's Free Spirit Trilogy and Stoic Therapy', *Journal of Nietzsche Studies* 38 (2009): 60–84; Keith Ansell-Pearson, 'For Mortal Souls: Philosophy and *Therapeia* in Nietzsche's *Dawn*', *Royal Institute of Philosophy Supplement* 66 (2010): 137–63. Nietzsche's approach is the principal inspiration for several subsequent attempts to rethink philosophical asceticism in the direction of relaxation, pleasure and embodiment. See Michel Foucault, *The History of Sexuality*. Vol. II. *The Use of Pleasure*, trans. Robert Hurley (New York: Random House, 1985), 'Technologies of the Self', in *Technologies of the Self: A Seminar with Michel Foucault*, eds. Luther H. Martin, Huck Gutman and Patrick H. Hutton (London: Tavistock, 1988), 16–51; Gilles Deleuze, *The Logic of Sense*, trans. M. Lester with C. Stivale (London: Continuum, 2004), 'The Exhausted', in *Essays Critical and Clinical*, trans. Daniel W. Smith and Michael A. Greco (Minneapolis: University of Minnesota Press, 1997), 152–74; Peter Sloterdijk, *Critique of Cynical Reason*, trans. Michael Eldred

(Minneapolis: University of Minnesota Press, 1987), *The Art of Philosophy: Wisdom as a Practice*, trans. Karen Margolis (New York: Columbia University Press, 2012); *You Must Change Your Life*.

21 Marilynne Robinson, *The Death of Adam: Essays on Modern Thought* (Boston: Houghton and Mifflin, 1998), 28–75; Stephen Jay Gould, *The Mismeasure of Man* (London: W. W. Norton, 1981).

22 On the gendering of passivity and its role in the development of modern philosophy, see especially Carolyn Merchant, *The Death of Nature: Women, Ecology and the Scientific Revolution* (San Francisco: Harper and Row, 1980), 127–91.

23 Pieper, *Leisure*, 36.

24 Pieper, *Leisure*, 36.

25 Pieper, *Leisure*, 31, citing Kant, 'Von einem neuerdings erhobenen vornehmen Ton in der Philosophie', *Akademie-Ausgabe* 8: 387–406 [Immanuel Kant, 'On a Newly Arisen Superior Tone in Philosophy', in *Raising the Tone of Philosophy: Late Essays by Immanuel Kant, Transformative Critique by Jacques Derrida*, ed. and trans. Peter Fenves (Baltimore, Maryland: Johns-Hopkins University Press, 1993), 51–81.]

26 On the nature of happiness in Aristotle and Thomas, see Pieper, *Leisure*, 53–5, and Pieper, *Happiness and Contemplation*, trans. Richard and Clara Winston (South Bend, Indiana: St Augustine's Press, 1998).

27 Pieper, *Leisure*, 30.

28 Pieper, *Leisure*, 38.

29 Martha C. Nussbaum gives a rich and detailed account of the critical role played by tranquillity in the Hellenistic philosophies, especially Stoicism: *The Therapy of Desire: Theory and Practice in Hellenistic Ethics* (Princeton: Princeton University Press, 1994), 316–401 and passim.

30 Hadot, *Philosophy as a Way of Life*, 88. The contemporary literature on Stoicism as a way of life is vast. I have in mind principally those works that argue (again, following Hadot) that Stoic exercises can be effective outside a Stoic belief system; on such readings, tranquillity and *otium* – ideals originally linked to beliefs concerning the superlunary world and the state of its celestial intelligences – naturally become considered principally in light of the techniques and daily regimens for self-improvement recommended by writers like Epictetus and Marcus Aurelius. For this approach to Stoicism, see for instance Richard Sorabji, 'Is Stoic Philosophy Helpful as Psychotherapy?' in *Aristotle and After*, ed. Richard Sorabji (London: Institute of Classical Studies, 1997), 197–209, and *Emotions and Peace of Mind: From Stoic Agitation to Christian Temptation* (Oxford: Oxford University Press, 2000), 159–302; D. Robertson, *The Philosophy of Cognitive-Behaviour Therapy (CBT): Stoicism as Rational and Cognitive Psychotherapy* (London: Karnac, 2010)

31 André Jean Festugière, *Epicurus and His Gods*, trans. C. W. Chilton (Cambridge, MA: Harvard University Press, 1956), 20–1, 40. For a more recent attempt to

recover Epicurean tranquillity as a spiritual exercise, see Howard Caygill, 'Under the Epicurean Skies', *Angelaki* 11, 3 (2006): 107–15. My thanks to the series editors for drawing my attention to Caygill's work.

32 Festugière, *Epicurus*, vii–viii.
33 Festugière, *Epicurus*, 21f. On the critical potential of Epicurean relaxation discussed here by Festugière, compare Eric Brown, 'Politics and Society' in *The Cambridge Companion to Epicureanism*, ed. James Warren (Cambridge: Cambridge University Press, 2009), 179–98.
34 Maine de Biran *Œuvres*, Vol. I. *Écrits de jeunesse*, ed. Bernard Baertschi (Paris: Vrin, 1998), 94.
35 Biran, *Écrits de jeunesse*, 94.
36 Biran, *Écrits de jeunesse*, 98.
37 Biran, *Écrits de jeunesse*, 96.
38 Romans 7.19.
39 Biran, *Écrits de jeunesse*, 98.
40 Biran, *Écrits de jeunesse*, 98.
41 Biran, *Écrits de jeunesse*, 98.
42 Biran, *Écrits de jeunesse*, 99.
43 Biran, *Écrits de jeunesse*, 99. The 'Jansenist adversary' mentioned here by Biran is most likely Cornelius Jansen (1585–38), the Bishop of Ypres and radical Augustinian against whom Fénelon often writes.
44 Charly Coleman, *The Virtues of Abandon: An Anti-Individualist History of the French Enlightenment* (Stanford: Stanford University Press, 2014), 203–41. See also Henri Gouhier, *Fénelon philosophe* (Paris Vrin, 1977); Denise Leduc-Fayette (ed.), *Fénelon, philosophie et spiritualité: actes du colloque* (Geneva: Droz, 1996); C. J. T. Talar, *Modernists and Mystics* (Washington, DC: Catholic University of America Press, 2009). For the concept of 'abandonment', see François Fénelon, *Spiritual Writings*, trans. Chad Helms (New York: Paulist Press, 2006), 235–35.
45 Félix Ravaisson, *La Philosophie en France* au XIXe siècle (Paris: Fayard, 1984), 320.
46 Paul Janet, *Les maîtres de la pensée moderne* (Paris: Calmann Lévy, 1883), 401. For the religious context of spiritualism I have relied on Henri Gouhier, *Les conversions de Maine de Biran* (Paris: Vrin, 1948), 397–410; Jacques Chevalier, *Histoire de la pensée*. Vol. IV. *La pensée moderne de Hegel à Bergson* (Paris: Flammarion, 1966); Frederick Copleston, *A History of Philosophy*. Vol. IX. *Nineteenth-Century French Philosophy* (London: Continuum, 2003 [1975]), 155–78; Rolf Kühn, *Französische Religionsphilosophie und -phänomenologie der Gegenwart: metaphysische und post-metaphysische Positionen zur Ehrfahrungs(un)möglichkeit Gottes* (Freiburg: Herder, 2013), 1–109. The term 'French spiritualism' or simply 'spiritualism' will serve to distinguish the philosophy inspired by Maine de Biran from the mostly unrelated phenomenon of spiritism. In France, the philosophy of *spiritualisme* is usually distinguished from the occult world of *spiritisme*, though, as in English, the two terms are sometimes used interchangeably.

47 Dominique Janicaud, *Ravaisson et la métaphysique: une génealogie du spiritualisme français*. 2nd ed. (Paris: Vrin, 1997), 4.
48 Marguerite Thibaud in *L'effort chez Maine de Biran et Bergson* (Grenoble: Allier, 1939), 137–60; René Violette, *La spiritualité de Bergson* (Toulouse: Éditions Édouard Privat, 1968); Harvey Hill, 'Henri Bergson and Alfred Loisy: On Mysticism and the Religious Life', in *Modernists and Mystics*, ed. Talar, 104–35. Bergson's mysticism is discussed at length in Chapter 4.
49 Janicaud, *Spiritualisme français*, 5.
50 Henri Bergson, *The Two Sources of Morality and Religion*, translated by R. A. Audra and C. Brereton with W. H. Carter (London: Macmillan & Co., 1935), 188.
51 Pierre Hadot, *Plotinus, or the Simplicity of Vision* (Chicago: University of Chicago Press, 1993), 71, 82. For Bergson, see *Philosophy as a Way of Life*, 253–4.
52 See for instance, Michel Foucault, *The History of Sexuality*. Vol. II. *The Use of Pleasure*, trans. Robert Hurley (New York: Random House, 1985), 9; Sloterdijk, *You Must Change Your Life*, 452.
53 Gouhier, *Les conversions*, 16–64, 397–411.
54 Jean-Jacques Rousseau, *Reveries of a Solitary Walker*, trans. Peter France (London: Penguin, 1979), 28.
55 Rousseau, *Reveries*, 28.
56 Rousseau, *Reveries*, 104.
57 Rousseau, *Reveries*, 104.
58 Rousseau, *Reveries*, 39.
59 Rousseau, *Reveries*, 89.
60 Coleman, *Virtues of Abandon*, 241–9.
61 Anne Hartle, 'Augustine and Rousseau: Narrative and Self-Knowledge in the Two Confessions', in *The Augustinian Tradition*, ed. Gareth B. Mathews (Berkeley: University of California Press, 1999), 263–85.
62 Rousseau, *Reveries*, 52.
63 Rousseau, *Reveries*, 103–4.
64 Catherine E. Rigby, *Topographies of the Sacred: The Poetics of Place in European Romanticism* (Charlottesville: University of Virginia Press, 2004), 46–47.
65 Biran, *Écrits de jeunesse*, 99.
66 Christopher Brooke, *Philosophic Pride: Stoicism and Political Thought from Lipsius to Rousseau* (Princeton: Princeton University Press, 2012), 1–11; Jean-Luc Marion, 'Resting, Moving, Loving: The Access to the Self According to Saint Augustine', *The Journal of Religion* 91, no. 1 (2011): 24–42. My reading of Augustine's dialectic of effort and repose is indebted to Marion.
67 Augustine of Hippo, *Confessions*. Vol. I., trans. William Watts (Cambridge, Massachusetts: Harvard University Press, 1912), 3 (1.1).
68 Augustine of Hippo, *Confessions*. Vol. II., trans. William Watts (Cambridge, Massachusetts: Harvard University Press, 1912), 471 (13.35).

69   Genesis 2.15.
70   Augustine, *Confessions*. Vol. II., 376–7 (13.1).
71   Augustine, *Confessions*. Vol. II., 423 (13.20).
72   Genesis 1.2.
73   Augustine, *Confessions*. Vol. II., 389 (13.8). Emphasis in the original.
74   Augustine, *Confessions*. Vol. II., 391 (13.9).
75   Augustine, *Confessions*. Vol. II., 391 (13.9).
76   Augustine, *Confessions*. Vol. II., 473 (13.37).
77   François Fénelon, *Selections from the Writings of Fénelon*, trans. and ed. Mrs Follen (Boston: Samuel G. Simpkins, 1844), 178.
78   Gouhier, *Les conversions*, 360–7.
79   Cf. Bernard Baertschi, *L'Ontologie de Maine de Biran* (Fribourg: Éditions universitaires, 1982). For Baertschi, Biran evinces a realist ontology which anticipates the subjective turn of phenomenology without relinquishing a commitment to corporeality.
80   *Sloterdijk, You Must Change Your Life*, 3.
81   Brooke, *Philosophic Pride*, 76–101; Julien-Eymard d'Angers, *Récherches sur le Stoïcisme aux XVIe et XVIIe siècles* (New York: G. Olms, 1976), 1–32.
82   Michel Spanneut, *Permanence du Stoïcisme de Zénon à Malraux* (Duculot: Gembloux, 1973), 317–90.
83   Victor Delbos, *Figures et doctrines de philosophes* (Paris: Plon, 1918), 285–327; Gouhier, *Les conversions*, 331–44; Spanneut, *Permanence du Stoïcisme*, 345–9.
84   Biran, *Écrits de jeunesse*, 39–42. 'Constancy' (a term that Seneca uses in relation to Stoic philosophy) is not quite the same concept as the older Greek notion of 'tranquillity' (*ataraxia*), but Biran is treating them as synonyms in this passage, where he also conflates Seneca and Cicero as equal representatives of Stoic philosophy (Cicero, though he admired many Stoic ideas was, strictly speaking, an Academician). For the French interpretation of Stoicism that seems to be influencing Biran here, compare Brooke, *Philosophic Pride*, 76–100.
85   Biran, *Écrits de jeunesse*, 99.
86   Jones, *French Introspectives*, 100.

Chapter 2

1   P. Mansell Jones, *French Introspectives: From Montaigne to André Gide* (Cambridge: Cambridge University Press, 1937), 2.
2   Charles Augustin Sainte-Beuve, *Causeries du Lundi*. Vol. XIII (Paris: Garnier frères, 1870), 305. The comparison between Biran's introspective style and the tradition of spiritual exercise taught by the Brothers of Christian Doctrine is my own, and relies

wholly on Jean de Viguerie's fascinating account of the Brothers' curriculum and its seminal influence on major philosophical figures during the 1780s: *Une œuvre d'éducation sous l'Ancien Régime: les Pères de la Doctrine chrétienne en France et en Italie, 1592–1792* (Paris: Nouvelle Aurore, 1976), 508–18. The Brothers of Christian Doctrine (*Doctrinaires*) were founded in 1597 and after the expulsion of the Society of Jesus were assigned to many colleges formerly under Jesuit administration, such as the one at Périgueux where Biran studied as a teenager. See Gouhier, *Les conversions*, 16.

3   Maine de Biran, *Œuvres*. Vol. X-2. *Dernière philosophie: existence et anthropologie*, ed. Bernard Baertschi (Paris: Vrin, 1989), 8.
4   Biran, *Influence of Habit*, 43.
5   Augustine, *De vera religione*, 39.72, *Bibliothèque Augustinienne 8*, ed. and trans. by Joseph Pegon (Paris: Desclée de Brouwer, 1951). My translation. 39.72.
6   Biran, *Dernière philosophie: existence et anthropologie*, 322.
7   Jones, *French Introspectives*, 42–56. For Biran and introspection I have also relied on Georges Gusdorf, *La découverte de soi* (Paris: Presses universitaires de France, 1948); Jerrold Siegel, *The Idea of the Self: Thought and Experience in Western Europe Since the Seventeenth Century* (Cambridge: Cambridge University Press, 2005), 248–94; Knud Haakonssen, 'The History of Eighteenth-Century Philosophy: History or Philosophy?', in *The Cambridge History of Eighteenth-Century Philosophy*, ed. Knud Haakonssen (Cambridge: Cambridge University Press, 2011), 2–25.
8   Gary Hatfield, 'The Senses and the Fleshless Eye: The *Meditations* as Cognitive Exercises', in *Essays on Descartes' Meditations*, ed. Amélie Oksenberg Rorty (Berkeley: University of California Press, 1986), 69.
9   Descartes, *Meditations on First Philosophy*, trans. John Cottingham (Cambridge: Cambridge University Press, 1996), 12 (AT VII, 17–18).
10 Étienne Bonnot de Condillac, *Treatise on the Sensations*, trans. Geraldine Carr (Los Angeles: University of Southern California Press, 1930), 59 (I.xi.1).
11 Condillac, *Treatise on the Sensations*, 205, 217 (IV.ii, IV.vi).
12 Condillac, *Treatise on the Sensations*, 227–36 (IV.viii).
13 Descartes, *Meditations*, 8 (AT VII p. 9).
14 Condillac, *Treatise on the Sensations*, 45 (I.vii.2).
15 Condillac, *Treatise on the Sensations*, 220 (IV.vi.6).
16 Gabriel Madinier, *Conscience et mouvement: étude sur la philosophie française de Condillac à Bergson* (Paris: Alcan, 1939), 1–38.
17 Marno, 'Easy attention'.
18 Charles Bonnet, *Essai analytique sur les facultés de l'âme* (Copenhagen/Geneva: Philibert, 1775), xv.
19 Bonnet, *Essai analytique*, xiii–xiv.

20 Bonnet, *Essai analytique*, xi.
21 Bonnet, *Essai analytique*, xiii.
22 Marno, 'Easy attention'.
23 Hatfield, 'The Senses and the Fleshless Eye', 55.
24 Hatfield, 'The Senses and the Fleshless Eye', 69.
25 Madinier, *Conscience et* mouvement; Alexis Bertrand, *Philosophie de l'effort et les doctrines contemporaines* (Paris: Alcan, 1889); Björn Sjövall, *Psychology of Tension* (Stockholm: Svenska bokförlaget, 1967), 169-93.
26 Augustine, *Confessions*. Vol. I, 7.10 (371).
27 Descartes, *Meditations,* 36 (AT VII, 52).
28 Marno, 'Easy Attention', 149. Cf. Marion, *Cartesian Questions,* 134-55.
29 Gouhier, *Les conversions,* 16-65.
30 Jean-Jacques Rousseau, *The Collected Writings*. Vol. XIII. *Émile, or On Education*, trans. Allan David Bloom (Hanover and London: University Press of New England, 2010), 431.
31 Rousseau, *Émile*, 438.
32 Rousseau, *Émile*, 439-40.
33 Coleman, *Virtues of Abandon,* 207. Rousseau, however, was also a friend and admirer of Condillac, and self-sufficiency is thus an important ideal in his approach to meditation. See Amélie Oksenberg Rorty, 'The Two Faces of Stoicism: Rousseau and Freud', *Journal of the History of Philosophy*, 34 (1996): 335-56.
34 Cf. Descartes, *Meditations,* 41-42 (AT VII, 60-61): 'I have reason to give thanks to him who has never owed me anything ... rather than thinking myself deprived or robbed of any gifts he did not bestow.' On the false autonomy of the meditator and the discovery of grace through introspection, see Gusdorf, *La découverte de soi*, 124-29.
35 The literature on Augustinian introspection and spiritual exercise is enormous, especially if we look at it from the perspective of a longer tradition as I am doing here. Among the interpretations which have influenced my reading of Biran are, aside from the seminal analysis by Gouhier (*Les conversions*): Marion, *Cartesian Questions,* 134-55; Sherman, *Partakers of the Divine,* 75-130; Jean-Luc Marion, *In the Self's Place: The Approach of Saint Augustine*, trans. Jeffrey Kosky (Stanford: Stanford University Press, 2012).
36 Bonnet, *Essai analytique*, xiii.
37 Lezsek Kolakowski, *God Owes Us Nothing: A Brief Remark on Pascal's Religion and on the Spirit of Jansenism* (Chicago, University of Chicago Press, 1995).
38 Marno, 'Easy attention', 148.
39 Romans 7.
40 Jacques Roger, *Buffon: A Life in Natural History*, trans. Sarah Lucille Bonnefoi (Ithaca: Cornell University Press, 1997), 250-52; François Azouvi, 'Homo duplex', *Gesnerus* 42 (1984): 229-44.

41 Jones, *French Introspectives*, 4.
42 Jones, *French Introspectives*, 1.
43 Jones, *French Introspectives*, 4.
44 Foucault, *Technologies of the Self*, 46.
45 Foucault, *Technologies of the Self*, 46.
46 Henri Gouhier, *Les meditations métaphysiques de Jean-Jacques Rousseau* (Paris: Vrin, 1970). See also Carole Dornier, 'L'écriture de la citadelle intérieure ou la thérapeutique de l'âme du promeneur solitaire', *Annales de la société Jean-Jacques Rousseau* 48 (2008): 105–24.
47 Coleman, *Virtues of Abandon*, 6.
48 Coleman, *Virtues of Abandon*, 12.
49 Haakonssen, 'The History of Eighteenth-Century Philosophy', 16.
50 Jeffrey Burson, *The Rise and Fall of the Theological Enlightenment: Jean-Martin de Prades and Ideological Polarisation in Eighteenth-Century France* (South Bend: Notre Dame University Press, 2010).
51 Biran, *Dernière philosophie: existence et anthropologie*, 194–5.
52 Jeremy Dunham, 'A Universal and Absolute Spiritualism, Maine de Biran's Leibniz', in Maine de Biran, *The Relationship between the Physical and the Moral in Man*, ed. and trans. Darian Meacham and Joseph Spadola (London: Bloomsbury, 2016), 157–92. Dunham's work, however, relates mostly to the early Biran. For Biran's spiritualism in the *Nouveaux essais*, I have relied heavily on Gouhier, *Les conversions*, 311f, still the best study of how Biran combines Augustinian introspection with the ideas of Leibniz and achieves a synthesis of spiritual exercise and scientific methodology.
53 Jules Lachelier, *Œuvres*. Vol. II (Paris: Alcan, 1933), 221.
54 Biran, *Dernière philosophie: existence et anthropologie*, 194–5.
55 Biran, *Dernière philosophie: existence et anthropologie*, 8.
56 Biran, *Dernière philosophie: existence et anthropologie*, 3.
57 Biran, *Influence of Habit*, 56, n. 2. The critique of Descartes' *cogito* is developed by Biran in the *Mémoire sur la decomposition de la pensée*. Here Biran argues that the primitive fact of existence cannot be thinking (which demands awareness *of* self) but (following Leibniz) an 'immediate apperception' that precedes any awareness of self and corresponds to a feeling of effort or what philosophers had called the movement of the will. Hence his riposte to Descartes: *je veux, donc je suis*. See Maine de Biran, *Œuvres*. Vol. III. *Mémoire sur la decomposition de la pensée*, ed. F. Azouvi (Paris: Vrin, 2000) and the discussion in Michel Henry, *Philosophy and Phenomenology of the Body*, trans. Girard Etzkorn (The Hague: Nijhoff, 1975), 35–51.
58 Biran, *Dernière philosophie: existence et anthropologie*, 196.
59 Biran, *Dernière philosophie: existence et anthropologie*, 7.

60 Biran, *Dernière philosophie: existence et anthropologie*, 195.
61 Biran, *Dernière philosophie: existence et anthropologie*, 195.
62 Biran, *Dernière philosophie: existence et anthropologie*, 25.
63 Biran, *Dernière philosophie: existence et anthropologie*, 26.
64 Biran, *Dernière philosophie: existence et anthropologie*, 324.
65 Biran, *Dernière philosophie: existence et anthropologie*, 323.
66 Biran, *Dernière philosophie: existence et anthropologie*, 322.
67 Biran, *Dernière philosophie: existence et anthropologie*, 322-3.
68 Maine de Biran, *Journal*. Vol. II, ed. Henri Gouhier (Neuchatel: Éditions de la Baconnière, 1955), 416.
69 Biran, *Journal* II, 416.
70 Gouhier, *Les conversions*, 367-422.
71 Maine de Biran, *Journal*. Vol. I, ed. Henri Gouhier (Neuchatel: Éditions de la Baconnière, 1954), 209.
72 On Biran and Stoicism, see Victor Delbos, *Figures et doctrines de philosophes* (Paris: Plon, 1918), 285-327; Gouhier, *Les conversions*, 331-44; Spanneut, *Permanence du Stoïcisme*, 345-49.
73 Favourite passages from Marcus Aurelius' *Meditations* cited by Biran in the *journal intime* include: *Meditations* 2.4; 3.1; 4.7; 5.21; 6.41; 7.2; 7.16; 7.47; 7.68; 9. 32; 10.24; 12.14.
74 François Fénelon, *Œuvres*, Vol. II (Paris: Lefevre, 1835), 318.
75 Biran, *Journal* II, 208. Aside from Fénelon, Biran also read Jacques-Bénigne Bossuet, Thomas à Kempis and Teresa of Ávila, among other spiritual writers.
76 Maine de Biran, *Journal*. Vol. III, ed. Henri Gouhier (Neuchatel: Éditions de la Baconnière, 1957), 214.
77 Biran, *Journal* III, 202.
78 Biran, *Journal* III, 202.
79 Gouhier, *Les conversions*, 367-422.
80 Biran, *Dernière philosophie: existence et anthropologie*, 183.
81 Biran, *Dernière philosophie: existence et anthropologie*, 322.
82 Biran, *Dernière philosophie: existence et anthropologie*, 25.
83 Victor Cousin, 'Préface de l'éditeur', in Maine de Biran, *Nouvelles considérations sur les rapports du physique et du moral de l'homme*, ed. Victor Cousin (Paris: Ladrange, 1834), i-xlii; Jules Simon, 'Philosophes modernes: Maine de Biran', *Revue des deux mondes* (15 November 1841), 653.
84 Biran, *Dernière philosophie: existence et anthropologie*, 184.
85 Biran, *Dernière philosophie: existence et anthropologie*, 185.
86 Biran, *Dernière philosophie: existence et anthropologie*, 186.
87 René Descartes, *Discours de la méthode* 62.
88 Georges Le Roy, *L'Éxpérience de l'effort et de la grâce chez Maine de Biran* (Paris: Boivin, 1937).

89 Biran, *Dernière philosophie: existence et anthropologie*, 322–3.
90 Biran, *Dernière philosophie: existence et anthropologie*, 322.
91 Janicaud, *Spiritualisme français*, 15–36.
92 Biran, *Influence of Habit*, 43.
93 Biran, *Influence of Habit*, 261.
94 Biran, *Dernière philosophie: existence et anthropologie*, 323.
95 Biran, *Influence of Habit*, 219.
96 Biran, *Influence of Habit*, 195.
97 Biran, *Influence of Habit*, 199.
98 Biran, *Influence of Habit*, 146.
99 Biran, *Influence of Habit*, 147.
100 Biran, *Influence of Habit*, 146.
101 Biran, *Influence of Habit*, 47.
102 Biran, *Influence of Habit*, 47–8.
103 Biran, *Influence of Habit*, 146.
104 Biran, *Influence of Habit*, 215.
105 Maine de Biran, *The Relationship between the Physical and the Moral in Man*, ed. and trans. Darian Meacham and Joseph Spadola (London: Bloomsbury, 2016), 134.
106 Biran, *The Physical and the Moral*, 134.
107 Biran, *The Physical and the Moral*, 136.
108 Biran is citing the eighteenth-century physician Herman Boerhaave, *Praelectiones Academicae de morbis nervorum*. Vol. II (Lugduni Batavorum, 1761), 496–7. See Azouvi, 'Homo Duplex'.
109 For the methodological unity of Biran's philosophy, see François Azouvi, *Maine de Biran: la science de l'homme* (Paris: Vrin, 1995), 10. Building on Gouhier's approach in *Les conversions*, Azouvi argues that because Biran's work passes through so many different 'conversions', the unity of his thought is not any one specific theme, but a method. Azouvi sees this method as the scientific method of observation. I propose that what is scientific about Biran's method derives its basic characteristics from the spiritual exercise of introspection.
110 Henri Bergson, *The Creative Mind*, trans. Mabelle Anderson (New York: Philosophical Library, 1948), 71.
111 Weil, *Waiting on God*, 55.
112 Biran, *Influence of Habit*, 206.
113 Gilles Deleuze, *Pure Immanence: Essays on a Life*, trans. Anne Boyman (New York: Zone, 2001), 28. It strikes me that in this one place Deleuze is a very accurate reader of Biran's *Nouveaux essais* in ways that have yet to be studied further; though a start has been made by Giorgio Agamben: *Potentialities* (Stanford University Press, 2000), 230.
114 Biran, *Dernière philosophie: existence et anthropologie*, 323.
115 Henry, *Phenomenology of the Body*, 9.

Chapter 3

1   Ravaisson, *Philosophie en France*, 320.
2   Mark Sinclair, 'Introduction', in Félix Ravaisson, *Selected Essays*, ed. Mark Sinclair (London: Bloomsbury, 2016), 6; Janicaud, *Spiritualisme français*, 16.
3   Raymond Lenoir, 'La doctrine de Ravaisson et la pensée moderne', *Revue de métaphysique et de morale* 26, no. 3 (1919): 357. In writing this chapter I have also consulted and relied on Lucien Lévy-Bruhl, *History of Modern Philosophy in France* (Chicago: Open Court, 1899), 436–82; Joseph Dopp, *Félix Ravaisson; la formation de sa pensée d'après des documents inédits* (Louvain, Éditions de l'Institut supérieur de philosophie, 1933); Chevalier, *La pensée moderne*; Janicaud, *Spiritualisme français*; François Laruelle, *Phénomène et différence: essai sur l'ontologie de Ravaisson* (Paris: Klincksieck, 1971); Copleston, *Nineteenth- and Twentieth-Century French Philosophy*, 1–215; Andrea Bellantone, 'Ravaisson: Le Champ Abandonné de la *Métaphysique*', *Cahiers philosophiques* 129, no. 2 (2012): 5–21; Tullio Viola, 'The Serpentine Life of Félix Ravaisson: Art, Drawing, Scholarship, Philosophy', in *Et in imagine ego: Facetten von Bildakt und Verkörperung*, eds. Ulrike Feist and Markus Rath (Berlin: Akademie-Verlag, 2012), 155–74; Clare Carlisle, 'Between Freedom and Necessity: Ravaisson on Habit and the Moral Life', in *A History of Habit: From Aristotle to Bourdieu*, eds. J. Bell, A. Hutchinson and T. Sparrow (Lanham: Lexington, 2013), 153–76; Clare Carlisle, *On Habit* (London: Routledge, 2014). The best detailed account, in English, of Ravaisson's metaphysics is now Mark Sinclair, *Being Inclined: Félix Ravaisson's Philosophy of Habit* (Oxford: Oxford University Press, 2019). Sadly this arrived as my book was going to press, and I have not been able to engage with it in what follows, though Sinclair's constructive account of inclination as a pre-reflexive tendency that is not contrary to but constitutive of the will's freedom parallels what I argue in this chapter regarding Ravaisson's definition of grace.
4   Cited in Dopp, *Félix Ravaisson*, 294.
5   Bellantone, 'Ravaisson', 12.
6   Lenoir, 'La doctrine de Ravaisson', 353.
7   M. Pidoux, *Le spiritualisme organique* (Paris: Asselin, 1969); Jean Cazeneuve, *Ravaisson et les médecins animistes et vitalistes* (Paris: Presses universitaires de France, 1958). The culture of effort is discussed in more detail in Chapter 4 below. For the intellectual background to Ravaisson's thought I have also found the following particularly useful: George Boas, *French Philosophies of the Romantic Period* (Baltimore: Johns Hopkins University Press, 1925); Louis Foucher, *La philosophie catholique en France au XIXe siècle, avant la renaissance thomiste et dans son rapport avec elle (1800–1880)* (Paris: Vrin, 1955).
8   Cousin, 'Préface de l'éditeur' in Biran, *Nouvelles considérations*, xli. Victor Cousin (1792–1867), during his long career Professor of Philosophy at the Sorbonne, Director of the École Normale Supérieur, Peer of France and Minister of Public

Instruction, was a prolific editor and translator internationally influential for his school of 'eclectic spiritualism', a reaction to the psychologism of Locke and Condillac. On the relationship between Cousin's philosophy and Ravaisson's spiritualism, see Patrice Vermeren 'Ravaisson en son temps et en sa thèse', *Les études philosophiques* 1 (1993): 71–81.

9 Biran, *Journal* II, 303.
10 Fénelon, *Spiritual Writings*, 235–9.
11 Biran, *Nouvelles considérations*, 147. These passages on Fénelon are not replicated in the modern critical edition since it is not clear whether Biran intended them to be part of the *Nouvelles considérations*; their inclusion in Cousin's edition is very much the result of Cousin's selective redaction. But as the passages are typical of Biran's thought and as it is the reception of his late philosophy that interests us here, their original context is of little importance and I refer to Cousin's edition for the sake of convenience. On the history of the text, see Maine de Biran, *Œuvres*. Vol. IX. *Nouvelles considérations sur les rapports du physique et du moral de l'homme*, ed. Bernard Baertschi (Paris: Vrin, 1990), vii–xx.
12 Biran, *Nouvelles considérations*, 163–4, citing Fénelon. English translation from *The Complete Fénelon*, eds and trans. Robert J. Edmonson and Hal M. Helms (Brewster, MA: Paraclete Press, 2008), 104–5, 112.
13 Cousin, 'Préface de l'éditeur' in Biran, *Nouvelles considérations,* xxxviii. On Cousin's critique of Biran cf. Victor Cousin, *Elements of Psychology*, trans. C. S. Henry (New York: Dayton and Saxton, 1842 [3rd edn]), 139–54; and the discussion in Nathan Truman, *Maine de Biran's Philosophy of Will* (New York: Macmillan, 1904), 81–7.
14 Cousin, 'Préface de l'éditeur' in Biran, *Nouvelles considérations*, vi, xlii.
15 In nineteenth-century French philosophy the doctrine opposed to materialism tended to be spiritualism rather than idealism.
16 Cousin, 'Préface de l'éditeur' in Biran, *Nouvelles considérations*, xvi, xlii.
17 Cousin, 'Préface de l'éditeur' in Biran, *Nouvelles considérations*, xii. See Victor Cousin, *Fragments de philosophie cartésienne* (Paris: Charpentier, 1845). Cousin was partly responsible for the revival of Descartes in French philosophy through his influential edition of the complete works of Descartes.
18 Cousin, 'Préface de l'éditeur' in Biran, *Nouvelles considérations*, xvi, xviii.
19 Cousin, 'Préface de l'éditeur' in Biran, *Nouvelles considérations*, xxx.
20 Cousin, 'Préface de l'éditeur' in Biran, *Nouvelles considérations*, xxxix, xlii.
21 Victor Cousin, *Lectures on the True, the Beautiful, and the Good*, trans. O. W. Wight. 3d edn (Edinburgh: T & T Clark, D. Appleton & co, 1854), 10. The *Lectures* were originally delivered in 1815–21.
22 Cousin, *The True, the Beautiful, and the Good*, 109. My emphasis.
23 Cousin, *The True, the Beautiful, and the Good*, 32.
24 Paul Ricœur, *Husserl: An Analysis of His Phenomenology*, trans. Edward G. Ballard and Lester E. Embree (Evanston: Northwestern University Press, 1967), 16.

25 Jean-Luc Marion, 'The Saturated Phenomenon', trans. Thomas A. Carlson, *Philosophy Today* 40, no. 1 (1996): 103–124.
26 Cousin, *The True, the Beautiful, and the Good*, 115.
27 Cousin, *The True, the Beautiful, and the Good*, 111.
28 Cousin, *The True, the Beautiful, and the Good*, 11: 'Whatever career you embrace, propose to yourselves an elevated aim, and put in its service an unalterable constancy (*une constance inébranlable*).' The Stoic philosophy associated with the term 'constancy' surely would not have been lost on Cousin.
29 Vermeren, 'Ravaisson', 71–81.
30 Victor Cousin, 'Du mysticisme', *Revue des deux mondes* 11, no. 3 (1845): 469–86; Alfred Fouillée, 'La Morale de la Beauté et de l'Amour, selon le mysticisme contemporain', *Revue des deux mondes* 52 (1882): 401–35; Fr. Paulhan, 'Le nouveau mysticisme', *Revue philosophique de la France et de l'Étranger* 30 (1890): 480–522. During the nineteenth century we see mysticism tackled in two distinct but interrelated ways: on the one hand the old sense of mysticism as a style of religious discourse; on the other hand the newly emerging, 'secular' sense of mysticism as a psychological phenomenon subject to scientific analysis. Spiritualism attempted to place philosophy somewhere in the middle between these two approaches, borrowing from religious mysticism its sense of the Absolute while using psychological methods for the description of the interior life. See Leigh Eric Schmidt, 'The Making of Modern "Mysticism"', *Journal of the American Academy of Religion* 71, no. 2 (2003): 273–302.
31 Michel de Certeau, *The Mystic Fable*. Vol. I. *The Sixteenth and Seventeenth Centuries*, trans. Michael B. Smith (Chicago: Chicago University Press, 1992).
32 Cousin, *The True, the Beautiful, and the Good*, 110–11. Cousin critiques Fénelon at 85–90.
33 Cousin, *The True, the Beautiful, and the Good*, 119.
34 C. J. T. Talar summarizes the negative attitudes taken to Fénelon and the Quietist controversy in 'Prayer at Twilight: Henri Bremond's *Apologie pour Fénelon*' in Talar (ed.), *Modernists and Mystics*, 39–61.
35 Certeau, *Sixteenth and Seventeenth Centuries*, 94–6.
36 Certeau, *Sixteenth and Seventeenth Centuries*, 20–1.
37 Jean-Philibert Damiron, *Essai sur l'histoire de la philosophie en France au XIXe siècle* (Paris: Hachette, 1834), 338. Certeau argues that the phrase 'natural mysticism', the same expression used by Damiron in this passage, originated in the eighteenth century, when it was used to describe an inborn awareness of the divine (*Sixteenth and Seventeenth Centuries*, 108).
38 Dopp, *Félix Ravaisson*, 225–45; Janicaud, *Spiritualisme français*, 15–35; Laruelle, *Phénomène et différence*, 178–87.
39 Dopp, *Félix Ravaisson*, 247–78.
40 Ravaisson, *Selected Essays*, 65.

41 Ravaisson, *Selected Essays*, 68–9. The piece referred to by Ravaisson here is 'Jugement de Schelling sur la philosophie de M. Cousin et sur l'état de la philosophie française et de la philosophie allemande en general', trans. Félix Ravaisson, *Revue germanique* 3, no. 10 (1835): 3–24.
42 Ravaisson, *Selected Essays*, 78.
43 Ravaisson, *Selected Essays*, 78.
44 Jacques Derrida, *Du droit a la philosophie* (Paris: Galilée, 1990), 185–94.
45 Laruelle, *Phénomène et différence*, 191.
46 Ravaisson, *Selected Essays*, 79.
47 Ravaisson, *Selected Essays*, 80.
48 Ravaisson, *Selected Essays*, 80.
49 Ravaisson, *Selected Essays*, 51.
50 François Fénelon, *A Demonstration of the Existence of God, Deduced from the Knowledge of Nature*, trans. Samuel Boyse (London: John Murray, 1796), 278. Augustine is cited at 276: 'But because thou art too intimately within them [intimior intimo nostro], and they never enter within themselves.' This is, as far as I can tell, the passage paraphrased by Ravaisson in *Of Habit* (cf. *Selected Essays*, 58, n. 61).
51 François Fénelon, *Œuvres*. Vol. II (Paris: Tenré & Boiste, 1822), 338.
52 Fénelon, *Spiritual Writings*, 235–9.
53 Ravaisson, *Selected Essays*, 81.
54 Ravaisson, *Selected Essays*, 81.
55 Ravaisson, *Selected Essays*, 81.
56 Ravaisson, *Selected Essays*, 81.
57 Ravaisson, *Selected Essays*, 80. My emphasis.
58 Paul Ricœur, *Freedom and Nature: The Voluntary and the Involuntary*, trans. Erazim Kohák (Chicago: Northwestern University Press, 1966), in particular 280–307, where Ravaisson's analysis of habit forms the starting point for a whole phenomenology of the human condition.
59 Ravaisson, *Philosophie en France*, 258.
60 Ravaisson, *Philosophie en France*, 317–19. Ravaisson cites: Athanasius, *De incarnatione* 54, 3; Psalms 82.6; Plato, *Symposium* 178c; 1 John 4.8. Ravaisson is using the David Martin translation of the Bible which gives *agape* as 'charité', hence his rendering of *ho theos agape esti* as 'Dieu est charité', where more recent translations have 'Dieu est amour' (thus the NRSV: 'God is love'). I have chosen to translate 'charité' as 'charity' rather than 'love' in order to reflect the importance given to the idea of love as 'gift', 'liberality' and 'grace' in this passage.
61 Fénelon, *Spiritual Writings*, 236.
62 Ravaisson, *Selected Essays*, 317.
63 Ravaisson, *Philosophie en France*, 142.
64 Étienne Vacherot, 'La situation philosophique en France', *Revue des deux mondes* 75 (1868): 951.

65 Weil, *Waiting on God*, 55.
66 Ravaisson, *Philosophie en France*, 319–20.
67 Ravaisson, *Selected Essays*, 295.
68 Ravaisson, *Selected Essays*, 295.
69 Ravaisson, *Selected Essays*, 296.
70 Ravaisson, *Selected Essays*, 297.
71 Ravaisson, *Selected Essays*, 325, n. 16.
72 Ravaisson, *Selected Essays*, 301, 308. On Ravaisson and art, see Viola, 'The Serpentine Life of Félix Ravaisson, 155–74.
73 Félix Ravaisson, 'Appendice: Fragments de Ravaisson' in Janicaud, *Spiritualisme français*, 264.
74 Ravaisson, *Selected Essays*, 315.
75 Ravaisson, *Selected Essays*, 315.
76 Ravaisson, *Selected Essays*, 304.
77 Ravaisson, *Selected Essays*, 304.
78 Ravaisson, *Selected Essays*, 312.
79 Ravaisson, *Selected Essays*, 320.
80 Charles Rénouvier, 'D'une forme moderne du Stoïcisme', *La Critique philosophique* 28 (1876): 25.
81 Antoine Adam, *Sur le problème religieux dans la première moitié du XVIIe siècle* (Oxford: Clarendon Press, 1959).
82 William J. Bouwsma (ed.), 'The Two Faces of Humanism: Stoicism and Augustinianism in Renaissance Thought', in *A Usable Past: Essays in European Cultural History* (Berkeley: University of California Press, 1990), 58.
83 Bouwsma, *A Usable Past*, 64.
84 Bouwsma, *A Usable Past*, 58.
85 Ravaisson, *Selected Essays*, 271.
86 Ravaisson, *Selected Essays*, 318.
87 Katerina Ierodiakonou, 'Introduction' in *Topics in Stoic Philosophy*, ed. Katerina Ierodiakonou (Oxford: Oxford University Press, 1999), 3; J.-B. Gourinat, 'La disparation et la reconstitution du Stoïcisme: éléments pour un histoire', in *Les Stoïciens*, eds. G. R. Dherbey and J. B. Gourinat (Paris: Vrin, 2005), 13–28.
88 Charles Rénouvier, *Manuel de philosophie ancienne II* (Paris: Paulin, 1844), 266.
89 Spanneut, *Permanence du Stoïcisme*, 342–66.
90 M. Jammer, *Concepts of Force: A Study in the Foundations of Dynamics* (Cambridge, MA: Harvard University Press, 1957), 24–57.
91 Gourinat, 'La disparition et la reconstitution du Stoïcisme', 22.
92 Félix Ravaisson, *Essai sur la* Métaphysique *d'Aristote* (Paris: Cerf, 2007 [orig. 1837–45]), 480–543; 568–81.
93 Ravaisson, *Selected Essays*, 118. Citing Epictetus, *Discourses* 2.18.

94   Ravaisson, *Selected Essays*, 95.
95   Ravaisson, *Selected Essays*, 126.
96   Ravaisson, *Selected Essays*, 91.
97   Ravaisson, *Selected Essays*, 95.
98   Ravaisson, *Selected Essays*, 118.
99   Ravaisson, *Selected Essays*, 124.
100 Ravaisson, *Selected Essays*, 125.
101 Sinclair, 'Introduction' in Ravaisson, *Selected Essays*, 11.
102 Simone Kotva, 'The God of Effort: Henri Bergson and the Stoicism of Modernity', *Modern Theology* 32 (2016): 397–420.
103 Émile Bréhier, *Histoire de la philosophie*. Vol. I. *L'Antiquité et le Moyen âge* (Paris: Alcan, 1928), 308.
104 Ravaisson, *Selected Essays*, 269–70.
105 Ravaisson, *Selected Essays*, 272.
106 Ravaisson, *Selected Essays*, 270.
107 Ravaisson, *Selected Essays*, 271.
108 Ravaisson, *Selected Essays*, 271.
109 Ravaisson, *Selected Essays*, 272.
110 For the connection between Ravaisson's critique of Pascal and his critique of Stoicism, compare Ravaisson, *Essai sur la* Métaphysique *d'Aristote*, 581, with *Selected Essays*, 269, where the description of Pascal's liking for 'grandeur and baseness' echoes the characterization of Stoicism as 'a singular assemblage of force and weakness, baseness and grandeur'.
111 Ravaisson, *Selected Essays*, 275.
112 Ravaisson, *Selected Essays*, 262; citing Blaise Pascal, 'On Mind and Style', in *Pensées*, trans. W. F. Trotter (New York: Dutton, 1958), 2.
113 Ravaisson, *Selected Essays*, 260.
114 Ravaisson, *Selected Essays*, 253.
115 Ravaisson, *Selected Essays*, 274.
116 Ravaisson, *Selected Essays*, 275.
117 Janicaud, *Spiritualisme français*, 4.
118 Janicaud, *Spiritualisme français*, 5.
119 The separation of introspection from religious meditation is argued elsewhere by Dominique Janicaud; see for instance *Phenomenology 'Wide Open': After the French Debate*, trans. Charles Cabral (New York: Fordham University Press, 2005).
120 Denise Leduc-Fayette, 'La métaphysique de Ravaisson et le Christ', *Les Études philosophiques* 4 (1984): 511–27.
121 James Frazer, *The Golden Bough: A Study in Magic and Religion*, abridged (London: Macmillan and Co., 1922). Hadot, *Philosophy as a Way of Life*, 126–44.

The contrast between the approaches of Frazer and Weil is pointed out by Marie Cabaud-Meany, *Simone Weil's Apologetic Use of Literature: Her Christological Interpretations of Ancient Greek Texts* (Oxford: Oxford University Press, 2007), 18–19; the link between Weil and Ravaisson is suggested by Maurice Nédoncelle in '*Félix Ravaisson, Essai sur la* Métaphysique *d'Aristote. Fragments du tome III (Hellénisme, judaïsme, christianisme)*, texte établi par Charles Devivaise, 1953', *Revue des Sciences Religieuses* 28/3 (1954): 323–4.

122 Paul Janet, 'Le spiritualisme français au XIXe siècle', *Revue* des *deux mondes* 75 (1868): 379. Janet (1823–99) was a philosopher and spiritualist who wrote several important pieces, this one included, that helped to redefine the movement along Ravaissonian lines.

123 Janet, 'Le spiritualisme français', 379.

124 Janet, 'Le spiritualisme français', 382.

125 Madinier, *Conscience et mouvement*; Rolf Kühn, *Französische Religionsphilosophie und -phänomenologie*, 30–57.

126 Thomas Carlyle, *On Heroes, Hero-Worship and the Heroic in History* (London: James Fraser, 1841), 22.

127 Carlyle, *On Heroes*, 17.

128 Carlyle, *On Heroes*, 18.

129 G. Karl Galinsky describes the shifting attitudes of Christian writers to Hercules in *The Herakles Theme* (Oxford: Basil Blackwell, 1972), 188–9, and observes how Hercules eventually became positively identified as a type of Christ after the first few centuries of Christian polemic against Hercules had abated.

Chapter 4

1 Bergson, *The Creative Mind*, 88–9.

2 Madinier, *Conscience et mouvement*, iii. On effort in Bergson and French philosophy, see Henri Bergson, *Mind-energy, Lectures and Essays*, trans. Herbert Wildon Carr (New York: H. Holt, 1920), 186–230; Thibaud, *L'Effort*, 137–60 and passim; Valentine Moulard-Leonard, 'The Sublime and the Intellectual Effort: The Imagination in Bergson and Kant', *Journal of the British Society for Phenomenology* 37, no. 2 (2006): 138–51; Matasaki Muramatsu, 'Les avatars de la "tension" dans le spiritualisme français', in *Considérations inactuelles: Bergson et la philosophie française du XIXe siècle*, eds. Shin Abiko, Hisashi Fujita, Yasuhiko Sugimura (New York: Georg Olms, 2017), 7–20; Anne Devarieux, 'La force de la volonté: Henri Bergson ou la "seconde vie" de l'effort biranien', in *Considerations inactuelles,* eds. Abiko, Fujia and Sugimura, 21–44.

3 Thibaud, *L'Effort*, 137–60.

4   Bergson, *Two Sources*, 188.
5   Gilles Deleuze, *Desert Islands and Other Texts, 1953–1974*, trans. Michael Taormina, ed. David Lapoujade (New York: Semiotext(e), 2004), 22–51; Gilles Deleuze, *Bergsonism*, trans. H. Tomlinson and B. Habberjam (New York: Zone, 1991).
6   Theodore Zeldin, *A History of French Passions*. Vol. II. *Politics & Anger* (Oxford: Oxford University Press, 1979), 880–1.
7   Xavier Bichat, *Physiological Researches on Life and Death*, trans. F. Gold (Washington, DC: University Publications of America, 1978); Elizabeth Williams, *The Physical and the Moral: Anthropology, Physiology, and Philosophical Medicine in France, 1750–1850* (Cambridge: Cambridge University Press, 1994); Michel Foucault, *The Birth of the Clinic*, trans. A. M. Sheridan (London: Routledge, 1989), 176–80. It should be pointed out, however, that the influence of Bichat was not received uncritically by Bergson, whose conceptualization of vitalism is distinct from that of the medical tradition. On Bergson's nuanced reception of Bichat, see Keith Ansell-Pearson, *Bergson: Thinking beyond the Human Condition* (London: Bloomsbury, 2018), 91–110. My thanks to Keith for reminding me of Bergson's complex relationship to medical vitalism.
8   Zeldin, *Politics & Anger*, 876. See also Guglielmo Ferrero, *Le Militarisme et la société moderne* (Paris: Stock, 1899); Paddy Griffith, *Military Thought in the French Army, 1815–51* (Manchester: Manchester University Press, 1989), 51–82.
9   Joan Tumblety, *Remaking the Male Body: Masculinity and the Use of Physical Culture in Interwar and Vichy France* (Oxford: Oxford University Press, 2012).
10 Spanneut, *Permanence du Stoïcisme*, 387.
11 Spanneut, *Permanence du Stoïcisme*, 380.
12 Spanneut, *Permanence du Stoïcisme*, 372.
13 Roger Gard, 'Introduction' to Alfred de Vigny, *Servitude and Grandeur of Arms*, trans. Roger Gard (London: Penguin, 1996), viii. See also Alfred de Vigny, *The Warrior's Life*, ed. and trans. Roger Gard (London: Penguin Books, 2013).
14 Spanneut, *Permanence du Stoïcisme*, 369–70; Marc Citoleux, *Alfred de Vigny: persistances classiques et affinités étrangères* (Paris: Champion, 1924), 495–546; Camilla H. Hay, 'The Basis and Character of Alfred De Vigny's Stoicism', *The Modern Language Review* 40, no. 4 (1945): 266–78.
15 Vigny, *Servitude and Grandeur*, 162.
16 Alfred de Vigny, *Œuvres*. Vol. II. *Prose* (Paris: Gallimard: 1948), 1326, 1000. Cited in Spanneut, *Permanence du Stoïcisme*, 346.
17 Kathleen Butler, *A History of French Literature: The Nineteenth Century and After* (New York: Russell, 1966), 299. Nietzsche's own sense of what the Stoic art of life represented, however, is more complex than the wider context of the 'cult of action

and energy' from which his ideas spring. See Ure, 'Nietzsche's Free Spirit Trilogy' and Ansell-Pearson, 'For Mortal Souls'.
18 Spanneut, *Permanence du Stoïcisme*, 369–70.
19 Bergson, *Two Sources*, 46–77. What follows builds on an earlier piece: Simone Kotva, 'The God of Effort', which studies the link between Bergson's mysticism and Stoicism. On Bergson's mysticism as a spiritual exercise and art of life more broadly, see Thibaud, *L'Effort*, 137–60 and passim; René Violette, *La spiritualité de Bergson* (Toulouse: Éditions Édouard Privat, 1968); Harvey Hill, 'Henri Bergson and Alfred Loisy: On Mysticism and the Religious Life', in *Modernists and Mystics*, ed. Talar, 104–35; Ansell-Pearson, *Bergson*, 153–72. For the *Two Sources*, see *Bergson et la religion: Nouvelles perspectives sur* Les Deux Sources de la morale et de la religion, ed. Ghislain Waterlot (Paris: Presses Universitaires de France, 2008).
20 Bergson, *Two Sources*, 46.
21 Bergson, *Two Sources*, 188.
22 Bergson, *Two Sources*, 188.
23 Bergson, *Two Sources*, 215.
24 Bergson, *Two Sources*, 275.
25 Henri Bergson, *The Creative Mind*, trans. Mabelle Anderson (New York: Philosophical Library, 1948), 232.
26 Cf. Simone Kotva, 'The Line of Resistance: Ravaisson and Bergson', *Journal of Religion and Literature* 49, no. 2 (2019): 228–39.
27 Nathalie Frieden-Markevitch, *La Philosophie de Bergson: aperçu sur un Stoïcisme inconscient* (Fribourg: Éditions universitaires, 1982); Vladimir Jankélévitch, *Bergson* (Paris: Presses Universitaires de France, 1959), 198, 182–200, 79.
28 Gilbert Murray, *The Stoic Philosophy: Conway Memorial Lecture* (New York: G. P. Putnam's Sons, 1915), 38.
29 Thomas Bénatouïl, 'Stoicism and Twentieth-Century French Philosophy', in *The Routledge Handbook of the Stoic Tradition*, ed. John Sellars (London: Routledge, 2016), 371.
30 Henri Bergson, 'Rapport sur le prix Bordin (8 Nov 1905)', in *Écrits philosophiques*, ed. Frédéric Worms (Paris: Presses universitaires de France, 2011), 295.
31 Henri Bergson, *Creative Evolution*, trans. Arthur Mitchell (London: Macmillan, 1911), 333.
32 Henri Hude and Françoise Vinel, 'Introduction', in Henri Bergson, *Cours IV: sur la philosophie grecque*, eds. Hude and Vinel (Paris: Presses Universitaires de France, 2000), 8.
33 Bergson, *Cours IV*, 130. See 'Cynisime et Stoïcisme', 115–36.
34 Bergson, *Cours IV*, 117–18.
35 Bergson, *Cours IV*, 136.

36 In 1884–5 Bergson had taught a survey course on Greek philosophy which also addressed Stoicism but crucially without mention of Ravaisson, whom it seems Bergson at that time had not read; consequently, the Stoics are accorded small attention. See Bergson, *Cours IV*, 147–52.
37 Hude and Vinel, 'Introduction,' in Bergson, *Cours*, 8.
38 Bergson, *Cours IV*, 131. When interpreting what Bergson says about the Stoic doctrine of effort or *tonos*, I found the following particularly useful: Thomas Bénatouïl, 'Force, fermeté, froid: la dimension physique de la vertu stoïcienne', *Philosophie antique* 5 (2005): 5–30; René Brouwer, *The Stoic Sage: The Early Stoics on Wisdom, Sagehood and Socrates* (Cambridge: Cambridge University Press, 2014), 51–91.
39 Bergson, *Cours IV*, 133.
40 Bergson, *Cours IV*, 118.
41 Bergson, *Cours IV*, 123.
42 Bergson, *Cours IV*, 131.
43 Bergson, *Cours IV*, 132.
44 Bergson, *Cours IV*, 134.
45 Bergson, *Cours IV*, 135–6.
46 Henri Bergson, *Time and Free Will: An Essay on the Immediate Data of Consciousness*, trans. F. L. Pogson (London: G. Allen, 1913 [3rd edn]), 13.
47 Bergson, *Time and Free Will*, 13.
48 Bergson, *The Creative Mind*, 243.
49 Bergson, *The Creative Mind*, 243.
50 Émile Bréhier, *La théorie des incorporels dans l'ancien Stoïcisme*, 9th edn (Paris: Vrin, 1997), 63.
51 Émile Bréhier, *The Hellenistic and Roman Age*, trans. Wade Baskin (Chicago: University of Chicago Press, 1969), 53.
52 Bréhier, *Hellenistic and Roman Age*, 53.
53 Léontine Zanta, *La renaissance du Stoïcisme au XVIe siècle* (Paris: Champion, 1914), 3.
54 The peculiarities of the French interpretation of Stoicism and its indebtedness to Bergson are discussed in an excellent article by John Sellars, 'Aiôn and Chronos: Deleuze and the Stoic Theory of Time', *Collapse* 3 (2007): 177–205.
55 Deleuze, *The Logic of Sense*, 149.
56 Joshua Ramey, *The Hermetic Deleuze: Philosophy and Spiritual Ordeal* (Durham: Duke University Press, 2012).
57 Bénatouïl, 'Stoicism and Twentieth-Century French Philosophy', 361.
58 Gustave Loisel cited in Spanneut, *Permanence du Stoïcisme*, 371.
59 Spanneut, *Permanence du Stoïcisme*, 372–9; Kotva, 'God of Effort', 419–20.
60 Sjövall, *Psychology of Tension*, 169–203; Gilbert Varet, 'Spiritualisme et philosophie réflexive', *Revue des sciences philosophiques et théologiques* 74, no. 1 (1990): 23–34;

Rolf Kühn, *Französische Religionsphilosophie und -phänomenologie*, 21–109; My thanks to Barnabas Aspray for sharing his insights on reflexive philosophy.

61 Jules Lagneau, 'Simples notes pour un programme d'union et d'action', in *Écrits de Jules Lagneau réunis par les soins de ses disciples* (Paris: Sandre, 2006), 121, 118.

62 Lagneau, *Écrits*, 121.

63 Gérard Monod, 'Pensée et action chez Jules Lagneau', *Revue de Métaphysique et de Morale* 57, no. 2 (1952): 117–48.

64 Alain (Émile Chartier), *La théorie de la connaissance des stoïciens*, ed. Louis Goubert (Paris: Presses universitaires de France, 1964), 60.

65 André Comte-Sponville, 'Alain entre Jardin et Portique', in *Une éducation philosophique*, ed. Comte-Sponville André (Paris: Presses Universitaires de France, 1998), 50. See also Bénatouïl, 'Stoicism and Twentieth-Century French Philosophy', 361–2.

66 Alain (Émile Chartier), *On Happiness*, trans. Robert D. Cottrell and Jane E. Cottrell (Evanston, IL: Northwestern University Press, 1989), 74 ('Hercules'). For Alain's concept of effort, see *Œuvres*. Vol. III. *Les Passions et la sagesse*, eds Georges Bénézé (Paris: Gallimard, 1960), 1168–91.

67 See for instance Alain, *The Gods*, trans. Richard Pevear (London: Quartet, 1988), 105.

68 The connection between Alain and Ravaisson is my own supposition. In fact, Alain does not discuss any commentators in his dissertation, and it is possible, of course, that he formulates a positive interpretation of *tonos* independently of reading Ravaisson or scholars influenced by Ravaisson (though this does seem unlikely, given Ravaisson's influence, which was considerable). Whatever the case, Alain's interpretation of 'effort' and 'tension' would have been mediated through the same late nineteenth-century culture of effort that influenced Bergson. Irrespective of whether Alain studied Ravaisson's *Essay on Stoicism*, then, his dissertation on the Stoics expresses perfectly the core tenets of the modern thought-world that produces the decisive shift in the philosophy of spiritual exercise that interests us here.

69 Alain, *La théorie*, 59.

70 Alain, *La théorie*, 60.

71 Alain, *La théorie*, 65–6.

72 Alain, *La théorie*, 69.

73 Alain (Émile Chartier), *Œuvres*. Vol. II. *Les Arts et les dieux*, ed. Georges Bénézé (Paris: Gallimard, 1958), 28.

74 Alain, *Les Arts et les dieux*, 30.

75 Alain, *Les Arts et les dieux*, 29.

76 Alain, *Les Arts et les dieux*, 31.

77 Lagneau, 'Simples Notes', 117. See also Alain, 'Souvenirs concernant Jules Lagneau' in *Les Passions et la sagesse*, 709–86.
78 Spanneut, *Permanence du Stoïcisme*, 366.
79 Alain, *La théorie*, 66, n. 1 (Editor's comment).
80 Thierry Leterre, *Alain, le premier intellectual* (Paris: Stock, 2006).
81 Alain, *Les Passions et la sagesse*, 1368.
82 André Maurois, *Alain* (Paris: Gallimard, 1950), 12.
83 Alain, *On Happiness*, 117.
84 Alain, *On Happiness*, 73.
85 Alain, *On Happiness*, 116.
86 Alain, *On Happiness*, 117.
87 Alain, *On Happiness*, 74.
88 See Seneca, *Hercules Oetaeus*.
89 Alain, *On Happiness*, 179.
90 Alain, *On Happiness*, 179.
91 Alain, *On Happiness*, 179, 178.
92 Alain, *On Happiness*, 179.
93 Alain, *On Happiness*, 50.
94 Alain, *On Happiness*, 50.
95 Alain, *On Happiness*, 52.
96 Alain (Émile Chartier), *Propos sur la religion* (Paris: Presses universitaires de France, 1938), 31–2. On Alain's religious philosophy, see Simone Pétrement, 'Sur la religion d'Alain: (avec quelques remarques concernant celle de Simone Weil)', *Revue de métaphysique et de morale* 60, no. 3 (1955): 306–30.
97 Alain, *Œuvres*. Vol. I. *Propos*, ed. Maurice Savin (Paris: Gallimard, 1956), 417–19.
98 Maurois, *Alain*, 125; Pétrement, 'Sur la religion d'Alain', 317.
99 Bénatouïl, 'Stoicism'.
100 Alain, *Les Passions et la sagesse*, 549. This foreword was omitted from the English translation.
101 Alain (Émile Chartier), *Mars: Or, the Truth about War*, trans. Doris Mudie and Elizabeth Hill (London: Jonathan Cape, 1930), 270.
102 Alain, *Mars*, 271–2.
103 Alain, *Mars*, 60.
104 Ronald F. Howell, 'The Philosopher Alain and French Classical Radicalism', *The Western Political Quarterly* 18, no. 3 (1965): 594–614.
105 Lago, 'Simone Weil and Nihilism', 111–38.
106 Nathalie Sarthou-Lajus, 'Du goût pour les stoïciens', *Études*, 410, no. 6 (2009): 775–86.

Chapter 5

1. Biran, *Écrits de jeunesse*, 94.
2. Fénelon, *Spiritual Writings*, 235–9; cf. Coleman, *Virtues of Abandon*.
3. Kolakowski, *God Owes Us Nothing*.
4. Biran, *Écrits de jeunesse*, 99.
5. Since Weil, the most significant theological critic of Descartes has been Jean-Luc Marion. See for instance *On Descartes' Metaphysical Prism: The Constitution and Limits of Onto-Theo-Logy in Cartesian Thought*, trans. Jeffrey Kosky (Chicago: University of Chicago Press, 1999). On Weil and Descartes, see Peter Winch, *Simone Weil: The 'Just Balance'* (Cambridge: Cambridge University Press, 1989), 5–17; Emmanuel Gabellieri, *Être et don: Simone Weil et la philosophie* (Louvain: Peeters, 2003), 54–82; Lissa McCullough, 'Weil's Phenomenology of the Body', *Comparative and Continental Philosophy* 4, no. 2 (2012): 195–218.
6. Simone Weil, 'Science and Perception in Descartes', in *Formative Writings, 1929–1941*, trans. Dorothy Tuck McFarland and Wilhelmina Van Ness (London: Routledge & Kegan Paul, 1987), 45.
7. Weil, *Formative Writings*, 55.
8. Weil, *Formative Writings*, 86.
9. Weil, *Formative Writings*, 78.
10. Weil, *Formative Writings*, 78.
11. Pieper, *Leisure*. On Weil's philosophy of work in the essay on Descartes, see McCullough, 'Weil's Phenomenology of the Body'; Gavin Flood, *The Ascetic Self: Subjectivity, Memory and Tradition* (Cambridge: Cambridge University Press, 2004), 37–63.
12. Weil, *Formative Writings*, 87.
13. Weil, *Formative Writings*, 62. It seems Weil has in mind Descartes, *Meditations*, 32–3 (AT VII, 47–8).
14. Weil, *Formative Writings*, 77. My reading of Weil as a thinker of the middle and of paradox, while it is presented in the context of Biran's method and as a late reinvention of spiritualist ideas, agrees in essentials with the view put forward by prominent Weil scholars such as Emmanuel Gabellieri and Lissa McCullough. See for instance Gabellieri, *Être et don*; Emmanuel Gabellieri, 'Reconstructing Platonism: The Trinitarian Metaxology of Simone Weil', trans. C. Bally and C. Callahan, in *The Christian Platonism of Simone Wei*, eds. J. Doering and E. Springstead (Notre Dame: University of Notre Dame Press, 2004), 133–58; Lissa McCullough, *The Religious Philosophy of Simone Weil: An Introduction* (London: I.B. Tauris, 2014), 13–50.
15. Biran, *Relationship between the Physical and the Moral*, 130–7; F. C. T. Moore, *The Psychology of Maine De Biran* (Oxford: Clarendon, 1970), 105f; Azouvi, 'Homo duplex'.

16 Weil, *Formative Writings*, 80.
17 Maine de Biran, *Mémoire sur la décomposition de la pensée*, 361.
18 Weil, *Waiting on God,* 42
19 The religious overtones of Weil's argument in *Science and Perception* are usually traced to the influence of Jules Lagneau, Alain's own teacher whose posthumous *De l'existence de Dieu* (Paris: Alcan, 1926) Alain had edited and, it seems, introduced to Weil. But the influence of Biran's own work should not be underestimated; the whole account of meditation resulting in the self-perception of a 'dual being' is taken straight out of Biran's Augustinian anthropology, and would have been familiar to Weil from the *Essai sur les fondements de la psychologie et sur ses rapports avec l'étude de la nature* (Essay on the foundations of psychology and on its relationships to the study of nature) (1811–12), a classic student text.
20 Weil, *Lectures on Philosophy,* 28
21 Weil, *Lectures on Philosophy,* 44.
22 Weil, *Lectures on Philosophy,* 44.
23 Weil, *Lectures on Philosophy,* 45.
24 Weil, *Lectures on Philosophy,* 45.
25 Weil, *Lectures on Philosophy,* 95.
26 Weil, *Lectures on Philosophy,* 97.
27 Weil, *Lectures on Philosophy,* 171.
28 Rowan Williams, 'The Necessary Non-Existence of God', in *Simone Weil's Philosophy of Culture: Readings Toward a Divine Humanity*, ed. R. H. Bell (Cambridge: Cambridge University Press, 1993), 52–77.
29 Weil, *Lectures on Philosophy,* 179. On Weil and Stoicism, see G. Kahn, 'Simone Weil et le Stoïcisme grec', *Cahiers Simone Weil* 5, no. 4 (1982): 270–84; Diogenes Allen and Eric Springstead, *Spirit, Nature, and Community: Issues in the Thought of Simone Weil* (Albany: State University of New York Press, 1994), 96–110.
30 See for instance Simone Weil, *First and Last Notebooks*, trans. Richard Rees (London: Oxford University Press, 1970), 22, and Weil, *Seventy Letters,* 82–7.
31 Weil, *Lectures on Philosophy,* 178.
32 Weil, *Lectures on Philosophy,* 179–80.
33 Weil, *Waiting on God,* 125–7.
34 Weil, *Waiting on God,* 126–7.
35 Weil, *Waiting on God,* 127.
36 Biran, *Journal* II, 416.
37 Weil, *Lectures on Philosophy,* 214.
38 Weil, *Lectures on Philosophy,* 214.
39 Weil, *Lectures on Philosophy,* 214.
40 Weil, *Lectures on Philosophy,* 215.
41 Weil, *Lectures on Philosophy,* 215.

42 Weil, *Lectures on Philosophy*, 215.
43 Biran, *Dernière philosophie: existence et anthropologie*, 323.
44 Weil, *Formative Writings*, 226.
45 Flood, *Ascetic Self*, 37–63.
46 Weil suffered for many years from a chronic sinus infection, the cause of violent headaches and nausea; she was also in the habit of refusing food and bodily comforts on account of others' suffering. Robert Burton connects Weil's willingness to increase her suffering to a widespread culture of vicarious suffering inspired by religious ideals. See Robert Burton, *Holy Tears, Holy Blood: Women, Catholicism, and the Culture of Suffering in France, 1840–1970* (Ithaca: Cornell University Press, 2004), 133–47.
47 This is what many commentators have wrestled with. In parsing the relationship between asceticism and suffering in Weil's philosophy, I have found the following particularly useful: David McLellan, *Simone Weil: Utopian Pessimist* (Houndsmills: Macmillan, 1989); Alexander Irwin, *Saints of the Impossible: Bataille, Weil, and the Politics of the Sacred* (Minneapolis: University of Minnesota Press, 2002); Flood, *Ascetic Self*, 37–63.
48 Weil, *Formative Writings*, 209.
49 Flood, *Ascetic Self*, 42.
50 Weil, *Formative Writings*, 196.
51 Weil, *Formative Writings*, 160
52 Weil, *Formative Writings*, 161.
53 Weil, *Formative Writings*, 163.
54 Weil, *Formative Writings*, 167.
55 Weil, *Formative Writings*, 171.
56 Weil, *Formative Writings*, 185.
57 Weil, *Formative Writings*, 187.
58 Weil, *Formative Writings*, 220.
59 Weil, *Formative Writings*, 223.
60 Weil, *Formative Writings*, 226.
61 Simone Weil, *The Need for Roots*, trans. Arthur Wills (London: Routledge, 2002), 94–5.
62 Simone Pétrement, *Simone Weil: A Life*, trans. R. Rosenthal (London: Mowbrays, 1977), 428.
63 Pétrement, *Simone Weil*, 446.
64 John of the Cross, *The Collected Works*, trans. Kieran Kavanaugh and Otilio Rodriguez (Washington, DC: Institute of Carmelite Studies, 1991), 692, 685 ('Living Flame of Love', 3.47, 3.32).
65 John of the Cross, *The Collected Works*, 87, 506–7 ('Sayings of Light and Love', 26; 'The Spiritual Canticle', 9. 6–7).

66 The following have been useful to me when studying Weil's concept of mystical attention: Joseph-Marie Perrin and Gustave Thibon, *Simone Weil as We Knew Her*, trans. Emma Crauford (London: Routledge & Kegan Paul, 1953), 51–64; Claire Wolfteich, 'Attention or Destruction: Simone Weil and the Paradox of the Eucharist', *The Journal of Religion* 81, no. 3 (2001): 359–76; Sharon Cameron, 'The Practice of Attention: Simone Weil's Performance of Impersonality', *Critical Inquiry* 29, no. 2 (2003): 216–52; Gabellieri, *Être et don*, 231–72; Vivienne Blackburn, *Dietrich Bonhoeffer and Simone Weil: A Study in Christian Responsiveness* (New York: P. Lang, 2004); Kuhn, *Leere und Aufmerksamkeit*; Lissa McCullough, 'Prayer and Incarnation: A Homiletic Reflection', in *The Phenomenology of Prayer*, eds. B. E. Benson and N. Wirzba (New York: Fordham University Press, 2005), 209–17; Philip Goodchild, 'Engaged Philosophy of Religion', *Journal for Cultural and Religious Theory* 12, no. 2 (2012): 52–68. The theme of this section is a theory of passive attention that evolved over many centuries in Catholic spirituality and which Weil encounters in the works of John of the Cross. I will be referring to passages from John's spiritual direction as they become relevant to Weil, but the interested reader may also find these modern presentations of John's tradition useful: Ludovic de Besse, *The Science of Prayer* (London: Burns Oates & Washbourne Ltd., 1925); Bede Frost, *The Art of Mental Prayer* (London: Philip Allan, 1935); Ruth Burrows, *Guidelines for Mystical Prayer* (Sheed and Ward: London, 1976), 118–40. The connection between John of the Cross' concept of passive attention and Weil's idea of 'waiting', though hinted at in numerous places, has not been explored at length (as far as I know) in the critical literature, and the comparisons introduced in this section are my own.

67 Weil, *Waiting on God*, 128. For the phrase *en hypomone*, which Weil translates as 'with endurance', see for instance Luke 8:15: 'But as for that in the good soil, these are the ones who, when they hear the word, hold it fast in an honest and good heart, and bear fruit with patient endurance.'

68 Bénatouïl, 'Stoicism and Twentieth-Century French Philosophy', 361–2.

69 Weil, *Waiting on God*, 43.

70 Weil, *Seventy Letters*, 140.

71 Weil, *Waiting on God*, 111.

72 Cf. McCullough, *Religious Philosophy of Simone Weil*, 233: 'There appears to be a contest in Weil's thought between her Platonic-Augustinian side and her Stoic side.'

73 Alain Paire (ed.), *Joë Bousquet dans les* Cahiers du Sud: *Anthologie* (Marseille: Rivages, 1981), 73–4. For this meeting between Weil and Bousquet, fascinating in its own right as a study in distinct performances of attention, see Édith de la Héronnière, *Joë Bousquet: une vie à corps perdu* (Paris: Albin Michel, 2006),178–89

74 Paire, *Joë Bousquet*, 74–5.

75 Paire, *Joë Bousquet*, 74. In one version of the story, this is the compassionate question that reveals the Knight to be the rightful inheritor of the Grail.

76 Weil, *Notebooks*, 630: 'Christ alone is able to ask a man '"What is it that torments thee?" … How many human beings are there whom I have neglected to ask "What is it that torments thee?" If all of them were to rise up one day, if Christ were to say: "I was suffering and you failed to ask me what it was that tormented me"'.
77 In *Parzifal* a king (Amfortas) suffering from an incurable wound guards the mysterious Grail, here not a cup or dish but a precious stone. In one of the lapidary oracles which the Grail produces on its surface, the stone has prophesied that the king will be healed only if a virtuous knight (Parzifal) arrives at the castle in which the Grail is kept and, without premeditation, recognizes its keeper's affliction, asking the 'Grail question': 'what is the nature of your distress?' See Wolfram von Eschenbach, *Parzifal*, trans. by C. Edwards (Oxford: Oxford University Press, 2006), 204 (para. 484). Parzifal's eventual recognition of Amfortas' affliction is what interests Weil. Cf. P. Boitani, 'Recognition: The Pain and Joy of Compassion', in *Recognition: The Poetics of Narrative: Interdisciplinary Studies on Anagnorisis*, eds. P. Kennedy and M. Lawrence (New York: Peter Lang, 2009), 213–27.
78 John of the Cross, *Collected Works*, 685 ('Living Flame of Love', 3.32).
79 Paire, *Joë Bousquet*, 74–5.
80 Gillian Rose gives a brilliant analysis of the discrepancy between Weil's aspiration that compassion should be always incognito, easy and effortless, and her failure to evidence such graceful behaviour in her own life. See Gillian Rose, *Judaism and Modernity: Philosophical Essays* (Oxford: Blackwell, 1993), 211–23. My own conclusions have been informed by reading Rose alongside Gabellieri, *Être et don*, 491–524, who does an admirable job of theorizing the 'incognito' in Weil's ethics.
81 Paire, *Joë Bousquet*, 77.
82 Paire, *Joë Bousquet*, 74.
83 Weil, *Waiting on God*, 22.
84 Weil, *Waiting on God*, 21.
85 Weil, *Waiting on God*, 56.
86 John of the Cross, *The Mystical Doctrine of St. John of the Cross*, ed. and trans. R. H. J. Steurt (London: Sheed & Ward, 1937), 35; cf. John of the Cross, *Collected Works*, 102 ('Ascent to Mount Carmel', 2.13.4).
87 Weil, *Waiting on God*, 57.
88 Weil, *Waiting on God*, 53.
89 Weil, *The Need for Roots*, 248.
90 Weil, *On Science, Necessity and the Love of God* (London: Oxford University Press, 1968), 168. See Maurice Schumann, 'Henri Bergson et Simone Weil', *Revue des deux mondes* 1993: 193–203; Gabellieri, *Être et don*, 435–40. Both Schumann and Gabellieri suggest ways in which Weil and Bergson could be reconciled; my interpretation, while not gainsaying such reconciliation, is interested in determining the conditions that made Weil's dislike of Bergson (whether justified or not) meaningful.

91 Weil, *Waiting on God*, 55.
92 Weil, *Waiting on God*, 55.
93 Weil, *Waiting on God*, 58.
94 Weil, *Waiting on God*, 58.
95 Weil, *Waiting on God*, 58.
96 Weil, *Waiting on God*, 59.
97 Weil, *Waiting on God*, 59.
98 Weil, *Waiting on God*, 53.
99 John of the Cross, *Collected Works*, 686 ('Living Flame of Love' 3.34).
100 Jacques-Bénigne Bossuet, 'Short and Simple Method of Prayer', in *Letters of Spiritual Direction*, trans. Geoffrey Webb and Adrian Walker (London: A. R. Mowbray & Co., 1958), 42.
101 Weil, *Science, Necessity, and the Love of God*, 151.
102 Simone Weil, *Notebooks*, trans. A. Wills (London: Routledge & Kegan Paul), 411, 406.
103 Susan Sontag, 'Simone Weil', *New York Review of Books*, 1 February 1963. Web. 11 October 2014. Available online: http://www.nybooks.com/articles/archives/1963/feb/01/simone-weil/?insrc=toc/ (accessed 25 July 2019); Rose, *Judaism and Modernity*, 211-23; George Steiner, *No Passion Spent: Essays 1978-1996* (London: Faber, 1996), 171-9.
104 Weil, *Seventy Letters*, 144. There are numerous accounts of Weil's final months; two of the more authoritative being: Jacques Cabaud, *Simone Weil: A Fellowship in Love* (London: Harvill, 1964), 295-354; Sylvie Weil, *At Home with André and Simone Weil*, trans. B. Ivry (Evanston: Northwestern University Press, 2010).
105 Flood, *Ascetic Self*, 59.
106 Flood, *Ascetic Self*, 49.
107 Flood, *Ascetic Self*, 247.
108 McCullough, *Religious Philosophy of Simone Weil*, 37.
109 McCullough, *Religious Philosophy of Simone Weil*, 218.
110 McCullough, *Religious Philosophy of Simone Weil*, 215.
111 McCullough, *Religious Philosophy of Simone Weil*, 215.
112 The exceptions being Gabellieri and Rolf Kühn, who both discuss Weil in relation to spiritualism and 'reflexive philosophy'. Gabellieri, *Être et don*, 71-82; Kühn, *Französische Reflexions- und Geistesphilosophie: Profile und Analyse* (Frankfurt am Main: Hain, 1993), 126-56; Kühn, *Französische Religionsphilosophie und -phänomenologie*, 110-40.
113 McCullough, *Religious Philosophy of Simone Weil*, 220.
114 But see Schumann, 'Bergson and Weil', and Gabellieri, *Être et don*, 435-40.
115 Hadot, *Philosophy as a Way of Life*, 86-7.
116 Hadot, *Philosophy as a Way of Life*, 84. Hadot refers to Ravaisson's *Essai sur la Métaphysique d'Aristote*.

117 Hadot, *Philosophy as a Way of Life*, 278.
118 Hadot, *Philosophy as a Way of Life*, 108.
119 Hadot, *Philosophy as a Way of Life*, 253–4.
120 Foucault, *The Use of Pleasure*, 3–13.
121 Cf. Foucault, *Technologies of the Self*, 16–51.
122 Michel Foucault, *The History of Sexuality*. Vol. III. *The Care of the Self*, trans. Robert Hurley (New York: Vintage, 1986), 43.
123 Hadot, *Philosophy as a Way of Life*, 211.
124 On Hadot as critic of materialism and of secular normativity, see Michael Chase, 'Observations on Pierre Hadot's Conception of Philosophy as a Way of Life', in *Philosophy as a Way of Life: Ancients and Moderns – Essays in Honour of Pierre Hadot*, eds. Michael Chase, Stephen R. L. Clark and Michael McGhee (London: Wiley, 2013), 263–86.
125 Hadot, *Philosophy as a Way of Life*, 238–50.
126 Hadot, *Philosophy as a Way of Life*, 242.
127 Hadot, *Philosophy as a Way of Life*, 88.
128 Hadot, *Plotinus*, 71, 82.
129 Hadot, *Philosophy as a Way of Life*, 82. The comparison between Ignatius and ancient Greek *askesis* was suggested to Hadot by Paul Rabbow, *Seelenführung: Methodik der Exerzitien in der Antike* (München: Kösel-Verlag, 1954).
130 Alexander Nehamas, *The Art of Living* (Berkeley: University of California Press, 1998), 167, 164.
131 Murdoch, *Sovereignty of Good*, 4.
132 Murdoch, *Sovereignty of Good*, 8.
133 Murdoch, *Sovereignty of Good*, 7.
134 Murdoch, *Sovereignty of Good*, 7.
135 Murdoch, *Sovereignty of Good*, 9
136 Murdoch, *Sovereignty of Good*, 39.
137 Murdoch, *Sovereignty of Good*, 17–23.
138 Murdoch, *Sovereignty of Good*, 40.
139 Murdoch, *Sovereignty of Good*, 43. On Murdoch and Weil, see Soskice, *Kindness of God*, 17–34.
140 Murdoch, *Sovereignty of Good*, 67.
141 Murdoch, *Sovereignty of Good*, 64.

Chapter 6

1 Bernard M. Folz, *The Noetics of Nature: Environmental Philosophy and the Holy Beauty of the Visible* (New York: Fordham University Press, 2013). Cf. Simone

Kotva, 'Attention in the Anthropocene: On the Spiritual Exercises of Any Future Science', in *Political Geology: Active Stratigraphies and the Making of Life*, eds. Amy Donovan and Adam Bobbette (London: Palgrave Macmillan, 2018), 239–61. What I say below relates to this work and a recent collaboration with Alice Tarbuck on spiritual exercise, philosophy and ecology: Simone Kotva and Alice Tarbuck, 'The non-Secular Pilgrimage: Walking and Looking in Ken Cockburn and Alec Finlay's *The Road North*', *Critical Survey* 29, no. 1 (2017): 33–52.

2 Thomas Merton, 'Reflections on the Character and Genius of Fénelon', in *Fénelon: Letters*, ed. and trans. John McEwan (London: Harvill Press, 1963), 9–30.

3 Merton, *Mystics and Zen Masters*, 91–112.

4 Jane Bennett, *Vibrant Matter: A Political Ecology of Things* (Durham: Duke University Press, 2010), 114.

5 Bennett, *Vibrant Matter*, 115.

6 Bennett, *Vibrant Matter*, 115.

7 Bennett, *Vibrant Matter*, 116.

8 Bennett, *Vibrant Matter*, 122.

9 Sallie McFague, *The Body of God: An Ecological Theology* (London: SCM Press, 1993), 49–55; Catherine Keller, *Clouds of the Impossible: Negative Theology and Planetary Entanglement* (New York: Columbia University Press, 2015).

10 Isabelle Stengers, *Another Science Is Possible: Manifesto for a Slow Science*, trans. Stephen Muecke (Cambridge: Polity, 2018), 34–6, 42–3.

11 Isabelle Stengers and Philippe Pignarre, *Capitalist Sorcery: Breaking the Spell*, trans. Andrew Goffey (Houndmills: Palgrave Macmillan, 2011), 138, 145.

12 Isabelle Stengers and Martin Savransky, 'Relearning the Art of Paying Attention: A Conversation', *SubStance* 47, no. 1 (2018): 136. Cf. Isabelle Stengers, *In Catastrophic Times: Resisting the Coming Barbarism*, trans. Andrew Goffey (Lüneburg: Open Humanities Press, 2015), 61–8.

13 Stengers and Savransky, 'Relearning the Art of Paying Attention', 136.

14 John of the Cross, *Collected Works*, 690 ('Living Flame of Love' 3.43).

15 Stengers, *Another Science Is Possible*, 57.

Bibliography

Adam, Antoine. *Sur le problème religieux dans la première moitié du XVIIe siècle.* Oxford: Clarendon Press, 1959.
Agamben, Giorgio. *Potentialities.* Stanford, CA: Stanford University Press, 2000.
Alain (Émile Chartier). *Œuvres.* Vol. I. *Propos*, edited by Maurice Savin. Paris : Gallimard, 1956.
Alain (Émile Chartier). *Œuvres.* Vol. II. *Les Arts et les dieux*, edited by Georges Bénézé. Paris: Gallimard, 1958.
Alain (Émile Chartier). *Œuvres.* Vol. III. *Les Passions et la sagesse*, edited by Georges Bénézé. Paris: Gallimard, 1960.
Alain (Émile Chartier). *Mars: Or, the Truth about War*, translated by Doris Mudie and Elizabeth Hill. London: Jonathan Cape, 1930.
Alain (Émile Chartier). *La théorie de la connaissance des stoïciens*, edited by Louis Goubert. Paris: Presses universitaires de France, 1964.
Alain (Émile Chartier). *The Gods*, translated by Richard Pevear. London: Quartet, 1988.
Alain (Émile Chartier). *On Happiness*, translated by Robert D. Cottrell and Jane E. Cottrell. Evanston, IL: Northwestern University Press, 1989.
Allen, D. and E. Springstead. *Spirit, Nature, and Community: Issues in the Thought of Simone Weil.* Albany: State University of New York Press, 1994.
Angers, Julien-Eymard d'. *Récherches sur le Stoïcisme aux XVIe et XVIIe siècles.* New York: G. Olms, 1976.
Ansell-Pearson, Keith. *Bergson: Thinking beyond the Human Condition.* London: Bloomsbury, 2018.
Ansell, Pearson: Keith Ansell-Pearson, 'For Mortal Souls: Philosophy and Therapeia in Nietzsche's Dawn'. *Royal Institute of Philosophy Supplement* 66 (2010): 137–63.
Augustine of Hippo. *Confessions.* 2 Vols., translated by William Watts. Cambridge, MA: Harvard University Press, 1912.
Augustine of Hippo. *City of God against the Pagans*, translated by R. W. Dyson. Cambridge: Cambridge University Press, 1998.
Azouvi, François. 'Homo duplex', *Gesnerus* 42, nos. 3–4 (1984): 229–44.
Azouvi, François. *Maine de Biran: la science de l'homme.* Paris: Vrin, 1995.
Baertschi, Bernard. *L'Ontologie de Maine de Biran.* Fribourg: Éditions universitaires, 1982.
Bellantone, Andrea. 'Ravaisson: le "champ abandonné de la métaphysique"'. *Cahiers philosophiques* 129, no. 2 (2012): 5–21.
Bénatouïl, Thomas. 'Force, fermeté et froid: la dimension physique de la vertu stoïcienne'. *Philosophie Antique* 5 (2005): 5–30.

Bénatouïl, Thomas. 'Stoicism and Twentieth-Century French Philosophy'. In *The Routledge Handbook of the Stoic Tradition*, edited by John Sellars, 360–73. London: Routledge, 2016.

Bennett, Jane. *Vibrant Matter: A Political Ecology of Things*. Durham: Duke University Press, 2010.

Bergson, Henri. *Time and Free Will: Essay on the Immediate Data of Consciousness*, translated by F. L. Pogson. London: George Allen & Unwin, 1910.

Bergson, Henri. *Creative Evolution*, translated by Arthur Mitchell. New York: Henry Holt, 1911.

Bergson, Henri. *Mind-energy: Lectures and Essays*, translated by Herbert Wildon Carr. New York: H. Holt, 1920.

Bergson, Henri. *The Two Sources of Morality and Religion*, translated by R. A. Audra and C. Brereton with W. H. Carter. London: Macmillan & Co., 1935.

Bergson, Henri. *The Creative Mind*, translated by Mabelle Anderson. New York: Philosophical Library, 1948.

Bergson, Henri. *Cours IV: Cours sur la philosophie grecque*, edited by Henri Hude and Françoise Vinel. Paris: Presses universitaires de France, 2000.

Bergson, Henri. *Écrits philosophiques*. Paris: Presses universitaires de France, 2011.

Bertrand, Alexis. *Philosophie de l'effort et les doctrines contemporaines*. Paris: Alcan, 1889.

Besse, Ludovic de. *The Science of Prayer*. London : Burns Oates & Washbourne Ltd., 1925.

Bichat, Xavier. *Physiological Researches on Life and Death*, translated by F. Gold. Washington, DC: University Publications of America, 1978.

Biran, Maine de. *Nouvelles considérations sur les rapports du physique et du moral de l'homme*, edited by Victor Cousin. Paris: Ladrange, 1834.

Biran, Maine de. *Journal*. Vol. I, edited by Henri Gouhier. Neuchatel: Éditions de la Baconnière, 1954.

Biran, Maine de. *Journal*. Vol. II, edited by Henri Gouhier. Neuchatel: Éditions de la Baconnière, 1955.

Biran, Maine de. *Journal*. Vol. III, edited by Henri Gouhier. Neuchatel: Éditions de la Baconnière, 1957.

Biran, Maine de. *Œuvres*. Vol. I. *Écrits de jeunesse*, edited by Bernard Baertschi. Paris: Vrin, 1998.

Biran, Maine de. *Œuvres*. Vol III. *Mémoire sur la décomposition de la pensée*, edited by François Azouvi. Paris: Vrin, 2000.

Biran, Maine de. *Œuvres*. Vol. IX. *Nouvelles considérations sur les rapports du physique et du moral de l'homme,*. edited by Bérnard Baertschi. Paris: Vrin, 1990.

Biran, Maine de. *Œuvres*. Vol. X-2. *Dernière philosophie: existence et anthropologie*, edited by Bernard Baertschi. Paris: Vrin, 1989.

Biran, Maine de. *The Influence of Habit on the Faculty of Thinking*, translated by M. Donaldson Boehm. London: Baillière, Tindall & Cox, 1920.

Biran, Maine de. *The Relationship between the Physical and the Moral in Man*, translated by Darian Meacham and Joseph Spadola. London: Bloomsbury, 2016.

Blackburn, Vivienne. *Dietrich Bonhoeffer and Simone Weil: A Study in Christian Responsiveness*. New York: Peter Lang, 2004.

Boas, George. *French Philosophies of the Romantic Period*. Baltimore: The Johns Hopkins Press, 1925.

Boitani, P. 'Recognition: The Pain and Joy of Compassion'. In *Recognition: The Poetics of Narrative: Interdisciplinary Studies on Anagnorisis*, edited by P. Kennedy and M. Lawrence, 213–27. New York: Peter Lang, 2009.

Bonnet, Charles. *Essai analytique sur les facultés de l'âme*. Copenhagen/Geneva: Philibert, 1775.

Botton, Alain de. *The Consolations of Philosophy*. London: Hamish Hamilton, 2000.

Botton, Alain de. *Religion for Atheists: A Non-Believer's Guide to the Uses of Religion*. London: Penguin, 2013.

Bossuet, Jacques-Bénigne. *Letters of Spiritual Direction*, translated by Geoffrey Webb and Adrian Walker. London: A. R. Mowbray & Co., 1958.

Bouwsma, William J. *A Usable Past: Essays in European Cultural History*. Berkeley: University of California Press, 1990.

Bréhier, Émile. *Histoire de la philosophie*. Vol. I. *L'Antiquité et le Moyen âge*. Paris: Alcan, 1928.

Bréhier, Émile. *The Hellenistic and Roman Age*, translated by Wade Baskin. Chicago: University of Chicago Press, 1969.

Bréhier, Émile. *La théorie des incorporels dans l'ancien Stoïcisme*. 9th edn. Paris: Vrin, 1997.

Brooke, Christopher. *Philosophic Pride: Stoicism and Political Thought from Lipsius to Rousseau*. Princeton: Princeton University Press, 2012.

Brouwer, René. *The Stoic Sage: The Early Stoics on Wisdom, Sagehood and Socrates*. Cambridge: Cambridge University Press, 2014.

Brown, Eric. 'Politics and Society'. In *The Cambridge Companion to Epicureanism*, edited by James Warren, 179–98. Cambridge: Cambridge University Press, 2009.

Burrows, Ruth. *Guidelines for Mystical Prayer*. London: Sheed and Ward, 1976.

Burson, Jeffrey. *The Rise and Fall of the Theological Enlightenment: Jean-Martin de Prades and Ideological Polarisation in Eighteenth-Century France*. South Bend: Notre Dame University Press, 2010.

Burton, Richard. *Holy Tears, Holy Blood: Women, Catholicism, and the Culture of Suffering in France, 1840–1970*. Ithaca: Cornell University Press, 2004.

Butler, Kathleen. *A History of French Literature: The Nineteenth Century and After*. New York: Russell, 1966.

Cabaud, Jacques. *Simone Weil: A Fellowship in Love*. London: Harvill, 1964.

Cabaud-Meaney, Marie. *Simone Weil's Apologetic Use of Literature: Her Christological Interpretation of Ancient Greek Texts*. Oxford: Oxford University Press, 2007.

Cameron, Sharon. 'The Practice of Attention: Simone Weil's Performance of Impersonality', *Critical Inquiry* 29, no. 2 (2003): 216–52.

Caputo, John D. *The Weakness of God: A Theology of the Event*. Bloomington: Indiana University Press, 2006.
Carlisle, Clare. 'Between Freedom and Necessity: Ravaisson on Habit and the Moral Life'. In *A History of Habit: From Aristotle to Bourdieu*, edited by J. Bell, A. Hutchinson and T. Sparrow, 153–76. Lanham: Lexington, 2013.
Carlisle, Clare. *On Habit*. London: Routledge, 2014.
Carlyle, Thomas. *On Heroes, Hero-Worship and the Heroic in History*. London: James Fraser, 1841.
Cazeneuve, Jean. *Ravaisson et les médecins animistes et vitalistes*. Paris: Presses universitaires de France, 1958.
Certeau, Michel de. *The Mystic Fable*. Vol. I. *The Sixteenth and Seventeenth Centuries*, translated by Michael B. Smith. Chicago: Chicago University Press, 1992.
Chase, M., S. Clark and M. McGhee (eds). *Philosophy as a Way of Life: Ancient and Modern. Essays in Honour of Pierre Hadot*. Wiley: Blackwell, 2013.
Chevalier, Jacques. *Histoire de la pensée*. Vol. IV. *La pensée moderne de Hegel à Bergson*. Paris: Flammarion, 1966.
Citoleux, Marc. *Alfred de Vigny: persistances classiques et affinités étrangères*. Paris: Champion, 1924.
Coleman, Charly. *The Virtues of Abandon: An Anti-Individualist History of the French Enlightenment*. Stanford: Stanford University Press, 2014.
Comte-Sponville, André. 'Alain entre Jardin et Portique'. In *Une éducation philosophique*, edited by André Comte-Sponville, 270–86. Paris: Presses universitaires de France, 1998.
Condillac, Étienne Bonnot de. *Treatise on the Sensations*, translated by Geraldine Carr. Los Angeles: University of Southern California Press, 1930.
Copleston, Frederick. *A History of Philosophy*. Vol. IX. *Nineteenth-Century French Philosophy*. London: Continuum, 2003 [1975].
Cousin, Victor. 'Préface de l'éditeur'. In *Nouvelles considérations sur les rapports du physique et du moral de l'homme*, edited by Maine de Biran, Victor Cousin, i–xlii. Paris: Ladrange, 1834.
Cousin, Victor. *Elements of Psychology*, translated by C. S. Henry. 3rd edn. New York: Dayton and Saxton, 1842.
Cousin, Victor. 'Du mysticisme'. *Revue des deux mondes* 11, no. 3 (1845): 469–86.
Cousin, Victor. *Fragments de philosophie cartésienne*. Paris: Charpentier, 1845.
Cousin, Victor. *Lectures on the True, the Beautiful, and the Good*, translated by O. W. Wight. 3rd edn. Edinburgh: T & T Clark, D. Appleton & co, 1854.
Damiron, Jean-Philibert. *Essai sur l'histoire de la philosophie en France au XIXe siècle*. Paris: Hachette, 1834.
Delbos, Victor. *Figures et doctrines de philosophes*. Paris: Plon, 1918.
Deleuze, Gilles. *Bergsonism*, translated by H. Tomlinson and B. Habberjam. New York: Zone, 1991.

Deleuze, Gilles. *Essays Critical and Clinical*, translated by Daniel W. Smith and Michael A. Greco. Minneapolis: University of Minnesota Press, 1997.

Deleuze, Gilles. *Desert Islands and Other Texts 1953–1974*, translated by M. Taormina. New York: Semiotext(e), 2004.

Deleuze, Gilles. *The Logic of Sense*, translated by M. Lester with C. Stivale. London: Continuum, 2004.

Deleuze, Gilles. *Pure Immanence: Essays on a Life*, translated by Anne Boyman. New York: Zone, 2005.

Derrida, Jacques. *Du droit a la philosophie*. Paris: Galilée, 1990.

Descartes, René. *Meditations on First Philosophy*, translated by John Cottingham. Cambridge: Cambridge University Press, 1996.

Devarieux, Anne. 'La force de la volonté: Henri Bergson ou la "seconde vie" de l'effort biranien'. In *Considérations inactuelles: Bergson et la philosophie française du XIXe siècle*, edited by Hisashi Fujita Abiko and Yasuhiko Sugimura, 21–44. New York: Georg Olms, 2017.

Dornier, Carole. 'L'écriture de la citadelle intérieure ou la a thérapeutique de l'âme du promeneur solitaire'. *Annales de la société Jean-Jacques Rousseau* 48 (2008): 105–24.

Dunham, Jeremy. 'A Universal and Absolute Spiritualism, Maine de Biran's Leibniz'. In Maine de Biran, *The Relationship between the Physical and the Moral in Man*, translated and edited by Darian Meacham and Joseph Spadola, 157–92. London: Bloomsbury, 2016.

Epictetus. *The Discourses as Reported by Arrian, the Manual, and Fragments*. 2 Vols., translated by W. A. Oldfather. London: Heinemann, 1928.

Eschenbach, Wolfram von. *Parzifal*, translated by C. Edwards. Oxford: Oxford University Press, 2006.

Falke, C. *The Phenomenology of Love and Reading*. London: Bloomsbury, 2016.

Fénelon, François. *A Demonstration of the Existence of God, Deduced from the Knowledge of Nature*, translated by Samuel Boyse. London: John Murray, 1796.

Fénelon, François. *Œuvres*. Vol. II. Paris: Tenré & Boiste, 1822.

Fénelon, François. *Œuvres*. Vol. II. Paris: Lefevre, 1835.

Fénelon, François. *Selections from the Writings of Fénelon*, translated and edited by Mrs Follen. Boston: Samuel G. Simpkins, 1844.

Fénelon, François. *Spiritual Writings*, translated by Chad Helms. New York: Paulist Press, 2006.

Fénelon, François. *The Complete Fénelon*, edited and translated by Robert J. Edmonson and Hal M. Helms. Brewster, MA: Paraclete Press, 2008.

Ferrero, Guglielmo. *Le Militarisme et la société moderne*. Paris: Stock, 1899.

Festugière, André-Jean. *Epicurus and His Gods*, translated by C. W. Chilton. Cambridge, Massachusetts: Harvard University Press, 1956.

Flood, Gavin. *The Ascetic Self: Subjectivity, Memory and Tradition*. Cambridge: Cambridge University Press, 2004.

Folz, Bernard M. *The Noetics of Nature: Environmental Philosophy and the Holy Beauty of the Visible*. New York: Fordham University Press, 2013.

Foucault, Michel. *The Birth of the Clinic*, translated by A. M. Sheridan. London: Tavistock, 1973.

Foucault. Michel *The History of Sexuality*. Vol. II. *The Use of Pleasure*, translated by Robert Hurley. New York: Random House, 1985.

Foucault. Michel. *The History of Sexuality*. Vol. III. *The Care of the Self*, translated by Robert Hurley. New York: Random House, 1986.

Foucault, Michel. 'Technologies of the Self'. In *Technologies of the Self: A Seminar with Michel Foucault*, edited by L. Martin, H. Gutman and P. Hutton, 16–50. London: Tavistock, 1988.

Foucher, Louis. *La philosophie catholique en France au XIXe siècle, avant la renaissance thomiste et dans son rapport avec elle (1800-1880)*. Paris: Vrin, 1955.

Fouillée, Alfred. 'La Morale de la Beauté et de l'Amour, selon le mysticisme contemporain', *Revue des deux mondes* 52 (1882): 401–35.

Frazer, James. *The Golden Bough: A Study in Magic and Religion*, edited by Abridged. London: Macmillan and Co., 1922.

Frieden-Markevitch, Nathalie. *La Philosophie de Bergson: aperçu sur un Stoïcisme inconscient*. Fribourg: Éditions universitaires, 1982.

Frost, Bede. *The Art of Mental Prayer*. London: Philip Allan, 1935.

Gabellieri, Emmanuel. *Être et don: Simone Weil et la philosophie*. Louvain: Peeters, 2003.

Gabellieri, Emmanuel. 'Reconstructing Platonism: The Trinitarian Metaxology of Simone Weil', translated by C. Bally and C. Callahan. In *The Christian Platonism of Simone Wei*, edited by J. Doering and E. Springstead, 133–58. Notre Dame: University of Notre Dame Press, 2004.

Galinsky, G. Karl. *The Herakles Theme*. Oxford: Basil Blackwell, 1972.

Ganeri, Jonardan. *Attention, Not Self*. Oxford: Oxford University Press, 2017.

Goodchild, Philip. 'Engaged Philosophy of Religion'. *Journal for Cultural and Religious Theory* 12, no. 2 (2012): 52–68.

Goodchild, Philip. 'Thinking and Life: On Philosophy as Spiritual Exercise'. In *Intensities: Philosophy, Religion, and the Affirmation of Life*, edited by K. S. Moody and S. Shakespeare, 165–76. Farnham: Ashgate, 2012.

Goodchild, Philip (ed.). *On Philosophy as a Spiritual Exercise: A Symposium*. Basingstoke: Palgrave Macmillan, 2013.

Gouhier, Henri. *Les conversions de Maine de Biran*. Paris: Vrin, 1948.

Gouhier, Henri. *Les méditations métaphysiques de Jean-Jacques Rousseau*. Paris: Vrin, 1970.

Gouhier, Henri. *Fénelon philosophe*. Paris Vrin, 1977.

Gouhier, Henri. 'Félix Ravaisson'. *Les études philosophiques* 4 (1984): 433–5.

Gould, Stephen Jay. *The Mismeasure of Man*. London: W. W. Norton, 1981.

Gourinat, J.-B. 'La disparition et la reconstitution du Stoïcisme: éléments pour une histoire'. In *Les Stoïciens*, edited by G. R. Dherbey and J.-B. Gourinat, 13–28. Paris: Vrin, 2005.

Griffith, Paddy. *Military Thought in the French Army, 1815–51*. Manchester: Manchester University Press, 1989.
Gusdorf, Georges. *La découverte de soi*. Paris: Presses universitaires de France, 1948.
Haakonssen, Knud. 'The History of Eighteenth-Century Philosophy: History or Philosophy?'. In *The Cambridge History of Eighteenth-Century Philosophy*, edited by Knud Haakonssen, 2–25. Cambridge: Cambridge University Press, 2011.
Hadot, Pierre. *Philosophy as a Way of Life: Spiritual Exercises from Socrates to Foucault*, edited by A. I. Davison and translated by Michael Chase. Oxford: Blackwell, 1995.
Hadot, Pierre. *Plotinus, or the Simplicity of Vision*. Chicago: University of Chicago Press, 1993.
Hartle, Anne. 'Augustine and Rousseau: Narrative and Self-Knowledge in the Two Confessions'. In *The Augustinian Tradition*, edited by Gareth B. Mathews, 263–85. Berkeley: University of California Press, 1999.
Hatfield, Gary. 'The Senses and the Fleshless Eye: The *Meditations* as Cognitive Exercises'. In *Essays on Descartes' Meditations*, edited by Amélie Oksenberg Rorty, 45–79. Berkeley: University of California Press, 1986.
Hay, Camilla H. 'The Basis and Character of Alfred De Vigny's Stoicism'. *The Modern Language Review* 40, no. 4 (1945): 266–78.
Henry, Michel. *Philosophy and Phenomenology of the Body*, translated by Girard Etzkorn. The Hague: Nijhoff, 1975.
Héronnière, Édith de la. *Joë Bousquet: une vie à corps perdu*. Paris: Albin Michel, 2006.
Hill, Harvey. 'Henri Bergson and Alfred Loisy: On Mysticism and the Religious Life'. In *Modernists and Mystics*, edited by C. Talar, 104–35. Washington, DC: Catholic University of America Press, 2009.
Howell, Ronald F. 'The Philosopher Alain and French Classical Radicalism'. *The Western Political Quarterly* 18, no. 3 (1965): 594–614.
Hughes, John. *The End of Work: Theological Critiques of Capitalism*. Oxford: Blackwell, 2007.
Hunter, Ian. 'Spirituality and Philosophy in Post-Structuralist Theory', *History of European Ideas* 35, no. 2 (2008): 265–75.
Huxley, Aldous. *Themes and Variations*. London: Chatto and Windus, 1954.
Ierodiakonou, Katerina (ed.). *Topics in Stoic Philosophy*. Oxford: Oxford University Press, 1999.
Ignatius of Loyola. *The Spiritual Exercises of St. Ignatius: A Literal Translation and Contemporary Reading*, translated by David L. Fleming. St. Louis: The Institute of Jesuit Studies, 1978.
Inglis, Brian. *The Unknown Guest: The Mystery of Intuition*. London: Chatto and Windus, 1987.
Irwin, Alexander. *Saints of the Impossible: Bataille, Weil, and the Politics of the Sacred*. Minneapolis: University of Minnesota Press, 2002.
Jammer, M. *Concepts of Force: A Study in the Foundations of Dynamics*. Cambridge, MA: Harvard University Press, 1957.

Janet, Paul. 'Le spiritualisme français au XIXe siècle', *Revue des deux mondes* 75 (1868): 353–85.

Janet, Paul. *Les maîtres de la pensée moderne*. Paris: Calmann Lévy, 1883.

Janicaud, Dominique. *Ravaisson et la métaphysique: une génealogie du spiritualisme français*. 2nd ed. Paris: Vrin, 1997.

Janicaud, Dominique. *Phenomenology 'Wide Open': After the French Debate*, translated by Charles Cabral. New York: Fordham University Press, 2005.

Jankélévitch, Vladimir. *Bergson*. Paris: Presses universitaires de France, 1959.

John of the Cross. *The Mystical Doctrine of St. John of the Cross*, edited and translated by R. H. J. Steurt. London: Sheed & Ward, 1937.

John of the Cross. *The Collected Words*, translated by Kieran Kavanaugh and Otilio Rodriguez. Washington, DC: Institute of Carmelite Studies, 1991.

Jones, P. Mansell. *French Introspectives: From Montaigne to André Gide*. Cambridge: Cambridge University Press, 1937.

Kahn, Gilbert. 'Simone Weil et le Stoïcisme grec'. *Cahiers Simone Weil* 5, no. 4 (1982): 270–84.

Kant, Immanuel. *Metaphysics of Morals*, translated by Mary Gregor. Cambridge: Cambridge University Press, 1991.

Kant, Immanuel. 'On a Newly Arisen Superior Tone in Philosophy'. In *Raising the Tone of Philosophy: Late Essays by Immanuel Kant, Transformative Critique by Jacques Derrida*, edited and translated by Peter Fenves, 51–81. Baltimore, Maryland: Johns-Hopkins University Press, 1993.

Keller, Catherine. *Clouds of the Impossible: Negative Theology and Planetary Entanglement*. New York: Columbia University Press, 2015.

Kolakowski, Lezsek. *God Owes Us Nothing: A Brief Remark on Pascal's Religion and on the Spirit of Jansenism*. Chicago, University of Chicago Press, 1995.

Kotva, Simone. 'The God of Effort: Henri Bergson and the Stoicism of Modernity', *Modern Theology* 32 (2016): 397–420.

Kotva, Simone. 'Attention in the Anthropocene: On the Spiritual Exercises of Any Future Science'. In *Political Geology: Active Stratigraphies and the Making of Life*, edited by Amy Donovan and Adam Bobbette, 239–61. London: Palgrave Macmillan, 2018.

Kotva, Simone. 'The Line of Resistance: Ravaisson and Bergson', *Journal of Religion and Literature* 49, no. 2 (2019): 228–39.

Kühn, Rolf. *Französische Reflexions- und Geistesphilosophie: Profile und Analysen*. Frankfurt am Main: Hain, 1993.

Kühn, Rolf. *Französische Religionsphilosophie und -phänomenologie der Gegenwart: metaphysische und post-metaphysische Positionen zur Ehrfahrungs(un)möglichkeit Gottes*. Freiburg: Herder, 2013.

Kühn, Rolf. *Leere und Aufmerksamkeit*. Dresden: Text & Dialog 2014.

Lachelier, Jules. *Œuvres*. Vol. II. Paris: Alcan, 1933.

Lagneau, Jules. *Écrits de Jules Lagneau réunis par les soins de ses disciples*. Paris: Sandre, 2006.

Lago, A. dal. 'On the Ethics of Weakness: Simone Weil and Nihilism', translated by
P. Carravetta. In *Weak Thought*, edited by G. Vattimo and P. A. Rovatti, 111–38.
Albany: State University of New York Press, 2012.
Laruelle, François. *Phénomène et différence: essai sur l'ontologie de Ravaisson*. Paris:
Klincksieck, 1971.
Leduc-Fayette, Denise. 'La métaphysique de Ravaisson et le Christ', *Les Études philosophiques* 4 (1984): 511–27.
Leduc-Fayette, Denise (ed.). *Fénelon, philosophie et spiritualité: actes du colloque*.
Geneva: Droz, 1996.
Lenoir, Raymond. 'La doctrine de Ravaisson et la pensée moderne'. *Revue de métaphysique et de morale* 26, no. 3 (1919): 353–74.
Leterre, Thierry. *Alain, le premier intellectuel*. Paris: Stock, 2006.
Madinier, Gabriel. *Conscience et mouvement: étude sur la philosophie française de Condillac à Bergson*. Paris: Alcan, 1939.
Marcus, Aurelius. *Meditations*, translated by C. R. Haines. London: William
Heinemann, 1916.
Marcuse, Herbert. *Eros and Civilisation: A Philosophical Inquiry into Freud*. Boston:
Beacon Press, 1955.
Marion, Jean-Luc. *Cartesian Questions: Method and Metaphysics*. Chicago: Chicago
University Press, 1999.
Marion, Jean-Luc. *On Descartes' Metaphysical Prism: The Constitution and Limits of Onto-Theo-Logy in Cartesian Thought*, translated by Jeffrey Kosky. Chicago:
University of Chicago Press, 1999.
Marion, Jean-Luc. 'Resting, Moving, Loving: The Access to the Self According to Saint
Augustine'. *The Journal of Religion* 91, no. 1 (2011): 24–42.
Marion, Jean-Luc. 'The Saturated Phenomenon', translated by Thomas A. Carlson,
Philosophy Today 40, no. 1 (1996): 103–24.
Marno, David. 'Easy attention: Ignatius of Loyola and Robert Boyle'. *Journal of Medieval and Early Modern Studies* 44, no. 1 (2014): 135–61.
Marno, David. *Death Be Not Proud: The Art of Holy Attention*. Chicago: Chicago
University Press, 2016.
Martz, Louis. *Poetry of Meditation: A Study in English Religious Literature*. 2nd edn. New
Haven: Yale, 1962.
Maurois, André. *Alain*. Paris: Gallimard, 1950.
McCullough, Lissa. 'Prayer and Incarnation: A Homiletic Reflection'. In *The Phenomenology of Prayer*, edited by B. E. Benson and N. Wirzba, 209–17. New York:
Fordham University Press, 2005.
McCullough, Lissa. 'Weil's Phenomenology of the Body'. *Comparative and Continental Philosophy* 4, no. 2 (2012): 195–218.
McCullough, Lissa. *The Religious Philosophy of Simone Weil: An Introduction*. London:
I.B. Tauris, 2014.
McFague, Sallie. *The Body of God: An Ecological Theology*. London: SCM Press, 1993.

McLellan, David. *Simone Weil: Utopian Pessimist*. Houndsmills: Macmillan, 1989.

Merchant, Carolyn. *The Death of Nature: Women, Ecology and the Scientific Revolution*. San Francisco: Harper and Row, 1980.

Merton, Thomas. 'Reflections on the Character and Genius of Fénelon'. In *Fénelon: Letters*, edited and translated by John McEwan, 9–30. London: Harvill Press, 1963.

Merton, Thomas. *Mystics and Zen Masters*. New York: Delta, 1967.

Monod, Gérard. 'Pensée et action chez Jules Lagneau', *Revue de Métaphysique et de Morale* 57, no. 2 (1952): 117–48.

Moore, F. C. T. *The Psychology of Maine de Biran*. Oxford: Clarendon, 1970.

Moulard-Leonard, Valentine. 'The Sublime and the Intellectual Effort: The Imagination in Bergson and Kant', *Journal of the British Society for Phenomenology* 37, no. 2 (2006): 138–51.

Muramatsu, Matasaki. 'Les avatars de la "tension" dans le spiritualisme français'. In Shin *Considérations inactuelles: Bergson et la philosophie française du XIXe siècle*, edited by Hisashi Fujita Abiko and Yasuhiko Sugimura, 7–20. New York: Georg Olms, 2017.

Murdoch, Iris. *The Sovereignty of Good*. London: Routledge, 1970.

Nédoncelle, Maurice. 'Félix Ravaisson, *Essai sur la métaphysique d'Aristote. Fragments du tome III (Hellénisme, judaïsme, christianisme)*, texte établi par Charles Devivaise, 1953'. *Revue des Sciences Religieuses* 28, no. 3 (1954): 323–4.

Nehamas, Aleaxander. *The Art of Living: Socratic Reflections from Plato to Foucault*. Berkeley: University of California Press, 1998.

North, Paul. *The Problem of Distraction*. Stanford: Stanford University Press, 2012.

Oksenberg Rorty, Amélie. 'The Structure of Descartes' *Meditations*'. In *Essays on Descartes' Meditations*, edited by Rorty, 1–20. Berkeley: University of California Press, 1986.

Onfray, Michel. *A Hedonist Manifesto: The Power to Exist*, translated by Joseph McClellan. New York: Columbia University Press, 2015.

Pascal, Blaise. *Pensées*, translated by W. F. Trotter. New York: Dutton, 1958.

Paulhan, Fr. 'Le nouveau mysticisme'. *Revue philosophique de la France et de l'Étranger* 30 (1890): 480–522.

Pétrement, Simone. 'Sur la religion d'Alain (avec quelques remarques concernant celle de Simone Weil)'. *Revue de Métaphysique et de Morale* 60, no. 3 (1955): 306–30.

Pétrement, Simone. *Simone Weil: A Life*, translated by R. Rosenthal. London: Mowbrays, 1977.

Pidoux, M. *Le spiritualisme organique*. Paris: Asselin, 1969.

Pieper, Josef. *Leisure: The Basis of Culture*, translated by Alexander Dru. London: Faber, 1952.

Pieper, Josef. *Happiness and Contemplation*, translated by Richard and Clara Winston. New York: Pantheon, 1958.

Ramey, Joshua. *The Hermetic Deleuze*. Durham: Duke University Press, 2012.

Ravaisson, Félix. *Essai sur la Métaphysique d'Aristote*. 2 Vols. Paris: Cerf, 2007 [orig. 1837–1845].

Ravaisson, Félix. *La philosophie en France au XIXᵉ siècle, 1867*. Paris: Hachette, 1889.
Ravaisson, Félix. *Selected Essays*, edited by Mark Sinclair. London: Bloomsbury, 2016.
Rénouvier, Charles. *Manuel de philosophie ancienne*. Vol. II. Paris: Paulin, 1844.
Rénouvier, Charles. 'D'une forme moderne du Stoïcisme'. *La Critique philosophique* 28 (1876): 17–25.
Ricœur, Paul. *Freedom and Nature: The Voluntary and the Involuntary*, translated by E. Kohák. Evanston: Northwestern University Press, 1966.
Ricœur, Paul. *Husserl: An Analysis of His Phenomenology*, translated by Edward G. Ballard and Lester E. Embree. Evanston: Northwestern University Press, 1967.
Rigby, Catherine E. *Topographies of the Sacred: The Poetics of Place in European Romanticism*. Charlottesville: University of Virginia Press, 2004.
Robertson, D. *The Philosophy of Cognitive-Behaviour Therapy (CBT): Stoicism as Rational and Cognitive Psychotherapy*. London: Karnac, 2010.
Robinson, Marilynne. *The Death of Adam: Essays on Modern Thought*. Boston: Houghton and Mifflin, 1998.
Roger, Jacques. *Buffon: A Life in Natural History*, translated by Sarah Lucille Bonnefoi. Ithaca: Cornell University Press, 1997.
Rorty, Amélie Oksenberg. 'The Two Faces of Stoicism: Rousseau and Freud'. *Journal of the History of Philosophy* 34, no. 3 (1996): 335–56.
Rose, Gillian. *Judaism and Modernity: Philosophical Essays*. Oxford: Blackwell, 1993.
Rose, Marika. *A Theology of Failure: Žižek against Christian Innocence*. New York: Fordham University Press, 2019.
Rousseau, Jean-Jacques. *Reveries of a Solitary Walker*, translated by Peter France. London: Penguin, 1979.
Rousseau, Jean-Jacques. *The Collected Writings*. Vol. XIII. *Émile, or On Education*, translated by Allan David Bloom. Hanover and London: University Press of New England, 2010.
Roy, Georges Le. *L'Éxpérience de l'effort et de la grâce chez Maine de Biran*. Paris: Boivin, 1937.
Sainte-Beuve, Charles Augustin. *Causeries du Lundi*. Vol. XIII. Paris: Garnier frères, 1870.
Sarthou-Lajus, Nathalie. 'Du goût pour les stoïciens', *Études*, 410, no. 6 (2009): 775–86.
Schlegel, Jean-Louis. 'La philosophie, un exercise spirituel'. *Esprit* 404, no. 5 (2014): 29–42.
Schmidt, Leigh Eric. 'The Making of Modern "Mysticism"'. *Journal of the American Academy of Religion* 71, no. 2 (2003): 273–302.
Schumann, Maurice. 'Henri Bergson et Simone Weil'. *Revue des deux mondes* (November 1993): 193–203.
Sellars, John. *The Art of Living: The Stoics on the Nature and Function of Philosophy*. London: Bloomsbury, 2003.
Sellars, John. 'Aiôn and Chronos: Deleuze and the Stoic Theory of Time'. *Collapse* 3 (2007): 177–205.

Sellar, John. *Stoicism*. London: Routledge, 2014.
Sherman, Jacob. *Partakers of the Divine: Contemplation and the Practice of Philosophy*. Minneapolis: Fortress Press, 2014.
Siegel, Jerrold. *The Idea of the Self: Thought and Experience in Western Europe since the Seventeenth Century*. Cambridge: Cambridge University Press, 2005.
Simon, Jules. 'Philosophes modernes: Maine de Biran'. *Revue des deux mondes* (15 November 1841): 634–58.
Sinclair, Mark. 'Introduction'. In Félix Ravaisson, *Selected Essays*, edited by Mark Sinclair, 1–30. London: Bloomsbury, 2016.
Sjövall, Björn. *Psychology of Tension*. Stockholm: Svenska Bokförlaget, 1967.
Sloterdijk, Peter. *Critique of Cynical Reason*, translated by Michael Eldred. Minneapolis: University of Minnesota Press, 1987.
Slojterdijk, Peter. *The Art of Philosophy: Wisdom as a Practice*, translated by Karen Margolis. New York: Columbia University Press, 2012.
Sloterdijk, Peter. *You Must Change Your Life: On Anthropotechnics*, translated by Wieland Hoban. Cambridge: Polity, 2013.
Sontag, Susan. 'Simone Weil'. *New York Review of Books*, 1 February 1963. Available online: http://www.nybooks.com/articles/archives/1963/feb/01/simone-weil/?insrc=toc/ (accessed 25 July 2019).
Sorabji, Richard. 'Is Stoic Philosophy Helpful as Psychotherapy?' In *Aristotle and After*, edited by Richard Sorabji, 197–209. London: Institute of Classical Studies, 1997.
Sorabji, Richard. *Emotion and Peace of Mind: From Stoic Agitation to Christian Temptation*. Oxford: Oxford University Press, 2000.
Soskice, Janet M. *The Kindness of God: Metaphor, Gender, and Religious Language*. Oxford: Oxford University Press, 2007.
Spanneut, Michel. *Permanence du Stoïcisme de Zénon à Malraux*. Duculot: Gembloux, 1973.
Steiner, George. *No Passion Spent: Essays 1978–1996*. London: Faber, 1996.
Stengers, Isabelle. *In Catastrophic Times: Resisting the Coming Barbarism*, translated by Andrew Goffey. Lüneburg: Open Humanities Press, 2015.
Stengers, Isabelle. *Another Science Is Possible: Manifesto for a Slow Science*, translated by Stephen Muecke. Cambridge: Polity, 2018.
Stengers, Isabelle, and Martin Savransky, 'Relearning the Art of Paying Attention: A Conversation'. *SubStance* 47, no. 1 (2018): 130–45.
Stengers, Isabelle, and Philippe Pignarre. *Capitalist Sorcery: Breaking the Spell*, translated by Andrew Goffey. Houndmills: Palgrave Macmillan, 2011.
Stillman, Anne. 'Distraction Fits'. *Thinking Verse* 2: 27–67.
Struck, Peter. *Divination and Human Nature: A Cognitive History of Intuition in Classical Antiquity*. Princeton: Princeton University Press, 2018.
Tarbuck, Alice, and Simone Kotva. 'The non-Secular Pilgrimage: Walking and Looking in Ken Cockburn and Alec Finlay's *The Road North*'. *Critical Survey* 29, no. 1 (2017): 33–52.

Thibaud, Marguerite. *L'effort chez Maine de Biran et Bergson*. Grenoble: Allien, 1939.

Thibon, Gustave, and Joseph-Marie Perrin. *Simone Weil as We Knew Her*, translated by Emma Crauford. London: Routledge & Kegan Paul, 1953.

Truman, Nathan. *Maine de Biran's Philosophy of Will*. New York: Macmillan, 1904.

Tumblety, Joan. *Remaking the Male Body: Masculinity and the Use of Physical Culture in Interwar and Vichy France*. Oxford: Oxford University Press, 2012.

Ure, Michael. 'Nietzsche's Free Spirit Trilogy and Stoic Therapy'. *Journal of Nietzsche Studies* 38 (2009): 60–84.

Vacherot, Étienne. 'La situation philosophique en France'. *Revue des deux mondes* 75 (1868): 950–77.

Vattimo, Gianni, Pier Aldo Rovatti, and Peter Carravetta (eds). *Weak Thought*. Albany, NY: Southern University of New York Press, 2012.

Vermeren Patrice. 'Ravaisson en son temps et en sa thèse'. *Les études philosophiques* 1 (1993): 65–86.

Vigny, Alfred de. *Servitude and Grandeur of Arms*, translated by Roger Gard. London: Penguin, 1996.

Vigny, Alfred de. *The Warrior's Life*, edited and translated by Roger Gard. London: Penguin Books, 2013.

Viguerie, Jean de. *Une œuvre d'éducation sous l'Ancien Régime: les Pères de la Doctrine chrétienne en France et en Italie, 1592–1792*. Paris: Nouvelle Aurore, 1976.

Viola, Tullio. 'The Serpentine Life of Félix Ravaisson: Art, Drawing, Scholarship, Philosophy'. In *Et in imagine ego: Facetten von Bildakt und Verkörperung*, edited by Ulrike Feist and Markus Rath, 155–74. Berlin: Akademie-Verlag, 2012.

Violette, René. *La spiritualité de Bergson*. Toulouse: Éditions Édouard Privat, 1968.

Wall, T. C. *Radical Passivity: Levinas, Blanchot and Agamben*. Albany, NY: Southern University of New York Press, 1999.

Weil, Simone. *Waiting on God*, edited by Joseph-Marie Perrin and translated by Emma Craufurd. London: Routledge and Kegan Paul, 1951.

Weil, Simone. *Seventy Letters*, translated by R. Rees. London: Oxford University Press, 1965.

Weil, Simone. *On Science, Necessity, and the Love of God*, translated by Richard Rees. London: Oxford University Press, 1968.

Weil, Simone. *First and Last Notebooks*, translated by R. Rees. London: Oxford University Press, 1970.

Weil, Simone. *Lectures on Philosophy*, translated by H. Price. Cambridge: Cambridge University Press, 1978.

Weil, Simone. *Formative Writings 1929–1941*, translated by Dorothy Tuck McFarland and Wilhelmina van Ness. London: Routledge, 1987.

Weil, Simone. *The Need for Roots*, translated by Arthur Wills. London: Routledge, 2002.

Weil, Sylvie. *At Home with André and Simone Weil*, translated by B. Ivry. Evanston: Northwestern University Press, 2010.

Williams, Elizabeth. *The Physical and the Moral: Anthropology, Physiology, and Philosophical Medicine in France, 1750–1850*. Cambridge: Cambridge University Press, 1994.

Williams, Rowan. 'The Necessary Non-Existence of God'. In *Simone Weil's Philosophy of Culture: Readings toward a Divine Humanity*, edited by R. H. Bell, 52–77. Cambridge: Cambridge University Press, 1993.

Winch, Peter. *Simone Weil: 'The Just Balance'*. Cambridge: Cambridge University Press, 1989.

Wolfteich, Claire. 'Attention or Destruction: Simone Weil and the Paradox of the Eucharist'. *The Journal of Religion* 81, no. 3 (2001): 359–76.

Zambala, Santiago (ed.). *Weakening Philosophy: Essays in Honour of Gianni Vattimo*. Montreal & Kingston: McGill-Queen's University Press, 2007.

Zanta, Léontine. *La Renaissance du Stoïcisme au XVIe siècle*. Paris: H. Champion, 1914.

Zeldin, Theodore. *A History of French Passions*. Vol. II. *Politics & Anger*. Oxford: Oxford University Press, 1979.

Index

abandonment 2, 12–13, 28, 37, 175–6
   Fénelon 131–2
   Ravaisson 65–6, 76–9, 86, 91
action 116–17
activity viii, 4, 18, 31, 33–5, 39, 51–3, 68, 71–4, 113, 125, 129, 161, 177, 179
   grace 77–80, 85
   passive 17, 21, 63, 142–3, 151, 171
   pure 134, 136, 138
Agamben, Giorgio 5
Alain x, 22–3, 133, 139, 145, 165
   on effort 121–2
   on prayer 124
   on Quietism 125, 180
   on Stoicism 117–25
   on war 123, 128–9
Anthropocene 174
Aquinas, Thomas 7
Aristotle 7, 68, 82, 110
asceticism 6, 89–91, 163
attention ix–x, 1, 16, 52, 58, 111, 138–41, 166, 170–2
   and ecology xi, 174–80
   and ethics 159–60
   and introspection 30–1, 35, 39–40, 54–5, 134
   and paradox 142–3
   passive 8, 30, 151, 155, 170
   and waiting (*l'attente*) 4–5, 153–63, 170–2
   see also John of the Cross, Murdoch, Weil, Marno
Augustine 24–5, 28, 32, 33, 39, 42, 56, 73, 80, 87, 177
   on introspection 28
   on work and repose 17–21, 151
   (*see also* Bouwsma, Fénelon, mysticism)
Ávila, Teresa of 105, 121

Bacon, Francis 143–4
Bellantone, Andrea 60
Bénatouïl, Thomas 115, 127
Bennett, Jane 176–7
Bergson, Henri x, 13, 22–3, 55, 95, 97–113, 121, 128–30, 139, 158–9, 165, 166, 168, 173
   on effort 14, 98–9
   on grace 112–13
   on mysticism 104–13
   on Stoicism 108–13
Bichat, Xavier 99
Biran, Pierre Maine de ix–x, 9–17, 20–1, 22–5, 27–8, 38–58, 59–61, 70, 74, 87, 91, 93, 97, 98, 101, 104, 105, 106, 127, 129, 144–5, 152, 165, 169, 173, 179
   on effort and grace 42–7, 52, 53–8, 131 133, 145
   on Fénelon 12, 62–3
   on habit 11–12, 48–9, 50–1, 55
   on happiness and repose 9–12
   on introspection 38–42
   on prayer 45, 156
   on Rousseau 12, 17
   on Stoicism and Christianity 23–5, 43–6, 100, 143, 152–3, 162
Blondel, Maurice 116
Bonnet, Charles 31, 34, 35, 50
Bossuet, Jacques-Bénigne 92
Bousquet, Joë 153–4, 151–6
Bouwsma, William J. xi
   on Augustinianism and Stoicism 80–1, 179
Bréhier, Émile 87, 114, 166
Brooke, Christopher 22
Brothers of Christian Doctrine 2
Buffon, Comte de (Georges-Louis Leclerc) 35

Cabanis, Pierre 31
Carlisle, Clare xi
Carlyle, Thomas xii, 95
Catherina of Siena 105

Certeau, Michel de 69
Chardin, Teilhard de 115
Chartier, Émile *see* Alain
Chase, Michael 167
Christ 43, 89, 143
Chrysippus 83
Cicero 24
Coleman, Charly xi, 12, 37
Comte-Sponville, André 117
Condillac, Étienne Bonnot de ix, 27, 31–2, 34, 39, 40, 47, 50, 98
    on introspection and attention 29–30
contemplation *see* introspection
Cousin, Victor 62–7, 68–9, 71, 73, 74, 75, 76, 87, 93, 95, 97, 100
    on mysticism and philosophy 62–7
    on Quietism 67, 68–9
Cynics xii, 7–8, 123

Darwin, Charles 61, 69
    evolution, theory of 99
Deleuze, Gilles 6, 56, 98, 115, 127
Derrida, Jacques 71
Descartes, René 1, 30, 34, 40, 64–7, 80, 87, 134–7
    on meditation and attention 28–39, 32–3, 134
Donne, John 5
double vision 54, 165

ecology xi, 174–80
ecstasy 40–1, 46–7, 49, 54, 105, 179
effort
    and French thought 95, 97–130, 139, 158, 165
    and heroism 77–8, 139, 154, 170
    and introspection 28–33
    and military virtues 99–104
    and modern philosophy viii–xii, 6–9, 139, 158–9, 173–4
    and social Darwinism 98–9
    and *tonos* 86, 107
    (*see also* Alain, Bergson, Hercules, Stoicism)
    and work 6–8, 135, 145–51
    energy 39–40, 45, 54, 61, 85, 104, 111, 115, 161–2
Epictetus 3, 84, 101
Epicureanism 7–8, 22, 120, 124
    ataraxia 112
    relaxation 8, 168

Fénelon, François ix, 4, 13, 16, 22, 24–5, 56, 60, 52, 67, 68, 69, 74, 79, 87, 91, 92, 106, 132, 175, 177
    on abandonment 12, 37, 63, 76, 132
    on passivity 44–5
    on prevenient grace 72–3
Festugière, André-Jean 8
Flood, Gavin xi, 163–4, 165, 167
Foucault, Michel 6, 36–7, 127, 167, 169
Francis of Assisi 141, 143
Frazer, James 93
French spiritualism ix, 1–2, 8–9, 13–14, 22, 28, 37, 39, 53, 59–95, 98, 144–5, 165, 169
    and mysticism 39, 68–80, 145, 132, 152
Frieden-Markievitch, Nathalie 106–7

Gabellieri, Emmanuel 163
gift 7, 18–19, 56, 73, 76–7, 91, 94, 116, 125–6
Goethe, Johann Wolfgang von 141
Goldschmidt, Victor 115
Gouhier, Henri xi
Gouyon, Jeanne 37
grace
    and attention 142–3, 151–63
    (*see also* Ravaisson, Weil)
    and charity 76–7
    and habit 51–53
    and movement 78–80, 112–13
    and nature 72–3
    and repose 7, 17–21
Guattari, Félix 176

habit 48, 49–53, 55–6, 72–4, 138–9, 160–3
Hadot, Pierre ix–x, 2–3, 6, 7–8, 14, 93, 115, 127, 132
    on attention 166–9
    on effort and relaxation 168
Hatfield, Gary 29, 32, 34, 179
Henry, Michel 6, 57
Heraclitus 83–5, 108, 113
Herbert, George 156
Hercules 7–8, 78, 80, 86, 97, 108, 114, 115, 123, 127, 128, 139
homo duplex 35, 53–4, 135–8, 143, 164 (*see also* Paul of Tarsus, paradox)
heroism xii, 23–4, 59–61, 77, 80, 95, 100–7, 122, 128–9, 139, 154, 170
Husserl, Edmund 66

Ignatius of Loyola 1, 3, 29, 32, 37, 56, 168
illumination 4, 32, 50, 54, 60, 140
inactivity ix, 73, 91, 103, 112, 136, 139, 155, 161
introspection
    dialectic of autonomy and abandon 52–3, 133, 139–40
    and mysticism 33–6, 139
    and philosophical method 29–32, 134–5, 137
    and Stoicism 100
intuition 3–4, 6, 63, 90–1, 113–15

Janet, Paul 13, 93–4
Janicaud, Dominique 13, 92, 93
Jankélévitch, Vladimir 107
Jansenism 35, 82, 118
Joan of Arc 105, 121
John of the Cross ix, 4, 8, 160, 161, 177
    on passive loving attention 151, 155, 157, 180
Jones, David 136
Jones, P. Mansell 36

Kant, Immanuel xii, 6–7, 111
Keller, Catherine 177

labour 7–8, 11, 24, 31, 41–2, 46–7, 85
    (*see* Weil)
Lachelier, Jules 39
Lagneau, Jules 116–17, 120, 121
Laruelle, François 71
Leduc-Fayette, Denise 93
Leibniz, Gottfried Wilhelm 39, 40
leisure xi–xii, 6–8, 30, 49, 159
Lenoir, Raymond 60, 61
Le Roy, Georges 48
Loisel, Gustave 115

Mably, Gabriel Bonnot de 12
Madinier, Gabriel 94–5
magic 48, 49, 178–9
Marcus Aurelius 3, 22, 44, 101, 102, 141
Marno, David xi, 4–5, 8, 34, 37, 179
    on attention 31
    on effort and grace 32–3, 36
Maurois, André 122, 126
Maximus the Confessor 175
McCullough, Lissa 163, 164–5
McFague, Sallie 177

meditation *see* introspection
Merton, Thomas 175
Montaigne, Michel de 12
movement 19–20, 23–5, 41, 50, 73, 78–83, 88, 98, 112–13, 119–20, 129, 159
Murdoch, Iris 8, 170–3, 174
Murray, Gilbert 107
mysticism
    Augustinian ix, 23, 25, 39, 59, 125, 129, 131–2, 151, 152–3, 159, 164–5, 180
    Christian 81, 93, 145, 151, 161, 179
    and ecology 173–80
    and French spiritualism 13, 59–95
    (*see also* ecstasy, prayer, Quietism)
    religious 55, 81, 95, 104, 121, 139

Nehamas, Alexander 169
Nietzsche, Friedrich 6, 104

paradox 136–8, 139–40, 146–51
    of effort and grace 19–21, 131–2, 142, 144, 156–63, 164–5, 173
    spiritual life as 162–3
    (*see also* homo duplex)
Parzifal 154–5, 159–60
Pascal, Blaise 12, 80, 82, 88–92
    on intuition and grace 90–1
passivity x, 129–30, 133–72
    active 109, 124–7, 129
    and attention 133–8, 146–63
    and grace 44, 63–7, 73–4
    and habit 48–52, 149–50
    and intuition 3–4, 6, 63
    and modern thought 2–5
Paul of Tarsus 10, 15–16, 102
peace 10, 13, 18–20, 46, 99, 121, 123–4
Pelagius 18, 22
Perrin, Joseph-Marie 153, 156
Pétrement, Simone 126
phusike theoria 174–5
Pieper, Josef xi–xii, 6–8, 136
Plato 12, 82, 107, 110 (*see also* Socrates)
Plotinus 105, 108, 168
prayer 4, 45, 49, 65–6, 110, 124, 151–63, 171–2
    mystical 8, 12–13, 60, 127, 131, 152, 177
    spiritual 16, 28, 44, 46, 93
    supplication 94, 110
psychic tension 116, 173

Quakers 139, 179
Quietism 12–13, 25, 71, 74, 75, 82, 87, 92, 125, 139, 164, 180
  Cousin's critique of 61–7, 68–9
  and grace as repose 13, 16

Racine, Jean 82
Ravaisson, Félix x, 13, 15, 59–62, 67–95, 97, 100, 101, 104, 106, 109, 118, 127, 129, 165, 166, 173
  on grace 72–80
  on habit 73–4
  on heroism 80, 100
  on Maine de Biran 70–4
  on Pascal 88–92
  on passivity 73–4
  on Stoicism 78–88, 100
Rénouvier, Charles 81
relaxation 147–9, 158–9
repose 17–21, 131–3, 151, 155, 157, 179–80
Ricoeur, Paul 66
Rose, Marika 5
Rousseau, Jean-Jacques ix, 6, 12, 27, 37, 56, 173
  on introspection 33–4
  on tranquillity 15–17

Sainte-Beauve, Charles Augustine 27
Sales, Francis de 4
Sartre, Jean-Paul 127, 166
Schelling, Friedrich 6, 71
secularity 21, 37, 179–80
Seneca 83
Sinclair, Mark 86
Sloterdijk, Peter 6, 21
Socrates 3–4, 12, 27, 63, 169
Spanneut, Michel xi, 83, 100–1
Spinoza 117
Starhawk (Miriam Simos) 178
Stengers, Isabelle
  on attention 178–80
Stoicism viii, 3, 7–8, 17, 19, 22–5, 43–6, 58, 61, 66–7, 82, 99–130, 165–6, 166–7
  and Christianity 22–5, 97, 101–2, 103, 128–30, 133, 138, 140–5, 152–3

  and French philosophy 80–4, 99–104, 113, 115
  and military virtue 99–104
  pantheism 109, 141
  resignation 103, 141, 143
  tonos and *anesis* 78–9, 84–6, 100, 108, 111, 113–15, 118
supernatural, the 20, 48, 69, 73, 124, 151

Tracy, Antoine Destutt de 31, 40
tranquillity 14–17, 23–5, 44, 131–2, 151

Vattimo, Gianni 5, 129
Vigny, Alfred de 102–3, 128
Vinci, Leonardo da 78, 80
vitalism 99 (*see* Bergson)

war 99–104, 123, 128–9
Weber, Max 6
Weil, Simone viii–xi, 4–5, 8, 23, 55, 58, 77, 88, 122, 126, 129, 131–72, 173–4, 177, 179
  on affliction 153–4
  on attention 134, 138–40, 153–63
  on Bergson 158–9, 165
  on Descartes 134–5
  on effort and grace 156–63
  on habit 149–50
  on John of the Cross 151–2
  on *Parzifal* 154–5, 159–60
  on passivity 133f
  on prayer 156–9, 161
  on Stoicism 138, 140–5, 152–3, 158–9, 160–2, 164
  on waiting (*l'attente*) 151–153, 157
  on work 144–51, 157–9

Witchcraft (religion) 178–9
wonder 1, 30, 32, 34, 51, 176
work 6–8, 18–19, 135, 144–51

Zanta, Léontine 114
Zeldin, Theodore 98–9
Zeno of Citium 83

www.ingramcontent.com/pod-product-compliance
Lightning Source LLC
Chambersburg PA
CBHW072147290426
44111CB00012B/1994